A PIRATE FOR LIFE

STEVE BLASS

WITH ERIK SHERMAN

TRIUMPH
BOOKS

This book is dedicated to Karen.
I couldn't have made this journey without her.

And to all of those who have touched my life,
your friendship means more to me than you know.

—S.B.

Library of Congress Cataloging-in-Publication Data
Blass, Steve.
   A Pirate for life / Steve Blass with Erik Sherman.
      pages cm.
   ISBN 978-1-60078-819-2
   1. Blass, Steve. 2. Baseball players—United States—Biography. 3. Sportscasters—United States—Biography. 4. Pittsburgh Pirates (Baseball team) I. Sherman, Erik. II. Title.
   GV865.B553A3 2013
   796.357092—dc23
      [B]   2012045873

This book is available in quantity at special discounts for your group or organization. For further information, contact:

Triumph Books LLC
814 North Franklin Street
Chicago, Illinois, 60610
Phone: (312) 337-0747
www.triumphbooks.com

Printed in the United States of America

ISBN 978-1-60078-819-2

Interior design by Sue Knopf

Photographs courtesy of Steve Blass unless otherwise noted

Contents

Foreword

I do not use the term *friend* lightly or carelessly. I actually get a bit annoyed at its overuse in our society because I think many have forgotten the word's true meaning and importance.

The French poet Jean de La Fontaine said it best: "Everyone calls himself a friend, foolish is he who believes it. Nothing is more common than the name friend, and nothing is more rare than the real thing."

Steve Blass *is* the "real thing," believe me! He's not just a great friend but also a great human being.

I got to know Steve when he joined hockey broadcasting legend Mike Lange to announce games on KBL, the fledgling cable network that televised Pirates baseball back in the mid-1980s. I was a rookie announcer who contributed with some pregame and postgame interviews. I spent a year traveling with Mike and Steve during that season, and what an education I got! I even learned a little something about broadcasting!

Almost 10 years later, I returned to Pittsburgh and joined Lanny Frattare, Steve, and Bob Walk to broadcast Bucco baseball on radio and television. I can honestly say that in the last 19 years I don't believe a week has gone by that I haven't seen or spoken with Steve. We've become pretty close.

I continue to marvel at what he does on a daily basis. He's my hero! *Nobody* has ever "lived" life to the max like Steve Blass.

Such joy. Such passion. Such enthusiasm.

What a pleasure it has been to get to know this modern-day Renaissance Man.

His on-field story, of course, is sensational and inspiring. He went from being an elite National League All-Star, World Series pitching hero, and *Sports Illustrated* cover boy, to a player felled by a sudden and inexplicable bout with wildness that ended his career in almost tragic fashion at its very peak.

The way in which Steve dealt with that bitter ending to his playing career is what makes him, to this day, an example to all. He didn't run away and hide from the relentless scrutiny and negative attention. He took it as a challenge and met it head-on. He dealt with it like a man. Like a pro. Like the stand-up guy that he remains today.

Can you imagine that, almost 40 years after retiring, he still gets questions about what happened?

And you know what? He still answers every one of those questions, whether they come from the reporters in New York or Los Angeles or the casual fan walking down the street in Pittsburgh. He answers with respect and kindness and almost certainly sprinkles in a little of that patented Blass humor.

Oh, that humor!

I swear, if Steve had so chosen, he could have made a career doing stand-up comedy. I've never met anyone so funny in my life. He's so quick and sharp that nothing gets past him. He absolutely loves an audience and lives to make people laugh.

But making others laugh is just one of Steve's favorite things.

Needless to say, Steve loves his Pirates and loves it even more when they are playing well. He especially enjoys seeing and calling a well-pitched game. I can't help but chuckle as I watch and listen to him get ultra-pumped as each out is recorded. But he is awfully proud, and rightfully so, of his longtime association with the ballclub, and he wears his passion for the team on his sleeve.

I'm so proud of Steve Blass and so honored and privileged to have gotten to know him and to call him a true friend. Enjoy reading the work of one of the all-time classic figures in sports.

Greg Brown
Pittsburgh, Pennsylvania
November 2011

Preface

For several years, I have felt that I had a book in me. The highs and lows that I have experienced in baseball since age eight are probably similar in many ways to those of other major leaguers. But I thought a combination of massive recall and the ongoing theme of an absolute fall from an above-average career, an ascent out of that abyss somewhat intact, followed by a reinvention of a life in broadcasting, might make for an interesting read.

My intent is not to inspire, but to tell the story of a boy who had a simple dream fulfilled. But that dream was lived out with bumps and bruises and much more complexity than he ever imagined.

Being extremely naïve about the publishing business, I thought I might be able to go right to the top and approach John Grisham, George Will, or even Roger Angell to write with or for me. That was before I met Erik Sherman. Erik sold me on the idea that I should tell my story myself, in my own words, hence an autobiography rather than a biography. The reasoning was that a biographer puts much more of himself in a book.

Erik went to Emerson College with Tim Neverett, who became a Pirates play-by-play announcer in 2009. In 2010, Greg Brown, our other play-by-play guy, mentioned to Tim that I thought I had a book in me. It struck a chord in Tim, because his college buddy Erik had already written a baseball book titled *Out at Home: The Glenn Burke Story*, which told the story of a ballplayer with the Los Angeles Dodgers and Oakland A's who died of AIDS.

I can't thank Erik enough for his hard work of not only transcribing hours and hours of recorded phone calls and face-to-face meetings but also capturing the feel of those interviews. Speaking of interviews, I've been overwhelmed by what some of my friends and teammates conveyed to Erik.

What I'd give to get those guys I played with out in my backyard for a few drinks—Willie, Maz, Dave, Bruce, Tony—and even try to explain to Roberto what I was going through when I struggled at the end of my career and how much the team meant to me. I wasn't able to do it then, but I'd give a million bucks to do it now.

Having completed the project, I think the timing couldn't have been better. Waiting past age 70 would have been too long. And last year's 40th anniversary of the 1971 World Series and those memories helped a lot.

Finally, in spite of my friends saying I have total recall of everything I ever made up, I have made an honest effort to be accurate. I hope you enjoy my story.

Steve Blass
Pittsburgh, Pennsylvania
October 19, 2011

Acknowledgments

Steve and I would like to thank the following for their valuable input, advice, and encouragement: Marty Appel, Tony Bartirome, Joe Billetdeaux, Karen Blass, David Blass, Chris Blass, Greg Brown, Tom Butters, Frank Coonelly, Richard Crowley, Lanny Frattare, Bob Friend, Frank Fuhrer, Marc Garda, Dave Giusti, Ginny Giusti, Richie Hebner, Jackie Hernandez, Ed Kirby, Bruce Kison, John Lamb, Don Leppert, Gil Lucas, Bill Mazeroski, Gene Michael, Bill Norbutt, Champ Perotti, Jim Rooker, Bill Virdon, and Bob Walk.

Sally O'Leary, a longtime Pirates public relations director and currently a major figure in the team's alumni association, provided invaluable help in not just proofreading the manuscript but also in supplying historical data, stories, and insight into Pirates baseball both during and after Steve's playing career. Sally was our greatest confidante and source for all things Buccos, and her enthusiasm for the project was never ending.

Tim Neverett made the introduction that brought Steve and I together to write this book. Without Tim, the opportunity to work with Steve may never have happened, and I will always be grateful to him for his help.

Jeff Pearlman, the best-selling author of several sports books, provided insightful feedback and direction, even as his own time was extremely limited in making deadline for his latest masterpiece.

Robert Wilson, literary agent, provided support throughout the project and gave nothing short of dead-on advice right to the end.

Habiba Boumlik, my bride, and Alex and Sabrina, our children, sacrificed months of family time and did their best to keep the house quiet and the coffee percolating so that the story of Steve Blass' riveting journey through a baseball life could be written.

Erik Sherman

Introduction

I t was September 22, 2011, an off-day for Steve Blass. But unlike so many of his broadcasting brethren who might just cool their jets on a rare regular season day off, Steve was, as usual, on the run. After a round of golf in a charity tournament, he raced over to Pittsburgh Airport to pick me up, already showered and changed into a jacket and tie.

We drove directly to a well-heeled Junior Achievement ceremony in a Victorian stone building where Steve was the guest of honor and was also being introduced as the 2012 co-chairman. He spoke eloquently and was an inspiration to a group of hand-picked fourth graders who were chosen to represent their schools. Then he said, "I brought some photos along if you're interested. The fee for one is $5. That's the most I can pay you to take one." He then signed as many autographs and posed in as many pictures as anybody wanted. It was classic Steve. Self-deprecating humor which, no doubt, helped get him through the tough times after his inexplicable loss of control effectively ended his career. The crowd, many of them bankers and executives imbibing glasses of Chardonnay and nibbling on catered hors d'oeuvres, loved him.

From there, a quick change of clothes into jeans, a T-shirt, and baseball cap and it was off to a "smoker" at a VFW Hall, filled to capacity with salt-of-the-earth, blue-collared men throwing back beer in plastic cups and chewing on dirty-water dogs, potato chips, and pretzels. If its working-class feel seemed like a scene out of *The Deer Hunter*, there was a reason for it. This event took place just a town away from Clairton, the setting of that Oscar-winning film. His act and language up on the dais was "colorful," which fit in perfectly with the other guest speakers and gritty crowd.

After Steve's requisite off-color jokes and stories were uproariously embraced by the all-male crowd, the emcee opened the event up for a question-and-answer session. The subject turned to the Pirates. Steve, ever the chameleon, now turned serious. He became all business and began breaking down the reasons why his beloved Buccos' promising summer was shot down in August.

The guys in the flannel shirts, jeans, and work boots loved him, just like the previous crowd of men in Brooks Brothers suits and women dressed in Ann Taylor. Of course they did. He was one of them. They were not unlike the dozens that I had interviewed in person or by phone about different portions of Steve's life. People who had played with him, worked with him, or had been touched by him in some way. Steve always seems to know exactly the right thing to say in any given situation. And he loves every minute of being the unofficial ambassador of the Pirates.

It could certainly have gone very differently for Steve. He loved every single thing about being a major league baseball player. And then, completely without warning, the All-Star and World Series hero could no longer find the strike zone in the prime of his career. In the decades that followed, whenever a pitcher or position player would have similar bouts of wildness, "Steve Blass Disease" was the diagnosis given by the baseball world.

It would have driven many men off the edge. It could have been tragic. But not for Steve, who was able to pull himself out of his self-proclaimed abyss and reinvent himself as a beloved broadcaster and better man than before.

Inspirational?

You bet.

Erik Sherman

CHAPTER 1

They Named a Disease After Me

"Warm up Blass. You're going in the game," pitching coach Mel Wright hollered over to me in the Pirates' bullpen on a typically balmy June night game in Atlanta's Fulton County Stadium.

Entering a ballgame in the fifth inning of a blowout was a strange thing for me, but these were strange days, indeed. Our manager, Bill Virdon, thought that maybe I might start pitching better again with some time out of the bullpen. No time to think, just go out there and pitch. So far, other experiments were not helping. I was inconsistent at best.

But on this particular night, my plight took a horrendous turn. I was no longer just walking guys or hitting batters or getting hit hard. I was throwing the ball in back of hitters and behind their heads. It was just god-awful. My night's pitching line: six walks, three wild pitches, and five hits in 1⅓ innings pitched. We mercifully got through that game, an 18–3 loss, but for me, it was just a horrific experience.

I was numb on the flight to Cincinnati after the game. We landed, and I went up to my room, dropped off my luggage, then walked the streets of Cincinnati all night thinking, *What the hell is this? What is going on?* In just a few weeks, I had gone from All-Star pitcher to bad starter to going to the bullpen and pitching badly. I got to thinking, *Well, where the hell do I go from here? This bullpen shit ain't working.*

I just walked the streets and wandered around. And this wasn't the first time. But this was certainly the bottom of the descent. The abyss.

Less than a year after finishing second in the Cy Young voting and less than two years after finishing off the mighty Baltimore Orioles with my second complete game win of the 1971 World Series, I was lost as a pitcher. Just dangling. Now the doubt was there. What is causing this? Am I going to get out of this? I was starting to feel anxious about going out on the mound. When I first started to struggle with the control, I thought, *Well alright, let's work it out.*

But now I had anxiety. Now I wasn't sure if I *wanted* to go out there. I had always lived a life of anticipation. I have always been excited about the next adventure, the next movie, the next ballgame, or the next experience. Now that anticipation, which was always a big part of my life, was being taken away from me.

The anticipation was my energy, my joie de vivre. When I was pitching well, on days I wasn't starting I still looked forward to going to the ballpark to shag some fly balls or fuck around with the guys in the clubhouse. We were all going to have a good time. On days that I did pitch, I had always counted the minutes until I could get out on the mound.

Now, it was different. I might go to have a good time, but it was almost like I was fraudulent. I was entertaining my teammates because I didn't want them to see me changing. So I masked it and tried to be exactly the same, knowing underneath that I wasn't having that much fun. I didn't think I was that funny anymore. I would drive home thinking, *Ah, you fuckin' fraud.* It was a kind of self-loathing. I thought, *Why am I doing it? I'm playing this game. Am I doing it for myself? Am I doing it for my teammates?*

I felt the need to be the life of the clubhouse, but I didn't feel great about doing it. It was like being on a train going down a track. I couldn't slow it down. It was out of control. But I was still on the train.

It was a different feeling for me than I had ever experienced before. I don't characterize it as fear, although maybe it was. I was very anxious about going out there when I knew I shouldn't be pitching in major league games. I was embarrassed and humiliated. Those are the worst two things a professional athlete can ever experience. I had hit the absolute bottom. I went out to pitch to an avalanche of doubt.

What a mind-boggling turn of events from the season before. I was very confident in my control in 1972. I had that string of good years starting in 1966. It was a hoot for me. I was having the time of my life. I expected to win. It was fun. I felt, to a degree, that I had mastered my craft. So I went out to the mound every fifth day, and knew I was going to do well. It wasn't going to be there every time out, but it was going to be there most nights. I was going to win a lot of games. I was going to pitch well. And I never had any health issues. That was never lurking in the back of my mind. I was throwing all my pitches the way I wanted to.

Hell, I won 19 games out of 32 starts. I might have won 25, but Bill was using five starters, somewhat of a novelty in the days of the four-man rotation. Bill's predecessor, Danny Murtaugh, felt the same way, believing that if he had five starters to count on, they would be fresher in September. We had no reason to argue with them, because the strategy worked.

Our Pirates ballclub was a very good baseball team. We were coming off a world championship and were pretty much still intact. Bill said it was the best baseball team he had been around, and he was with the Pirates, Yankees, Expos, and Astros as a player, manager, or coach. After a couple of Scotches, I tried to make him admit we might have kicked his 1960 world champion Pirates' ass. But it took a lot of Scotches. He was reluctant to admit that.

There was a brief strike at the beginning of 1972 and, hell, the last thing we wanted was to not get started on time. During the strike, I went home and threw some batting practice to some kids at my old school, Housatonic Regional High. That was so much fun! I felt like a million bucks. I felt like a conquering hero coming back to my high school, pitching off the mound, showing them what I was doing while pitching batting practice to them. But it was still a delay I wasn't really happy about.

One of the best things about the 1972 season was that we did not hope to win—we expected to win. During the 1971 season, we were finding out how good we were. In '72, we knew how good we were. That made a huge difference in how we approached the game. It was probably my most consistent year because I thought I pitched well from beginning to end. It was a wonderful ride, a breeze for me on the baseball field.

It was also a great year off the field. It was the year my wife Karen and I decided to move permanently to Pittsburgh with our two boys, David and Chris. For seven years, I had spent the off-season at our primary residence in Connecticut, and then it was off to spring training in Florida for two months, followed by the six-month regular season in Pittsburgh. Karen and I felt that once both the kids reached school age, making a permanent home in Pittsburgh made sense.

The genesis of the move came when I received an early-morning phone call one day at my room at the Viking Inn in Pittsburgh from our closer Dave Giusti's wife, Ginny. She told me that their friends down the street had been transferred and they were selling their house. I called Karen and told her to come to Pittsburgh and we did a great deal of house hunting. After all was said and done, we told the Giustis over dinner that we were going to take their friends' house. So everything was going so well in '72 that we actually found a house four homes away from Dave and Ginny, who remain our neighbors and dear friends to this day.

By mid-season, I was going to my first All-Star Game. What a great experience that was. We had a bunch of guys who went down to Atlanta, including Roberto Clemente, Willie Stargell, Al Oliver, and Manny Sanguillen. The night before the game, Karen and I had dinner with Roberto and Vera Clemente down in an area of the city called Underground Atlanta. We had never had dinner together before as couples. An "honor" is too strong a word to describe it, but it was really neat to go out and have dinner with Mr. and Mrs. Clemente. That sounds kind of simple, but it was truly a big deal for us. It was also a validation for me of sorts, because being invited out by the Clementes for dinner made the steak "prime" instead of "choice." It made the All-Star experience pretty sweet.

Another great memory about going for the first time was to walk into a clubhouse with a major league All-Star team. I'm walking in and there's Tom Seaver, Steve Carlton, Johnny Bench, Tony Perez, Billy Williams, and all these great, great players. Walking into that National League All-Star clubhouse was one of the neatest things I had ever experienced. Then, later, to go out in the bullpen and see Ferguson Jenkins and all these other All-Stars like Bob Gibson was surreal. It was like a fantasy land.

Before the game, I sat down by my locker, and Bench came over and said, "Steve, I understand you're pitching in the third inning. What signs do you want to use?"

I said, "Well, Johnny, every time I pitch against you, you seem to know what's coming, so why don't we just wing it?" We both had a good laugh.

When I entered the game in the third inning, I was both nervous and excited. I was throwing the ball all over the place and immediately walked Bill Freehan, the first hitter I faced. Thankfully, the pitcher's spot was next, and Jim Palmer sacrifice bunted Freehan to second. The great Rod Carew then ripped a single to center to score Freehan. I got out of the inning after Bobby Murcer lined a bullet to our first baseman, Lee May, who stepped on first to double up Carew to end the frame. On the walk to the dugout I said, "Whoa! These guys are good!"

After the game, a 4–3 National League victory in 10 innings, I found out that NBC had some technical difficulties and never showed the third inning. So, to this day, a lot of my relatives joke with me that they don't believe that I actually pitched in an All-Star Game.

The 1972 season continued to go very well for the Bucs the rest of the regular season, as we cruised to the National League East division crown by 11 games over the second-place Cubs. I even had a chance to be a 20-game winner. I had 19 wins going into my last start against the Mets at Three Rivers Stadium. But in the very first inning, John Milner hit a line drive right off the tip of my elbow. That scared the hell out of me. When you get hit by a batted ball and get hit on soft tissue, there is going to be bruising, and you are going to miss a lot of time. That happened to me when Joe Torre hit me on the soft tissue slightly below the elbow, bruised it badly, and I missed five weeks. But if you are hit on a bone, like Milner's shot off my elbow, it is either going to break the bone or you will be able to pitch soon after that because there is not the swelling that comes with the soft tissue damage.

I went to the hospital for X-rays, but they showed that it wasn't broken. I was so close to seeing my season end right then and there in a meaningless, playing-out-the-string kind of game just days before the playoffs were to begin. When I did come back to the clubhouse from the hospital, I had trainer Tony Bartirome bandage me up from head to toe like I had been in a train wreck. I waited in the clubhouse until after the game, and the beat writers came in and asked me, "How are you? How did it go at the hospital?"

I just stood there like I had fallen out of an airplane, all bundled, wrapped, and bandaged up with stuff around my head. You know, you have to have a little fun. And I can't help myself. I have to entertain. It's what I do.

As for the shot at what would have been my first and only 20-win season, I probably was not going to get it anyway because when Milner hit me, we were already losing 3–0. I didn't win my 20th, but going into the playoffs you are fueled by the fact that you proved what you are capable of doing.

I didn't miss any time. I would pitch Game 1 of the NLCS six days later against the Cincinnati Reds in Pittsburgh. Going into that series against the Big Red Machine, we didn't just think we would do well; we knew we would because of what we did the previous year. Confidence is great, but it has to be backed up by success, not the reverse. If it isn't backed up, then it is just a word. You've got to have a degree of confidence to be successful, but to really have true confidence you must have succeeded. So I think success comes before confidence, because now you know you can instead of thinking you can. So we felt good because we had won the World Series the year before and thought we could match up favorably with the Reds.

As both a player and a fan of the game, I always enjoyed playing the Reds. Pete Rose said it best, calling the Reds-Pirates games of the 1970s the highest quality brand of baseball he had ever been around. Regardless of what one thinks of Pete Rose, he knows the game. And he doesn't just remember every hit he ever got but probably every *pitch* he ever saw. Rose and I had battled one another for years by that point.

Years later, when I was broadcasting, I had a wonderful series of interviews called, "Blass' Best." When Rose was managing the Reds, I had him on the show one Saturday afternoon right around home plate at Riverfront Stadium. He was giving a bunch of cliché answers and going through the motions when finally I got to the end and said, "Well, Pete, I want to ask you something to test your memory here," knowing full well he remembered every pitch he ever saw.

I said, "Do you know how many people struck you out three times in one game?"

Rose said, "Two."

And I said, "Yeah, I was one of them."

Rose shot back, "Yeah, but on an *NBC Game of the Week*, I got four hits off you on four different kinds of pitches." Rose started getting animated, and that's when the interview got great. He had total recall of his career. He was also one of the few players whom I made sure my boys came to see because he played the game the way it was supposed to be played.

Rose and I are from a bygone era. The No. 1 thing on my pet peeve list today is fraternization. I always respected Rose and other opponents, but I never felt like I wanted to have a lot to do with them or make them my best friends. I was trying to beat them. Friendships and relationships were for later on.

I went out to pitch Game 1, and the second batter I faced was Joe Morgan. I had two fastballs in my repertoire, a sinking fastball and a riding fastball. I threw Morgan a sinking fastball down and away, and he turned it back around and hit a home run to right-center. After he pulled my fastball like that I said to myself, *Oh shit. Is this what they're going to do with my fastball today?* So for the next seven-plus innings, they probably saw about five fastballs. What they mostly saw the rest of the way from me was a variety of sliders and slop-shit, change-ups and curveballs, to the point where Rose was hollering out of their dugout, "Eat a fucking steak. Throw the ball like a man." That game was a good example of my ability to adapt to a good fastball-hitting team. I wound up going eight and a third innings and winning 5–1. That Morgan home run was the only run they got off me.

The most valuable lesson I learned about pitching in the postseason was in Game 1 of the 1971 NLCS against the San Francisco Giants. I had a good year and we made it to the playoffs, but I had not pitched at all in the playoffs in 1970 and had no postseason pitching experience. But in the 1971 NLCS, I started the first game. I thought I had to be better than I was in the regular season because it was postseason, but that was a trap, as I tried to do things I wasn't capable of doing. The Giants just kicked my ass all over the field in both starts that I had, so in the World Series I went back to being myself and pitched well, winning both games.

Going into the '72 playoffs, I told myself, *Well, alright, you learned your lesson in the '71 NLCS. Don't try to be Superman, because that's not your style of pitching.* So I prepared like I did in the regular season and tried not to do too much. Plus, I had pitched a lot against the Reds. They were a great fastball-hitting team. I knew what they were capable of doing and I knew what I was capable of doing, so the preparation wasn't any different because of the lesson I had learned in '71.

We were on the verge of knocking off the Reds and advancing to our second straight World Series appearance in Game 5 when we went into the bottom of the ninth inning with a 3–2 lead. I had pitched into the eighth inning, having given up just four hits before being relieved by Ramon Hernandez, who got the final two outs of the inning. Giusti was brought in in the ninth to slam the door on the Reds. Giusti was perhaps the best closer in the game at that time. In '71, he had the most saves in the National League and in '72 had a 1.93 ERA, the lowest of his great career.

Bench led off the inning for the Reds and promptly slammed a home run to tie the game and send the Riverfront Stadium crowd into a frenzy. Perez followed with a single up the middle, and after Denis Menke singled to left, Virdon took the ball from Giusti and summoned Bob Moose. Moose would retire the next two hitters before facing Hal McRae with runners on the corners. We were praying for extra innings. But that was not to be after Moose threw a wild pitch that scored pinch runner George Foster from third to give the Reds the National League championship.

Nobody felt worse than Dave. It was gut-wrenching for him. Dave has always known how I feel about his contributions to our ballclub, the saves he got, and the way he shut down ballgames. Dave had very decent major league stuff but was not overpowering. However, Dave was as mentally tough when a ballgame was on the line as anybody I have ever been around.

On Clemente's recommendation to Joe Brown, Dave came to us from St. Louis after scuffling through a mediocre 1969 season. He didn't pitch very much with the Cardinals, but he certainly found a home with us. He started off as just kind of a long man in the bullpen, but when closer Chuck Hartenstein struggled, Dave got his chance in that role and the rest is history.

His signature pitch was the palm ball, a devastating off-speed pitch, and he could make it do whatever he wanted to. In both the playoffs and World Series in '71, nobody scored on him in seven appearances. Zero runs. So he knew how we felt about him. After he gave up the home run to Bench, some of us on the Pirates reminded him that those things happen. But we as teammates can be a little more objective because all of us had had ups and downs of our own.

Perhaps in this case his was tremendously dramatic, but we all felt like he was The Man in our bullpen. He was our closer, and you don't take your closers lightly. Still, we were all horribly disappointed in the clubhouse. That's when Clemente came in and told us, "Get your fucking heads up! We had a great year!"

Clemente then went around to everybody's locker to congratulate them on what a great season we all had. As it turned out, that would be the great Clemente's last game he would ever play, as he would die tragically in a plane crash on a mission to deliver food and relief supplies to earthquake-torn Nicaragua less than three months later.

Despite our best efforts, Dave was almost inconsolable for a while. The team flew home, and I had my car there at the airport. Dave, his wife Ginny, Karen, and I drove back to Upper St. Clair from the airport. In the car there was both silence and anger. Nobody said anything.

Finally, I decided that being pissed about the Series loss wasn't helping anybody. So I pulled up to a red light in Mt. Lebanon and yelled, "Fire drill!" We all got out of the car, running around it, screaming every obscenity we had ever heard in the early hours of the morning. Mt.

Lebanon was the adjoining township to Upper St. Clair, and I picked that area for the fire drill because I didn't know if that kind of behavior was allowed in Upper St. Clair. Anyway, just before we got out of Mt. Lebanon, we did some really good work to relieve the tension of that dreadful Game 5. We all felt much better.

I couldn't wait for the winter to pass and for spring training to begin. Nobody loved the baseball life more than I did. I don't remember details or my numbers, but spring training in 1973 would be one of the best I ever had. I wasn't used to having good springs. At that point in my career, I was just trying to get in shape. I knew I was a good pitcher. I had proven that by having several good years in a row. The stats bear it out. Between '68 and '72, I won 78 games. That's an average of a little better than 15 wins a year. But that was a particularly good spring. I thought, *Okay, maybe I am going to just start having good springs instead of just pissing around.*

After the season started, however, I was not as sharp or consistently as good as I was in Florida. It was not bad at the beginning by any stretch, and my struggles were more of a gradual decline. I had had slumps before. I didn't have any particular anxiety early in the season, and I don't remember a particular game. The only statistic I remember early on before things got bad was that I had a record of 3–3 with one complete game on June 1. Every pitcher gets knocked around. I know I didn't walk 10 guys in those early games, so I thought, *Okay, it's not working right now, but we'll get it straightened out. We'll be fine.*

Back in 1968, on June 1 I was 1–2, but I wound up being 18–6. I had been through times when I wasn't doing a heck of a lot, so there was no panic in those early games. *Just keep throwing and it'll click. It'll take care of itself,* I kept telling myself.

I wasn't a kid. I had been around a long time, so I might have to tweak something in my pitching delivery. I might have been dropping down a bit or some other mechanical thing. I usually could find that kind of stuff in the bullpen between starts. So I kept reminding myself as the season progressed, *Okay, I'm not pitching well right now, but it'll come. We'll be fine.*

What followed was what proved to be a fateful trip to Atlanta for a three-game series with the Braves. I started the opening game on a

Monday night, and when I wasn't walking Braves hitters, they were hitting my strikes real hard. Bill came to get me during the fourth inning after retiring just one hitter. I had given up five runs on eight hits and two walks on the night. Following the game, Bill decided to experiment by putting me in the bullpen. Two nights later, on June 13, a complete meltdown left me with no answers.

Bill, like Murtaugh, was a big supporter of mine. Having won 19 games for Bill the year before, he showed a great deal of patience in me before moving me to the bullpen. As a matter of fact, Virdon had waited until my ERA climbed to 8.50 following my Monday night start. Because he had watched me over the years, he wasn't going to send me to the bullpen unless he was convinced that it was just the right thing to do. By the time he sent me to the bullpen, I couldn't have agreed with him more. One of the first things you did with a struggling starter back then was put him in the 'pen. The theory was: put him in the bullpen and don't give him so much time between starts to worry or wonder.

Because I never had arm problems, the thinking was that my issue was between the ears. Pitchers can be a little bit like kickers or free throw shooters. The game stops until they attempt a field goal, shoot a foul shot, or pitch the ball. You are on your own out there, and if you let negative things get in your mind, it can greatly affect your performance.

Mel Wright and our first-base coach, Don Leppert, were roommates on the road in 1973 and would stay up nights at the edge of their beds discussing my control problems. They both watched videotapes of the two wins I got in the 1971 Series literally more than 100 times, trying to find the smallest of differences in the way I pitched. They analyzed them to no end. If my cap was a little bit off to the side, they took note. It got to be ridiculous, but because they cared so much about me, they did everything they could. Like "Lep" would say years later, "If you were a prick, we wouldn't have worked so hard to get you right again."

Bill had brought Mel in as pitching coach that spring. I got along very well with him. My theory up until I started pitching badly was that by the time you got three, four, or five years in the big leagues and you're successful, you're almost your own pitching coach. You can recognize most of what you need to do for tinkering or adjustments, and you know what's happening when you're not pitching well. You have a pretty good handle on that yourself, so when Mel came in, I had no problem with him. I had a good sense of what I was doing.

When I began to struggle, he was tireless in working with me. I couldn't have had a better guy in my corner trying to help me figure my problems out. He passed away many years ago, but every time I see Bill, I tell him that Mel had nothing to do with my situation and nobody could have worked harder with me to try to get it turned around. Mel and I both had the same philosophy. *Let's try everything, because you don't want to be sitting on a chair on a back porch when you're 85 years old saying, "Boy, I wonder why we didn't try this? It might have made a difference."* The solution to my problems might have been one small thing that clicked and my troubles would have been gone. So, we did everything. What made it tough for Mel in his attempts to help me was the fact I had always pitched on gut instincts and by the seat of my pants. I was never a "method" pitcher, so when I went bad, I had no set of standard mechanics to come back to and maybe break down in sections.

A week went by before I came into another game, another relief appearance, this time against the Cubs. I had always pitched very well against the Cubs in my career and actually did relatively well in this outing, giving up just two hits and not walking anyone in two innings of work. We lost the game 5–3, but my stint earned me a start two nights later against the Mets. I saw it as a potential step forward and something to build on. That hope proved to be short-lived as I lasted only 1⅔ innings after giving up five runs on seven hits and two walks in a 5–4 loss.

Over the next month and a half or so, Bill would start me two more times with similar results. In both of my losses to the Cardinals and Mets, I walked four batters in one inning, and I didn't make it past the third inning in either game.

I was trying hard to figure everything out and what was happening to me. I didn't want to dump it all on my family or my teammates. There were a lot of nights when I would just come home and sit in the backyard, wondering why all this stuff was going on and what was happening. I'd try to find out in quiet times if I could sort it all out, but I just couldn't do it. There were some nights where it was emotional, tears coming down my cheeks, because I was thinking this might be it. I might not be a Pittsburgh Pirate anymore.

I started thinking about all the good times my teammates and I had had winning a World Series together. Or my life way back in the minor leagues. It might all be over. That made me very sad.

One of the things I regret about that whole period was not opening up more to Karen. Even if I knew I couldn't pitch anymore, it would have helped both of us if I had shared more of my thoughts with her. She had little idea of what was going on with me. I was so internal and angry. I was thinking about getting rid of my bathroom mirror because I didn't like what I saw. At the time, I didn't think anybody could understand what I was going through because I figured if I didn't understand it, how the hell could anybody else? I had trouble imagining what I could say to them.

Karen told me, in later years, that watching my pitching career unravel was the toughest thing she ever witnessed. On the rare occasions when we did talk about it, she became very emotional. That was another reason I wouldn't bring up the subject and would internalize instead. It was a Catch-22. I didn't want to make her sad, but if I didn't tell her, it brought about confusion.

Having these pitching woes was far worse at Three Rivers Stadium games because I knew people at the ballpark and around the city. Plus, the whole setting was so familiar for me, the site of so much glory in the recent past. When I pitched badly, there was some light booing, the occasional mock cheering, but mostly silence. I think people felt sorry for me, and that bothered me. You don't want to be embarrassed, and you don't want people feeling sorry for you.

Baseball is supposed to be a fun game. You're not supposed to be feeling sorry for a major leaguer. That was another negative for me when it was going badly. Having people feel sorry for me was just as bad as getting booed. I felt horrible pitching at home knowing that I shouldn't be out there, but I wasn't giving up yet. I was still trying. I was caught in an emotional crossfire. You want to go out and keep trying, but you know you shouldn't be out there, and the fans deserved more than what I was producing.

It got to the point where I didn't want to go to the grocery store, didn't want to go out, because I was so humiliated. Despite all of these troubles, the Pirates' fans were terrific to me. Throughout this gray period, I received around 100 letters of support per week, four-leaf clovers, crosses, all kinds of things. Hardly anything negative. That made me feel a little better about things. That told me I had been decent to people when it was going good. I never held myself any higher than I should have.

There was a guy from Virginia who sent me a letter, and it said, "Steve, I'm a great hunter. My aim is always perfect. The only time my aim is off is when my underwear is too tight." I showed all my teammates, and they all laughed like hell. But you better believe I went out and bought some loose underwear.

I tried to keep my outside demeanor the same throughout this period. It wasn't easy. I wasn't as comfortable because I was hurting so much inside. But I tried. I wanted to be that same person for them. I made an ass of myself like I always had. But life in the clubhouse and in the dugout was funnier and more fun when I was pitching well.

Being on the road was, perhaps, a little easier. On the road, it was kind of quiet when I struggled because the worse I got, the better the opposing team did. There was certainly no booing as I started walking or hitting their hitters. Fans on the road were never like the people at the Roman Coliseum rooting for the lions against the Christians. It was strangely quiet, a display of indifference to my struggles. I could also get out more with my roomie and drinking buddy Dave Giusti. Even when it was going good, we would go out and grab a couple of beers after road games. That was pretty standard procedure.

But at this point more than ever, Dave felt trying to get me drunk was especially important to ease some of the pain I was going through emotionally. The problem was, Dave would always get drunk first. But I always made sure I caught up with him. Dave was with me every night on the road, and I will never forget his support and friendship. It sounds funny to be grateful for getting drunk, but it did get me away from the whole situation for a few hours. Of course, the drinking certainly never solved any of my problems.

I got a chance to start in the annual Hall of Fame Game at Doubleday Field in Cooperstown, and the result was just awful. It didn't seem to make a difference where I was pitching or against whom. Sixty feet six inches was the monster in game situations. After that exhibition game, Bill announced I would be working out of the bullpen for the remainder of the season. I was going to the ballpark every day standing in the bullpen dreading that I'd get into a ballgame. I would have gone in, but I was dreading it because I felt I didn't belong out there and would hurt the team.

A little more than a month after Bill's announcement, in early September, he was fired by general manager Joe Brown. Murtaugh was brought back to manage the club for the third time in his career. The Pirates may have been playing only around .500 baseball, but we were still only three games out when the decision was made. It was a surprising move to make in the thick of a pennant race.

One of the reasons Bill got fired in 1973 was that Joe Brown thought Murtaugh could rescue me. When Murtaugh came back, he had me start right away. I kid with Bill about a lot of things. We'll go to dinners now and I'll say, "Bill Virdon's here and, you know, Bill, if you had kept me in the rotation, I'd still be pitching." Well, of course, that is bullshit. We have so much respect for each other that we can joke about it all now. The fact is that Bill supported me as much as Murtaugh did because he knew how hard I was trying. Bill is one guy that if he knows you are giving him all your efforts, you would never have a problem. It sounds like a cliché, but he respects a player who gives maximum effort more than anything.

Taking me out of the rotation was tough for him for another reason. He knew what I was capable of doing. Hell, I won 19 games for him in 1972. He didn't want to quit on me. I am sure he agonized over the decision. But that's all he could do, and I'm sure he was aware that part of the reason he was let go was because Joe Brown thought Murtaugh could pull a miracle out of his hat. Otherwise, you wouldn't fire a manager who is three games out in September.

Joe Brown always had faith that Danny Murtaugh could bring a spark to the ballclub because he had done it before, like when he came back out of retirement to guide us to the 1971 championship. Brown and Murtaugh were friends to the point where I almost had the feeling that Joe said, "Danny, do you want to do this? Can you come back and help me?" Or Danny would come to Joe and ask, "Do you need my help?" They had that kind of relationship.

Murtaugh started me on September 11, a 2–0 loss to the Cubs. I went five innings, walking five, but gave up only two hits and one earned run, easily my best start since the beginning of the season and one that offered a glimmer of hope.

That hope was shattered again 10 days later at Shea Stadium. We had battled all season long from being a season-high 11 games out of first place as late as June 29 to enter this huge game against Tom Seaver in first place by one-half game. It was a golden opportunity for me to win another big late-season game. But it was not to be. I never made it out of the first inning, yielding four hits and a walk and leaving the game down 4–0. The Pirates would not see first place again for the rest of the season and would finish at 80 wins and 82 losses, two and one-half games behind the Mets. Later in life, Joe Brown would say firing Bill was a mistake. Not only did it not turn me around, but it did not help the team, either.

I finished the season at 3–9 with a 9.85 ERA. Had I been anything but awful, we would have easily won the division. *How did it ever come to this?* I thought.

Nothing would ever be worse for me than the 1973 season. The following two years would be numbing. But 1973 was a fresh wound. Shortly after the season ended, I went down to the Instructional League at Pirate City in Bradenton. Toward the end, I called Karen and told her I needed her down there for support because nothing had changed and my wildness continued.

The Instructional League had allowed me the chance to get more game experience in while working on fundamentals in a relaxing setting that wasn't under the scrutiny of a major league schedule. With my pitching still awful, it bothered me more than usual because I'm saying to myself, *If I can't do it down here, it doesn't matter where I am. I could be pitching Little League and it would be the same.*

I was just reinforcing negatives at that point. It's like a golfer who goes out to the driving range and does the wrong things over and over again. If you're not doing anything correct, all you're doing is locking in the bad shit. It seemed like that was exactly what was happening in my case.

Unlike the year before, I was back home for the winter *not* looking forward to spring training. My concern was not just for myself but also what my problems were doing to the family. I had it in my mind that I didn't want it to disrupt my home life with Karen and the boys. I realize now that there was no way of avoiding it. My problems on the mound had an effect that I wanted badly to minimize. I didn't talk a lot about baseball at home. I thought the less I talked about it, the more I could keep David, Chris, and Karen away from it, so it wouldn't intrude on them too greatly.

I was quiet at home. I had my times of rage in the beginning, throwing things and breaking things, but never at home. My rage took place at the ballpark, in the car, or at a bar when I started drinking too much. I tried to protect my family as best as I could. Looking back, there was no way I could completely protect them because my downfall was out there in the headlines.

After David, around 10 years old at the time, got into a fight at his school for defending my honor against a boy who told him that his father thought I was a bum, I had a talk with my boys. I told them that the same kids who wanted to talk to you or who had you come home and get an autograph from me, are not going to be the same. I explained to them that this is how life works. The kids are not trying to be cruel, but it's easy to not be very nice when their own father or some radio or TV host is calling me a bum. People that speak disparagingly like that don't realize how cruel that can be not just to the person they are speaking about but also to their wife and children. Shit happens, and as an adult, I understand that. But it's not as easy for children to process.

From that point on, I tried as hard as I could to leave the baseball crap at the ballpark and play with them. I would take them to the pool, play catch with them, take them to the movies, get involved in their Little League stuff as much as I could, things like that.

I tried harder than anyone could possibly know to keep aspects of that part of my life as normal as possible, knowing that the so-called elephant in the living room was looming over our lives. Despite my efforts, what I was going through on the mound was the start of some very difficult times we had with David. During this period, while both our sons were affected, Chris tended to internalize his struggles like I do, while the issues with David were on the surface. David stopped playing Little League baseball and football, got involved with the wrong crowd, and would start drinking a couple of years later at just 12 years old. He had gone from being a happy kid to becoming a very angry one.

We tried everything, including a psychologist and counseling. We came to realize that his anger, apart from his father going into the tank, was also a combination of the move to Pittsburgh and the shock of leaving a small-town atmosphere where everyone knew everybody to being thrown into this high-end suburb with many more people, many more kids in class, and exposure to more temptations.

His anger issues escalated over the next three years, and we reached the point where we told him we had to change his environment. It was heartbreaking to tell your son, at age 15, that he can't live with his family anymore. But, in hindsight, it was the right move.

We sent him to stay for the summer at my Uncle Bill's place back in Falls Village, where I had grown up. Through Uncle Bill, he ended up working on a farm for a guy named Bill Holcomb, who had two or three other boys working there and had zero tolerance for any bullshit. He then came back to attend Linsly, a small private school in West Virginia, for two years, and worked his way back to Upper St. Clair High School to graduate with his class. David, to this day, feels that Reno DiOrio, the headmaster at Linsly, had a significant impact on his life.

The entire experience helped change his life. I am so proud of David that he got on the other side of his problems without doing some real damage to his life. He is now one of the hardest workers I have ever known.

I went down to Bradenton, Florida, for spring training in 1974 looking for answers from wherever and whomever I could find them. I tried every possible remedy for my control problems. There were times when we had two projectors showing me pitching good and showing me pitching bad side-by-side, looking for clues on how to improve my mechanics. I pitched on my knees. I pitched halfway between home and the mound. I pitched from second base. I tried to pitch from the outfield.

I tried pitching every day in the bullpen as well as a couple of times when I pitched entire ballgames from the bullpen. I would throw when our Pirates pitcher pitched as well as the innings when our Pirates pitcher got up to bat. If our pitcher threw 115 pitches, I threw 115 pitches, plus the number of pitches it took in the half-innings he batted for the Pirates.

I tried pitching after not even picking up a ball for 10 days.

I saw Dr. Bill Harrison, a hypnotist, and took part in his visualization program that he used with the Kansas City Royals and some golfers, actually staying in his home in Davis, California, for a week. Basically, with Dr. Harrison's help, I visualized the ball going where I wanted it to go out of my hand. That's kind of an oversimplification of the technique, but at least it got me to try to pitch correctly again. Although I saw credence in that, it ultimately was not the answer.

Dodgers great Maury Wills suggested I see Dr. Arthur Ellen, a psychologist in L.A., who had worked with his teammate, Hall of Fame pitcher Don Sutton. I went out and worked a few days with Dr. Ellen, but nothing we did helped.

The Pirates tried everything we were aware of back then. I jokingly tell people now that if this happened to me today, I would just take my ass up to the Harvard Medical School and say, "Here I am boys, fix me." Despite all of their efforts, our team trainers and doctors were of no help because there were no physical issues. Trainer Tony Bartirome couldn't have been more supportive and remains one of my best friends today. Hell, he didn't know what to do with me.

Almost 40 years later, I have more of an appreciation of how many different people tried to help me so many different ways. From teammates, to doctors, to psychologists, to friends, to family, I couldn't have the appreciation for them that I have now, because while I was going through it all I was so internalized. Back then, I really had no real perspective of the big picture. All things considered, just two and a half bad years out of a charmed life is pretty good, but I was so deep into this thing I was not able to pull up that perspective. I was so deep inside my own personal abyss that I wasn't able to obtain the perspective that I had later on. I was not able to appreciate that at the time.

Now I wonder how tough it was for my teammates to get ready to play a major league game while dealing with a friend and teammate who was hurting. Do you say a lot? Do you say nothing? Do you kid around? Don't kid around? Do you get angry? Do you not get angry? Do you ignore me? Do you not ignore me? It must have been so frustrating for them all to not know how to help me.

What was so baffling about the whole thing was that I never had any arm problems. Not even in Little League. I can still give full extension of my right arm as well as anybody who pitched for five years can. When I pick up a ball at Pirates Fantasy Camp now, I'll go out there and throw eight innings. Once per year, I pick the ball up and do that. So my issues were clearly in my head.

Joe Brown came up with the concept of giving transcendental meditation a try, which was pretty popular back in that era. It included different forms of relaxation exercises and techniques. He decided to make that a project of his, but rather than have it just spotlighted on me doing it, he collected quite an eclectic group to get involved as well. The group included our team doctor, Dr. Joe Finegold, Willie Stargell, Dave Giusti, Bruce Kison, and Joe himself.

One of the main things needed to get started in transcendental meditation was to make an offering before getting into the actual program. This enabled you to get your mantra, which is a word or phrase to help you relax throughout a 20-minute session. You are supposed to make your offering to the people who are putting this program together for you. It could be a piece of fruit, a flower, or something else to do with nature.

When we found out that we had to bring an offering, Dave, Willie, and I drove out to Anna Maria Island where we were staying. We decided to get some wild flowers growing beside Manatee Avenue on the way to the meditation group event. So here you have Stargell, a future Most Valuable Player and Hall of Famer, rooting around the side of the road through the litter and beer cans trying to find some flowers. Then there was Giusti, a Fireman of the Year reliever, and me, winner of a couple of World Series games, doing the same. We all looked like vagrants. We would have been better dressed if we had those picks and a garbage bag, taking care of the litter.

Anyway, we got our flowers and we all went into the group session individually and got a mantra. Once we had our mantras, we went off by ourselves to a spot in the room and repeated this mantra again and again. It is supposed to be your relaxation exercise. To this day, I still use it when I am not able to sleep or if I want to relax. I find it to be really good and effective.

At the first meeting, the leader began, "Alright, we are all going to close our eyes and repeat our mantra to ourselves for 20 minutes and see where that takes us." Three minutes into the program, Joe Finegold falls asleep and starts snoring. Bruce Kison, always vigilant, out of the corner of his eye sees Finegold sleeping and snoring, so he starts snickering. Now we've got a whole new ballgame. Bruce, during every session we had, which was two or three times a week during that spring training, without fail, would catch Dr. Joe falling asleep, and he would have to try to keep from laughing. After this same scenario played out a few times, it was hard for any of us to concentrate on our mantra because we were waiting for Kison to break up or Finegold to start snoring. So, as a group, it was less effective than we thought it might be.

Yet another approach to fix me, if drastic, was tried by Jim Rooker. Rooker had been with the club only a year, so he and I didn't have the history I had with most of the other Pirates. We had just gotten out of a long spring training workout and stopped to grab a few beers at someplace going out toward Anna Maria Island. It was brutally hot outside, so we moved inside to a bar where it was air conditioned. It felt like 50 degrees in there with the AC pumping.

It may have been the beer talking, but Rooker started trying to bait and antagonize me about my control problems in an attempt to get me pissed off. He thought by making me angry, I wouldn't give a shit anymore and start pitching well again. Rooker ultimately blurted out, "What the fuck is wrong with you?"

Despite the AC blasting, I started sweating like a pig because of my anxiety and frustration over pitching poorly again that spring. He was just amazed that between the strong air conditioning unit and our drinking cold beers that I could possibly be perspiring. Rooker later told me he thought I might slug him because of the wild look in my eyes and all the sweating. Actually, at that very moment in the bar, I was relieved to be away from the ballpark. That would become a continuing theme for me.

Anyway, I calmly looked at him and could only say, "I'm trying, Jim. I'm trying." What Jim didn't realize was that I had gone through rage where I broke things in the clubhouse. Been there, done that. Maybe subconsciously I was starting to accept my fate to a degree at that point. He didn't know I had gone through all that shit where I wanted to tear someone's head off, including my own. It was confronting me every day. I was sitting in there with him having a couple of beers. I didn't want to confront this shit anymore. I came in there wanting to get away from it all.

What baffled many in the organization was how well I pitched in the bullpen. I just dreaded going into games with a hitter in the batter's box. When I was pitching well, I had tunnel vision. Complete focus. Now, everything was bleeding in. With a game on the line, I heard everything. I heard the crowd and became aware of the enormity of pitching in the big leagues. All of a sudden, that shell that I was in when pitching well was gone, shattered, and completely eliminated. I felt completely exposed out there, hearing it all.

There was no focus. I couldn't lock in any longer. So it was all psychological because of how I just let it ride in the bullpen versus what I did in the games. The bullpen was a comfortable place to be. It was a bullpen with no one watching as opposed to being on a pitcher's mound throwing in front of thousands of people. Pitching in front of big crowds became really intimidating to me. So the bullpen was kind of an obscure thing compared to the game. The game was actual competition, whereas the bullpen's not competition. It was more comfortable, so I can accept the fact I pitched better in the bullpen.

It's like being on the driving range at the golf course. Everybody's a scratch player. I was a scratch player in the bullpen. But when I pitched in live games, I stopped believing I could do it anymore. I just locked up physically and psychologically.

Before my control problem, I had the ability to just concentrate on the immediate task at hand, which is a wonderful thing for an athlete. I could block out family, world hunger, or anything that was going on, because of that focus. That focus all went away, and everything was occurring in my mind. I was like an antenna.

During spring training, it is normal for all the pitchers to throw batting practice as a way of getting their work in and helping the hitters get prepared for the season. I was very much aware of the fact that some Pirates wouldn't get in the batting cage against me because they were afraid of getting hit by a pitch. I agreed with them. I understood exactly why someone was reluctant to do that. These were my teammates, and it just made me feel terrible. I didn't resent any of them for it. Instead, I thought, *How far have I fallen when I used to pitch 20 minutes of batting practice to my teammates in spring training without blinking an eye, and now they don't even want to get into the cage to face me?* It was another terrible negative, another spike driven into me.

In fact, the situation of pitching batting practice didn't get any better after the Pirates called me up to the 40 man roster that September after a stint in the minors. Just ask poor Miguel Dilone. Miguel was a very slender, short, and speedy Pirates outfielder who made his major league debut on September 2, 1974. He was used sparingly that month because we were so loaded with talent. There was a time on the road that month when the Pirates wanted me to go out in the morning to whichever ballpark we were going to be playing at and pitch with no one around. I would be out there pitching at 9:00 AM when there was a night game, trying to work through my control problem. Whenever we did this, we needed someone to stand up there at the plate.

It was the manager and the coaches who decided on Miguel facing me, because they were not going to send one of the regulars. It was like,

"Tag! You're it, Miguel! Get in the taxi and get out there." He was the designated target. It's funny now but anything but that then. At 8:30 in the morning, I had to meet whatever coaches I was working with, along with Miguel, and we would get in a cab and go to the ballpark.

Miguel knew he was going to get plunked for about an hour. Not every pitch, but he always had a good chance of getting nailed. So it almost got to the point where I would go down to the lobby at 8:30 and he would be hiding behind a palm tree or something, not wanting to go. But the coaches made him go, just so he could get up there with a bat and, ultimately, get hit several times each time we went out. He was so skinny. I just imagined him going back to the hotel with a bunch of knots on his legs and side. It was almost cruel. I don't know how he feels about me to this day, but he couldn't have been happy those mornings at 8:30, thinking, *Well, here I am, target practice again.*

I was always a cutup in the clubhouse, and I loved that part of big-league life almost as much as the thrill of pitching. I think I helped the club stay loose, and that gave us an edge. Despite all of my troubles that spring, I did a striptease in the clubhouse to the delight of one and confusion of all and got them all going and revved up. But it was more for their benefit then mine. I didn't want them feeling sorry for me. I wanted to try to act as much like I had been in the past so it would be easier on them. I was trying to convey to them that I was still fun to be around.

I finished spring training in 1974 with 25 walks in 14 innings, including a game in which I walked eight in one inning. In that particular game, I think Murtaugh wanted to keep me out there because he thought if I stayed out there long enough, I would get exhausted and something might suddenly click. He never would have done that in the regular season, obviously, but because it was spring training, he was willing to try anything and everything to get me back on track.

As it turned out, I would have plenty of time to rest. Despite losing our first six games of the regular season, I did not see action until the 10th game. Already behind 10–4 to the Cubs at Wrigley, I came into that game in a mop-up role in the bottom of the fourth. Right away, I could not find the plate, walking my first two batters in what would prove to be an omen for how my five innings of work that day would go. My pitching line: five innings pitched, five hits, eight runs (five earned), seven walks, and one wild pitch (which scored a run). The 18–9 loss was followed by a 1–0 defeat the following day, and we flew to New York with a record of 2–9, six games out.

The Pirates' hierarchy had to make some moves to right the ship before the season got away from them. Not long after we arrived at the hotel in New York, Joe Brown asked that I meet with him in his room. He needed my permission, as a veteran player, to send me to Charleston, West Virginia, home of the Pirates' Triple A team. I always had so much respect for Joe, and he always treated me extremely well, so this must have been very hard for him to do. "I don't belong with the Pirates," I told him. "I'm not going to help the Pirates right now. Maybe I can find it in Charleston."

Of course, getting sent down to the minors in what should have been the prime of my career, at age 32, felt like another dagger into my heart. Playing for Charleston was like a carnival. Everywhere I went, it was an easy story for a non–major league town sports writer. I was great copy. It wasn't easy, but I gave those guys time for a couple of reasons. First of all, they were legitimate, honest people trying to do their jobs. You've got to respect that. And second, because of the fact that I had the time for the writers and the media when I was the life of the party and was going good, I figured it was the decent thing to do.

All the interviews were painful, because it was just rehashing the same bad stuff. In the minor leagues, it was all fresh to them, and I was fresh meat. I couldn't blame them for that. I blamed myself for putting myself in that position.

Perhaps the perfect storm between my angst of being in the minors and needing to deal with the media blitz occurred during the depths of my awful season for the Charlies. We had left Charleston one morning on a bus and drove all the way to Toledo, Ohio, where we had a doubleheader. I pitched the first game and was just awful. I started drinking during the second game, just pounding it. I was just so lost.

After the second game was over, I didn't even shower or take my uniform off. I just got on the bus and drank some more. I drank all the way from Toledo to Pawtucket, Rhode Island, halfway across the country and where we had to play the next evening. The bus stopped four or five times on the way and, I guess having drank so much, I collected as much silverware as I could at roadside restaurants, or places we stopped at on the turnpike and the parkway, and stuck them in my uniform.

By the time we got to Pawtucket at around 7:00 AM, it felt like I was in a suit of mail, clinking and clattering. I thought it was hilarious because I was so drunk at the time. As I stepped off the bus, there was a writer and a photographer from *People* magazine whom I had agreed to talk with and get photographed for a story. That's how I greeted them, drunk and clattering, still in my Charleston Charlies uniform filled with silverware. Just ridiculous.

They took pity on me and gave me a couple of hours to go in and shower and shave. The interview went alright. The things I did to maybe get outside of myself, like getting drunk and socking away silverware. It was just awful. Just awful.

Charleston was very, very difficult on Karen and the kids. We wound up renting our house in Pittsburgh to Daryl Patterson, who was pitching for the Pirates. So when I went on the road in Triple A, Karen couldn't go home. She was down there in what was then a chemical town she didn't really care for and was unfamiliar with, with two little kids. I wasn't pitching very well, so it was not really much fun for any of us.

There were, at least, some familiar faces on the Charleston Charlies. There was my brother-in-law and pitcher John Lamb, as well as the Bucs' shortstop the previous three seasons, Jackie Hernandez.

Also on the team was a budding nucleus for the Pirates' next world championship team of 1979, which included John Candelaria, Omar Moreno, Kent Tekulve, and Ed Ott. And last, but not least, a journeyman infielder who would grow up to do some managing, a fellow named Tony La Russa.

Despite my efforts and the coaching staff's best intentions, I was not able to find my control and practically mirrored what I did with the Pirates the previous season by posting a 2–8 record with an ERA of 9.74 and an average of almost two walks per inning. Worse yet, I also hit 16 batters in just 61 innings pitched.

I missed my Pirates' teammates terribly. That I couldn't have the fun that I was used to having with them, making guys laugh and being a good teammate, absolutely broke my heart. Nobody ever had more fun in the majors than I did. And I hated that it was being taken away from me by this control problem I could not fix. It was almost like the pitching was secondary to how much fun I had. The joy I had was doing exactly what I wanted to be doing, playing major league baseball. I went home to Pittsburgh following the season at Charleston hurting deeply, contemplating my next move. I had a lot of time to reflect and to search for the reasons why this gut-wrenching reversal of fortune could happen.

There were several popular theories out there. The most universally accepted of them was an effect that the sudden death of Roberto had on me. I gave the eulogy at his funeral in what was an incredibly trying time for the entire organization. Roberto and I were friends, but we were not best buddies. However, with Roberto gone, I started wondering if it meant I needed to take on more of a leadership role to fill his large void, to become sort of a figurehead. But then there were Stargell and other vocal stars like Al Oliver and Richie Hebner. We still had a great ballclub with great leaders. So I was able to dismiss this theory.

Another theory was that I must have hit a batter really badly in 1972, and it subconsciously had made me afraid to hit another one. Well, I actually did hit Brooks Robinson with a pitch during spring training in '72. We had gone over to Miami to play the Orioles the spring after we played them in the World Series. Brooks was up, and I hit him right in the helmet with a fastball. He was down on the ground, and we all came running in to make sure he was okay.

Brooks told us, "Okay, I'll get up."

I said, "Goddammit, stay down there. People won't think I have a decent fastball if you get right up."

We didn't start that banter until we knew, of course, that he was alright. But even if there was another time that I hit a batter with a pitch and injured him, I consistently pitched so well that whole regular and postseason in 1972 that it certainly had no effect.

Superstitious theorists believed my problems were related to the infamous *Sports Illustrated* jinx, because I appeared on the cover during the '72 season. But that's bullshit. Plenty of athletes have appeared on the cover numerous times without seeing their abilities diminish.

Besides the theories, there were also rumors flying around as to what was causing my wildness. One of them was that Karen was having an affair, which was complete bullshit and completely groundless. I knew better than that. I've known her my entire life. Another was about problems I was allegedly having with my parents. I absolutely loved my mother and father, but that gives you an idea of the groundless stuff, like with the affair.

And then there was the sore arm rumor, but I never had a sore arm in my life.

Danny, Joe Brown, and I had decided that we were going to give it one more shot in spring training in 1975. It would be a group decision as to how it was going to play out. If we got things right, obviously things would move on. But if things continued to go badly, it would be a group decision and we would shut it down.

As usual, I was in good shape, and my arm felt strong. Murtaugh was going to give me a shot to start an exhibition game. The game was against the White Sox, and it was just another one of those awful performances. I pitched into the third inning, having walked eight batters, when Murtaugh came out to the mound to get me.

On his way back to the dugout, he just started screaming at the home plate umpire and got himself ejected. He argued balls and strikes until he got thrown out, whether he truly felt I had gotten squeezed by the umpire or not. His getting tossed was a personal gesture to me, I feel to this day, from Danny. Managers don't ever get thrown out of spring training games.

Roland Hemond was the general manager of the White Sox and would call it the saddest thing he'd ever seen in baseball.

After that game, I spoke to Danny and Joe and said, "Uncle. I've had enough. I don't want to go through it anymore." I had decided to shut it down. I was succumbing to what would later become a part of the

American lexicon—*Steve Blass Disease*, the inexplicable loss of control when throwing a baseball.

Karen and the boys were there in Bradenton with me. In spring training, it's so casual. Like so many times before, the boys met me at the end of the grandstand down the right-field line after I got through pitching and walked with me until we got to the clubhouse. On the occasion of this last game, Karen and I left with my back to the ballpark, with my sons on each side of me, holding my hands. And that was my last walk out of a major league setting, with my wife and two little toe-head sons with me, walking away from the game, as it were.

The next day, I requested a team meeting from Joe and Danny. I said, "I need to tell them personally. I don't want them to hear it or read about it from you guys."

Joe and Danny assembled the team in the lunch room. I addressed them by saying, "You guys mean the world to me. You were in my corner the whole way; I can't thank you enough for how tall you have all stood for me. I will never forget the help and support you've given me."

I didn't want it to be long. I just wanted to express how much they meant to me and what their support had meant to me going through all this. I wanted them to go about their business, because they were still going to be Pirates and I was moving on. Reaction from my teammates varied. Some actually wept. Others were completely solemn, like at a funeral. A few of them actually waited for a punch line. I can understand some of them thinking that because I was always coming up with some crazy shit, trying to be funny.

All I was doing was just trying to get through it, to let them know personally that I was leaving the game. I was just so broken-hearted I was going to be left out. I wasn't going to have the fun I had always had or be a part of that group any longer. I knew they were good, so I wasn't thinking about team results. I was thinking about relationships and how this was the end. This team and game were a huge part of my life, and it was going to be over. It was devastating. And it was devastating making that decision. It was even more devastating after the meeting thinking how much I was going to miss everything about baseball life.

Leading up to the farewell address, I didn't want any more pain. I didn't want to hurt anymore. So from that standpoint, I thought, *Okay, I'm going to make this decision because I'm going to feel better afterward.* But I didn't feel a helluva lot better afterward because I wasn't going to be doing something that I had done all my life. Nobody had more fun than I had doing it.

Before I made that final decision, I kept thinking whether there were things I could do to review my mechanics. The whole thing crystallized to me that I always pitched by gut instinct.

I didn't go *Step A: here's my set of mechanics, Step B: here's my release, and Step C: here's my arm slot.* None of that occurred to me. By pitching with my gut instincts like I always had, when it went bad, I really didn't have anything to come back to. When it wasn't there, it was just a free fall. It wasn't a foundation of pitching mechanics or anything else.

So ironic, isn't it, that I was always so locked in, and then locked up, progressing to being locked out? That was the essence of the physical manifestations I had when facing a hitter. When I started a windup, it was like the beginning of a tightening, like of a screw or a bolt, which hit its peak when I was releasing the ball. It was just as tight as a drum. And you just can't pitch that way. That's probably an oversimplification, but looking back on it now, objectively, after so much time, it almost covers what happened when I started to wind up.

When I finished saying my goodbyes, I told Karen and the kids that I wanted them to take the station wagon and drive home to Pittsburgh. I said I would take the Volkswagen and drive to a cabin we had about 60 miles from our home. I told Karen I needed some time alone.

It only took me a day or so to drive all the way up from Florida. Once I arrived at the cabin, I spent the next four days trying to sort everything out, drinking my brain loose and feeling sorry for myself. My intent was, *Alright, I'm going to go up there to the cabin and drink and sulk and pout and all that stuff and hope I can get over it by the time Karen and the kids are home.*

There was never any period of time where I thought about hurting myself or committing suicide. I'm too selfish for that. I would have missed spending time with myself. As my friends say, I'm my own best entertainment. I just hung around the cabin, went for walks, and tried to sort it all out and get on the other side of this turning point in my life. Without them even knowing it, I had clung to my family for those two years. I was in such a state that, had I not been around them, who the hell knows what I would have done?

I was heartbroken that I couldn't pitch anymore, but the part that was more of a problem was that I was no longer a part of The Show. I had been such a big part of it all. I loved the whole cauldron of pitching, the chemistry in the clubhouse, the road trips, the interviews, and the appearances. All that stuff was a mix, and I kept stirring it. It was a wonderful mix, and it was always warm.

Of course, there was the joy of pitching itself. When I was pitching well, I was going out there having a hoot. I was having the time of my life. I was getting all that positive feedback and not hoping to do well but expecting to do well. I thought, *My God, I've got this whole thing working!*

I never lost track of how good I had it. I'd had an appreciation of baseball since I was 10 years old and loved it to death. And now, it was gone forever. I was in a very bad place emotionally. I kept thinking, *Where am I now? Why did this happen? How did it happen? What's going to happen now?*

CHAPTER 2

Just a Skinny, Baseball-Obsessed Kid

"You're going away, Steve, and you'll be able to do whatever you want," my father told me as I got ready to board a flight to Kingsport, Tennessee, to start my professional career. "Work hard, and don't forget where you came from."

Where I came from was 1950s Falls Village, Connecticut, a veritable Norman Rockwell setting of American flags, hilltop churches, fishing streams, the corner candy store, a one-movie cinema, Little League fields, and one of the oldest train stations in the nation. In autumn, the foliage allowed for the appearance that the surrounding mountains were ablaze in red and orange, and the smell of burning leaves permeated the air. It was a place where our fathers and grandfathers left to defend our country in the World Wars. It was an environment where walking along the quaint sidewalks often meant running into a friend with a warm smile.

It was, very simply, a perfect little town near the banks of the Housatonic River that represented innocence, a pride in one's self, and all that was good.

I was one of five children but, as the oldest, often felt quite alone. When it came to playing, I often did so by myself because my sister Bonnie was next in line and didn't care much for baseball or football.

The separation of six years between my brother Warren's age and mine was just too great. Plus, he was more of an outdoorsman with very little interest in team sports. Then there was Terry, who actually did like sports but was eight years my junior, so young that we never seriously played together. And the youngest, Jeffrey, was 12 years younger than I was.

So I did a lot of individual, creative stuff, with most of it played out in the back of our house. Among the array of imaginary sports games I created was one that involved a rubber ball and the side of a barn. The balls would take different bounces off the barn, so I could imagine different scenarios.

I created baseball games and kept detailed accounts, including fly balls, ground-outs, and errors, all duly recorded on scorecards I had drawn up on yellow legal tablets. I played nine-inning games—often fictitious Game 7s of the World Series—incessantly in my summers as a kid.

Another baseball game I created for myself was with the aid of a pile of small stones just over the fence outside our yard. There must have been thousands of them. With a wooden bat, I would pick up those rocks, one after another, and hit them out into a pasture where cows grazed. I judged if the hit was a single, double, triple, home run, or an out based on how well I hit them.

I even had an indoor baseball game that drove my mother crazy because it involved me throwing the ball against the inside of our Dutch door which, naturally, separated halfway up. I would get all kinds of bounces.

The problem was that some of the bounces took out some of the knickknacks my father had brought or sent home to her when he was in the service. A lot of stuff from Hawaii just got crushed from my game because I couldn't field every bounce.

I had another game in the back of the same barn that had a peach basket that could be used for basketball games. One of the great things about it was the fact that I could dunk on command, making it a perfect complement to the athletic campus that was our house.

In the fall, I had a tiny gray football that I would throw up in the air, run down under it, and catch for imaginary receptions and touchdowns.

Not all of my imaginary creations were sports-related. Another of them was cowboys and Indians. I always took the side of the Indians. I had a toy gun and defended the Indian lands against the "sneaking white cowardly settlers." I pulled so hard for the Indians that I even wanted my first car to be a Pontiac, because it was named after the chief that bears its name.

So it kind of naturally evolved that I would love the Cleveland Indians. Also, with everybody so gaga over the Yankees, it was a little bit of a backlash. My Indian infatuation really took on a life of its own when I went to my first major league game in 1952. I saw the Cleveland Indians take on the Bronx Bombers at Yankee Stadium.

I'd never been to a major league game before. In fact, as a 10-year-old, I had hardly been on a train that went more than 20 miles. But we drove to Brewster, New York, and then took the train the rest of the way to Yankee Stadium.

As I walked through the turnstiles and then through one of the tunnels leading to the grandstand, my first glimpse inside Yankee Stadium looked like a bed of emeralds under the major league lights. I abruptly left my father's side and ran down the steps toward the field box seats, half scared to death, and got Indians reserve infielder Hank Majeski's autograph. It would be the first of hundreds of autographs I would amass over my lifetime.

After the game, I bought every souvenir I could find related to the Indians—the little pencils that had their logo, a cap, and a pennant. I became obsessed with all things Indians.

I get a lot of autograph requests now through the mail. I sign every one, stick them back into their self-addressed stamped envelopes, and return them. I am still flattered by these requests and I consider each one a compliment.

Well, I did that to Early Wynn, the future Hall of Fame Indians pitcher, not long after that season ended. I sent him a letter to Nokomis, Florida, his home in the winter.

When I received his autograph back, that sealed the deal. The Indians became my team to the degree where I would set up a scorecard with my yellow legal tablet with a ruler for the games that the Indians would play against the Yankees. Legendary announcer Mel Allen and Jim Woods worked the games on radio, and Les Keiter did the pregame and postgame shows.

Two years later, in 1954, I kept a scrapbook of the Indians' remarkable season when they won 111 out of 154 games. I can still name all the players from that team. Besides Wynn, they had a pitching staff for the ages with Bob Lemon, Mike Garcia, Bob Feller, Art Houtteman, and Hal Newhouser. I knew the whole damn group.

And Herb Score, who would come up the next year, was already being highly touted in the media as one of those players of the future. All I kept hearing about was what a fireballer he was on the mound. So my love of all things Indians started innocently enough out in the back of our house in Falls Village as a youngster but continued to escalate well into my early teens.

I was a very ambitious youngster and I loved having a few bucks in my pocket. I was one of the busiest entrepreneurs in Falls Village. When I was 10 and 11 years old, I believe I probably mowed half the lawns in town at one time or another.

I also was a pretty good salesman. I helped Betty Mansfield sell apples at her produce stand on Route 7. There were various types of apples, but I didn't bother learning about the differences, so every apple that I sold was a McIntosh. Later on, I would learn that there were Golden Delicious, Baldwins, and several other types.

I also sold vegetable and flower seeds. I found that business opportunity on the back of a comic book. If you sold so many packets of seeds, you could get a BB gun from the company. That's how I got my first BB gun.

My first exposure to an organized style of baseball was at eight years old. But before I even played my first game, I became the only player ever to have been traded in the Falls Village Canaan Little League. My problem was that because I was so little, when they passed out uniforms the evening before the first game, the Yankees team I was assigned to didn't have one small enough to fit me. So I was traded to the Giants before the night was over.

A nice man named Jerry Fallon was my first Little League coach. I'll never forget, at eight years old, being a little bit frightened playing in my first Little League game. But I was put at ease by Fallon when he brought the team in for a quick pregame talk.

"We're going to have a lot of fun," Fallon said. "And I hope you also learn a little baseball along the way."

It couldn't have been a better introduction to the game. Willie Stargell always said it best when declaring, "The umpire doesn't shout 'Work ball!' He says, 'Play ball!'" That's never left me, either.

I was not a prominent factor as a tiny eight-year-old in Little League. I started out 0-for–the first bunch of games. Eventually I would get my first hit, but I paid a big price for it.

In a subsequent game, I was on the on-deck circle getting ready to hit with the expectation of striking out as usual. Suddenly, I had an urge to pee. Rather than call attention to myself by calling time before I had to hit, I figured I could hold it. After all, I assumed I was almost certainly going to strike out like I usually did, so I would then easily be able to go behind the dugout, take care of business, and nobody would notice.

After making that decision, damned if I didn't get up there and flop a ball over the first baseman's head. Nobody was near the ball, so I scampered easily into second base with a double.

Once at second, I realized that I still had to take a piss. *And I did.* I just couldn't hold it any longer. It felt so good for a moment. It always does. But then "it" got a little bit chafed, and that feeling of relief went away. I was so embarrassed, but the good thing was that no one seemed to notice. Back in 1950, we had heavy wool, dark gray uniforms that felt like they weighed about 40 pounds, so it hid the evidence well. With my peeing, I suppose I have come full circle now. In my teenage and early adult years, I could hold it in. But before then as a Little Leaguer and, now, at 70, I can't. As they say, it's the circle of life.

I may have been a little skinny kid in grammar school, but I possessed a very good arm even then that helped me create a little name for myself. When I was in second grade, I had a little exercise to write for school. The question that we had to answer in a short essay was what we wanted to do when we grew up. I wrote down a fireman, because I didn't think they would have believed me if I said baseball player.

To compound that, years later my son Chris was asked to do a similar essay, only this time he had to write about what his father did for a living. He handed in a blank page. The teacher asked him about it, and he told her, "My Dad doesn't work. He plays baseball." That's a true story.

The ballfield at Lee H. Kellogg Elementary School where we played was unique to say the least. Its most obvious novelty was that it was a slanted field. For instance, if you hit the ball in play, you had to run uphill to first base. Nobody ever got an infield hit. You were pretty much on your own going from first to second, because that was level. But, damn, did we ever fly going from second to third base, because that was straight down hill. It was dramatically tilted that way. It was the most bizarre yet interesting baseball field I have ever been on in my life.

At this point, I would like to recognize a fellow native of Falls Village, Steve Schneider. He was a year older than me and was not only my friend, but my catcher throughout Little League, grammar school, and through my junior year of high school. Furthermore, by being the battery mate of Tom Parsons, Art Lamb, and me, he holds the Connecticut state high school record for most no-hitters caught by a catcher (10).

I just loved playing the field, and that didn't always allude to baseball. In Falls Village, we had four different churches—Methodist, Catholic, Presbyterian, and Congregational. It was a period in my life that was the closest I had ever gotten to really being seriously involved in religion, because I was trying to date a different girl from each church. So I got to know as much about religion in the eighth grade as any other time in my life. If I go to heaven, it will probably be a result of all the exposure I had to churches at 13 years old, even though it was for no good purpose.

I was excited to enter Housatonic Regional Valley High School the next year. I never would really apply myself to my studies, but I embraced the school's more than adequate athletic complex that catered to all of the major scholastic sports. As a freshman that first fall, despite still not being very big, I made the football team as a reserve quarterback.

But my fatal mistake was taking a call from somebody who said, "We have tickets to a Yale game this coming Saturday. Would you like to go?" I said to myself, as a freshman, *Hell, I ain't gonna play on the high school team this year anyway.* So I said yes.

The mistake was magnified when the car we were driving to New Haven to watch the Yale game passed right by the high school football bus. Some of the players and coaches saw me in the car driving by, and that was it. I got kicked off the team. I should have at least been smart enough to notify the driver to take a different route down to Yale.

It all worked out, though, because I wound up running cross country and that became one of the three sports I participated in at school. When winter rolled around, I made basketball my second sport. Our freshman coach was Ed Kirby, who was also the varsity baseball coach. I had met Ed several years before when he coached baseball at one of the elementary schools in the district.

We had a helluva record that freshman year. I was a good shooter. The problem was, so was everybody else. In our basketball games, after the other team scored, nobody on our side wanted to take the ball out because, if he did, he would never see it again. Everybody wanted to shoot. I would continue playing basketball all four years, quickly getting bumped up to varsity to play in a decent Class B basketball program under coach Roland Chinatti, who also was our athletic director. I did well enough to ultimately be named to the All-State Class B second team.

But before spring had even arrived, I couldn't wait for the start of my third sport and true passion, baseball. I was so obsessed with the game of baseball, many times at the cost of relationships. It's a forerunner of getting into pro ball where you have to have such tunnel vision and be locked in to the point where the cost is sacrificing other things far more important to the big picture in one's life. And that started for me in earnest in high school.

Looking back, I wish I hadn't been obsessed with baseball to the degree that I was. It created a life where I was self-absorbed and kept me from being closer to my brothers and sister. I think another reason why I am not as close with them as I should be is because of the special treatment I received from our mother. I was only three months old when our father started his three-year tour of duty in the army. During that time, Mom and I moved from place to place, creating a feeling that it was us against the world. It created a special bond that was great for my mother and me. But in reflection I can see how it may have created some jealousy.

I was also a lucky boy to have been just as close with my dad. I missed out when he was in the service, but I was very fortunate to catch up on lost time with him later. My father raised five kids on a salary of a hundred bucks or so a week as a plumber. That was a pretty damn good accomplishment. To supplement his income, he would do side jobs at night in the cellar of people's homes, usually replacing old and worn-out pipes. I often went with him, sat in the corner, and polished fittings for the gunk he would put on the copper pipes to connect them. It gave us a chance to talk while he worked, and I look back fondly at those moments we shared. I hope he knew how much they meant to me. I think he did.

It was also during that period that he coached some of my Little League teams. Despite his pitching experience, he never really worked with me on mechanics. We just simply enjoyed the time together.

With my Dad as my second Little League coach, I got an education on negotiating baseball deals. One afternoon I hid the keys to his car, and when it was time to go to the Little League field, I boldly told him I wasn't going to give him the keys unless he said I could pitch that night. Needless to say, it didn't work. He told me that unless I gave him the keys, I might never play any position ever again.

Years later with the Pirates, Joe Brown also called my bluff as a result of my failings in this area. I held out one spring but made the terminal mistake of going to Florida and hanging around the chain-link fence watching the Pirates work out.

Joe came up to me and said, "Boy, looks like a lot of fun, doesn't it, Steve?"

And I said, "Yeah, it does Joe. You know, we're only $2,500 apart. How about we cut cards?"

He said no and I said, "Alright, give me the pen. Where do I sign?"

It's too late for me to connect with my youngest brother, Jeff, who tragically died in a car accident when he was just 24 years old. To this day, it bothers me a great deal that we never got closer. He was so important to my boys, in fact, that my son David named his own son Jacob Jeffrey.

I keep thinking that when I retire from broadcasting, I'm going to have a lot of time to get closer with my other siblings, but that's kind of delusional. I need to do that now even though I'm not retired. I hope to do it, but hope has to translate into action. I can't say that I'm unhappy that I was very absorbed in baseball, because it's turned out so well. Like I've always said, to be a major league baseball player you have to have an obsession with it, and many times, that comes at the expense of some aspects of your personal life. Still, at age 70, I am trying to catch up with them now. I am, after all, the oldest, so I feel that responsibility lies a great deal with me.

My intensity also affected my relationships with girls. For example, I broke up with Karen on a regular basis. I would tell her that I was very sorry, but it was baseball season, and I didn't have time to date and care for her the way I should. The first thing I did every morning after getting out of bed would be to look out the window and check to see if the weather was going to be alright to play ball that day. That was a habit that started when I was eight years old.

State regulations mandated that we play just 14 scheduled regular season baseball games in the spring, but Kirby and our other coaches got very creative by adding games through scrimmages, intra-squad games, and, later on in my high school career, interstate semipro games for the better players.

The Housatonic baseball program was traditionally rich in success, particularly in the pitching department. By the time I got there, there had already been two or three guys that had been signed to pro contracts. One of them, Pete Lamb, was Karen's oldest brother. Karen's family was nothing short of a baseball incubator, which started with her father George, who had played some semipro ball in Sharon. Pete had an opportunity to sign with the Yankees, but he decided to go to the University of Connecticut instead.

As a freshman, I had two pitchers ahead of me, a senior and a sophomore, who were getting ready to be signed. Tom Parsons, who was Karen's cousin, was 6'5" as a senior with a curveball that probably could have been effective in the major leagues. He was being scouted heavily. One of Karen's other older brothers, Art Lamb, was a year ahead of me. He had to wait for Parsons to graduate before he could pitch a lot. And I had to wait for Art, who would sign with the Pirates, to graduate before I was going to get my chance.

So you knew you had to wait your turn to assume the ace role of the pitching staff. But because it was such a good program, I didn't mind waiting. Parsons may very well have been the best high school pitcher Housatonic ever had. He fired four no-hitters as a senior and, because he was the first one at the school to really attract major league scouts, put Housatonic on the map. He would go on to pitch briefly in the majors with the Pirates and the Mets.

A few years later, Karen's younger brother, John Lamb, would also come along and establish himself as a dominating high school pitcher. He would go on to become a teammate of mine with the Pirates for parts of three seasons. I still believe John would have had a very good major league career had he not been hit in the head by a line drive during batting practice by Dave Cash. The impact created a fracture in his skull. He wound up pitching some after that but was never quite the same.

John and I quite possibly were the only brothers-in-law to earn a win and a save in the same game. It happened over two days, September 4 and 5, 1970, in a game against the Phillies at Three Rivers Stadium. Rain suspended a game I had started the night before, and the next day George Brunet and John finished the final three innings.

It's amazing how intertwined Karen's family and I were with baseball. Hell, even another one of her cousins, Martin Whelan, became my catcher in my senior year. As a result, we thought when we got married, if we had boys, they would certainly grow up to be major league bonus babies. I coached both boys in Little League, but apparently I didn't pass on any big-league magic.

So the baseball scouts were very much aware of Housatonic Valley Regional High School and its baseball program. It's an incredible story that this little high school produced the pitchers and baseball players that it did. Much of the credit, of course, had to go to Kirby, our tough-love manager. He saw a lot of potential in some of his players but would tell me years later that I had more desire to succeed in baseball than anyone he had ever coached.

He gave me a team handbook early in my freshman season that seemed thicker than *War and Peace*. I really wanted to impress him, so I learned that damn thing inside and out. I think that got his attention. Ed is now one of my oldest and dearest friends, but I didn't like him my first couple of years of high school. He *worked* my *ass* off.

The baseball field is still situated down along the Housatonic River's flood line, 55 feet below where the school sits on top of a hill. Kirby made us run up that damn bank countless times, and it nearly killed me. Looking back now, I know why he did it. He used that drill to make me physically tough, believing all along that I had a chance to become a professional baseball player. And when that time would eventually come to pass, that toughness I developed under Ed would be needed to handle challenges in pro ball.

He mentally toughened us, too. One of the drills he used to help alleviate game-like pressures involved the suicide squeeze. To better prepare us for opposing crowd noise with a game on the line, he had each of our hitters take turns getting into the batter's box and square around for the sacrifice squeeze, while the rest of the team surrounded him in a semi-circle and just started screaming as loud as they could as the pitch came in. The idea was that the hitter would never have to deal with a scenario that difficult in a real game. He was remarkably thorough, committed, and dedicated, and that rubbed off on me. After a couple of years of playing in his system, I had an epiphany that if he was that committed, I should be that way, too.

Looking back now at the time I entered my junior year reminds me of that old parlor game question, "If you had to spend the rest of your life at one particular age, what would it be? For me, it would be hard to deny it was age 16. I had no responsibilities or leash from my parents and was having the time of my life.

People probably would say, "Sure, Steve, that sounds nice, but what about the time you spent in the major leagues?" It's a valid question, but nothing can compare with the whole experience of growing up in that atmosphere, that geographical region, and around the people that I did. There were the simple pleasures of playing catch with my pal Steve Schneider or going fishing with my Uncle Bill. As a later child of my grandparents, Bill was only three years older than I was and was my absolute hero. Uncle Bill and I were like Tom Sawyer and Huck Finn the way we made sandwiches, got on our bikes, and went fishing every day in the summer.

It was also the year I began dating Karen, my wife of 48 years. Karen and I met through The Grange Youth Organization, which provided a relaxed, informal atmosphere for young people looking to socialize with their peers. Karen and I were masters, which were leaders, in our respective Grange Clubs in Sharon and Falls Village. I saw a brochure that was sponsoring a regional Grange meeting that showed pictures of all the area masters. I saw her picture in that brochure, and it looked great to me. And the rest is history.

During my junior year, Karen and I wound up having driver's ed together, and I flunked the class. You've got to work your ass off to flunk driver's ed, but I still maintain the fact that I did it because of her. She denies this story, but I will back it up until the day I die. Every student had time sitting next to the instructor while the other two or three sat in the back seat. I would sit in the back with Karen and, because I was so busy paying attention to her, I missed much of the instruction needed to learn how to drive. I guess that was in line with my baseball obsession, always trying to get to first base.

Anyway, I eventually got my license, which was critical, because out in rural Falls Village, you have to drive everywhere. Another thing we did together was babysit for Kirby's kids. I don't remember much about them, but I do recall being able to be alone in the house with Karen. I have to assume the kids didn't light the house on fire, because it's still there. Taking my girlfriend babysitting was a great opportunity, because eventually, those kids had to go to bed. And when that happened, it was our time. Boy, did we hope that Ed and Mary Kirby were having a great time and would stay out for a while. And, of course, we had to position ourselves so we could see the car lights coming back into the driveway.

From the people who are familiar with the Lamb family's almost inconceivable success in baseball, I often get asked if I felt like I had to prove myself to them as a pitcher to gain a level of acceptance into their family. To that, I typically say, "Damn right!" I was very much aware of their success, from Karen's father on down through the boys. There wasn't added pressure, but it was important to me to show them how good I was. But there was never any hesitation by them in welcoming me into their family.

As it turned out, my cribbage-playing abilities were far more important. Cribbage is a very popular New England game, and they were all quite accomplished at it. At first, I didn't know what the hell it was, but over time I turned out to be a pretty good player. That was how I truly earned my stripes when entering that Lamb house.

When the spring rolled around, it was finally my time to shine. And shine I did. Despite being slight of build and still weighing less than 160 pounds, I pitched two no-hitters in establishing myself as the ace of the staff. I may have been a skinny kid, but I got every ounce of my body into every pitch with my herky-jerky delivery. It was like I was flinging myself toward home plate, the momentum carrying me over toward first base. The motion was a major plus for me when pitching against high school hitters who had never seen such a thing. The exertion from my violent windup made it difficult for them to pick up where and how I was releasing the ball.

Most pitchers, especially at high school age, are much more fluid, so the batter has a pretty good sense of how to time his motion. I knew that I couldn't achieve success just with my arm because I wasn't that big. I had to utilize whatever body I had to help me get zip on my fastballs.

After the school year was over, Kirby set it up so that I could play for the Kent team in the semipro Pomperaug League, which was south of the area where I grew up. Ed had relatives down there and somehow finagled to get me on the team. I got to pitch most Sundays that summer, and it turned out to be my first professional experience. That was because, one time, after I came out of a game following a really good outing, I went to take my spikes off and, when reaching for my shoes, looked inside and found a $10 bill. That was pretty slick. I got $10 to pitch a baseball game.

I was pitching against grown men now, so it really helped me when I was paired up with a very good catcher named Ray Wisniewski. What was interesting about Ray was that he was in the "big house" and was only let out of prison on the weekends to play ball. So it was an interesting battery. Only in New England would you have a high school kid pitching to a convict. Norman Rockwell could have painted this scene. A grizzled 30-something convict catching a baby-faced 17-year-old. But Ray was always very nice to me, and it was great to pitch to a guy who had experience.

There were actually two semi-pro interstate leagues in the northwest corner of New England. There was the Pomperaug, which I played in, and the Interstate Baseball League, which covered the towns in the Canaan area. Baseball was very popular in those small New England towns. They loved being represented, and just about each one of them had a team that played on Sundays. They would often get big crowds that would either pay admission or toss money into a hat. There was also quite a lot of betting that took place in the stands.

Pitching in that environment following both my junior and senior years was very important for both my mental and physical development as a young pitcher. It was a stepping stone toward becoming a professional ballplayer. The talent was very good and, at times, was as intense as some minor league games I later played in.

Several years before I started playing in the Pomperaug League, I was a batboy for the Canaan team. For three years, starting when I was 10, I would hitchhike to Canaan from Falls Village and ride with some of the players to whatever town they were going to play in. After each of the away games, they would stop at some gin mill and drink as much beer as they possibly could. Back in those days, kids weren't allowed in those little small-town bars, so they would leave me out in the car. One of the players would bring me a Coca-Cola every 20 minutes or so. I drank more freaking Coca-Cola than any kid in Connecticut during that time. But that was the way it worked, and I was fine with it.

In my senior year, we won our third straight Housatonic Valley Schoolmen's League Championship with a 14–2 record. Personally, I was just dealing. I went 9–2 with 164 strikeouts in less than 100 innings pitched. I threw three more no-hitters to set a lifetime school record of five that still stands today. I also had a game in which I struck out 18 opposing hitters.

Back then, the Connecticut State Tournament selected only four teams from each of the Class A, B, and C divisions. So there were only 12 teams that were competing for titles in the entire state. Despite all the pitching and overall talent we had at Housatonic, we never won a Class B State title.

I would put up a lot of money and say we played more tournament games than any other team in the state without winning. And it was a good level of baseball. When we were playing, future major league All-Star shortstop Dick McAuliffe, among others, was playing at Farmington to headline a very good crop of ballplayers in our area.

One of our last games of that senior year was an out-of-conference contest against Class A Torrington. We played them once per year as kind of a reward for having such a strong baseball program. Because I was smoking batters that season, there were 15 scouts in the stands for that game, by far the most there had ever been to come see me pitch.

Perhaps trying to be too fine and being a little nervous, I managed to walk one batter for each of those 15 scouts. On the upside, I also struck out 15, so the game took forever. By the time the game ended, at least 12 or 13 of those scouts were gone.

Bob Whalen, a primary scout with the Pirates, was one who stayed until the bitter end. Whalen was more than just a scout who was interested in signing me. I think he also saw me as a project, and I started to see him show up at the next few games I pitched. He was only about 5'7" at the most; a former decorated military man, he was so intense about having me become a professional baseball player that he would hold private pitching sessions with me on the side.

One of the things he did to improve my follow-through, for example, would be to put his pack of cigarettes out in front of the mound and make me, after I released the ball, bend down enough to pick them up with my pitching hand. He helped me quite a bit with exercises like that.

A couple of days after graduation, I flew out to Pittsburgh with my Dad, Kirby, and Whalen for my tryout at Forbes Field. We flew out of Hartford's Bradley Field. I had never been on a plane before. I was so naïve that when the plane banked to the left, I leaned to the right thinking that I could help balance the plane. Later, a stewardess came over to us and asked if we would like to have a cocktail. I said, "Sure, I would love a shrimp cocktail." We didn't see her for the rest of the flight. I guess that was the country boy in me going to the big city.

We arrived at Forbes Field on a Sunday morning before the Pirates took batting practice. The clubhouse manager took me to a little supply room where they had a uniform for me. With little fanfare, the clubhouse guy said, "Put this on and get out on the field."

My workout basically consisted of me throwing pitches to the Pirates' third-string catcher, Bob Oldis. I guess I didn't make a lasting impression on him. Forty years later, at a reunion-themed fantasy camp for the 1960 Pirates, I walked up to Bob and asked, "Do you remember catching me when I tried out in high school in 1960?"

Oldis replied, "Fuck no. What are you talking about?" He didn't have a clue, which really disappointed me.

I said, "Bob, I thought I made a big impression on you."

"Not really," he replied. I suppose his memory of that day was somewhat understandable. The Pirates signed about 40 boys that year, and three years later there were only about seven of us left. The attrition was something else.

We stayed to watch a doubleheader, and the Cubs beat them in both games. I still wonder if the Pirates were so pissed about being swept that it cost me a couple hundred bucks in bonus money.

We sat up in the stands and, by the fifth inning of the second game, there were little streams of beer going down the aisles at the different levels of the ballpark. That left a lasting impression on me. Those were the days when you had to bring your own beer because they didn't sell it at Forbes Field. The fans didn't seem to have a problem with that, as many bus groups would actually buy a ticket for a beer cooler!

We flew back home and, on June 27, 1960, with my grandfather, Dad, Ed, and my high school principal around me at our kitchen table, I signed a contract with the Pirates. It was truly a cherished moment in my life.

I had also received an offer from my beloved Cleveland Indians for a signing bonus of $2,500 to start the following spring, but I accepted the Pirates' offer of $4,000 with the opportunity to play in the minor leagues right away. It was a no-brainer. Fifteen hundred bucks was a big difference in those days, and I really didn't want to wait until the next year to start my professional career. Plus, in those days, they gave prospects conditional contracts, so if I ever made it to the big leagues, I would get an additional $4,000.

Another special part of getting that signing bonus was that it enabled me to pay off my folks' bills. Doing that made me feel very proud.

I was now officially a professional baseball player on my way to Kingsport, Tennessee, the Class D affiliate of the Pirates, to begin living my dream.

I was on my way!

CHAPTER 3

Life in the Bush Leagues

66 **H**ey Steve, just throw your shit over the plate and find out if
it's good enough," Don Osborn told me during one of my
first games as a minor leaguer. "And if it's not," he continued,
"you're still young enough to go out and get a real job."

When I signed in 1960, "Ozzie" was the minor league roving pitching
instructor for the Pirates. Ozzie dealt with me in the Rookie League
and as I advanced through the Pirates' minor league system. As luck
would have it, Don would eventually become the Pirates' pitching
coach on the major league club around the same time I was called up
to the big leagues.

That piece of advice he gave me about seeing if my stuff was good
enough was the greatest I ever received as a pitcher. It's a wonderful line
in its simplicity because, eventually, you've got to believe in your stuff
enough to see if it's good enough. The earlier you find out if you can pitch
in the big leagues, the better.

If you're scared, tentative, or a nibbler, it is extremely hard to be
successful as a pitcher. Case in point: for six years Sandy Koufax didn't
throw his shit over the plate, and he was not very good. The next six years
he threw his shit over the plate, and the rest is history. Classic example
of that philosophy times 10.

Besides having about as much to do with my development as a pitcher as anyone else in the Pirates' organization, Ozzie also liked to have some fun with me. Realizing I was from a small town in Connecticut where there were very few, if any, Latin people, Ozzie once had me pitching in the bullpen during my first Instructional League in Arizona and began fooling around with languages.

Don said, "Throw me a fastball." So I threw the catcher a fastball. Then he said, "Throw a curve." So I threw a curve.

Ozzie then goes, "Alright, now throw the combio," which is Spanish for change-up.

For me, the best I could come out with from what he said was "combination." So I went back to the fastball and I almost took that damned catcher's head off, who was waiting for the change-up. Ozzie never let me forget that story.

Earlier that year, I began my professional baseball career for the Bucs' Kingsport team in Tennessee. Having never been away from home, I was picked up at the airport by Lance Lewis, the young business manager for the club, and he took me over to a rooming house operated by a widow.

There were about five or six guys from the team who stayed there, and the place was like a revolving door. It seemed like almost every few days there was a new prospect signed who would come in to stay there while another one of them would get released or shipped out. It was a good situation for us, though. Because you were with other kids in rooming houses, you weren't ever completely alone. Staying in rooming houses with other prospects was standard in the low minor leagues in those days.

One of my first nights after arriving in Kingsport, realizing that I still had some significant signing bonus money left over in my pocket, I thought to myself, *Man, I'm on my own. I can do whatever I want.* Excited, and very hot from the Tennessee summer, I enthusiastically went out and bought a six pack of beer and half a watermelon.

The result of my newfound freedom? I spent the better part of the next three days in the bathroom. Not weighing more than 160 pounds at the time, it turned out to be a particularly poor choice of how to spend some of my bonus money. But I was still able to pitch and do well under the circumstances.

I learned another valuable lesson—besides not to mix beer with watermelon—during my first weeks away from home. I went to the laundromat for the first time with a bag of six pairs of underwear and dirty socks. I walked in and saw a vending machine with little boxes of soap. I figured that, naturally, because I had 12 items, I should probably get 12 of those little boxes of soap.

I threw the underwear and socks in all by themselves with the boxes of soap when, all of a sudden, the suds came out of the goddamn machine. I panicked and just ran away. I left everything there. I didn't know what to do. I panicked. I just went out and bought new underwear.

For the rest of that summer, I mailed my laundry back to Connecticut for my mom to do, and she would mail it back to me. The system worked to perfection until, in August, when I was in Dubuque, Iowa, she sent my clean clothes back to me along with some chocolate chip cookies she had made, which had melted all over the damn clean clothes.

So it turned out to be a somewhat flawed system because the clothes looked like I had shit myself. And the little Nestle chocolate bits didn't help the whole visual. So we had to upgrade the laundry system the next year. We found a way to do that.

Playing for a manager named Jim Gibbons, who was also the freshman baseball coach at the University of Notre Dame, I went 4–1 and spent just one month in Kingsport before getting sent up to Class D Dubuque. Quite simply, I got my clock cleaned at Dubuque. My struggles there were my first little doses of reality.

I thought, *Oh shit, maybe I'm not quite as good as I thought I was.* Actually, that was the right reaction to have because, as I would discover later, practically every player struggles at some level. Very few guys run the table and go right from high school to Cooperstown. You just have to learn how to deal with the challenges of moving up through the various classes of competitive ball.

After several weeks of getting hit hard, I called home and told my father, "Dad, this ain't working. I don't know if this is going to work."

He said, "Well, you've got to hang in there and give it time. You've got to find out if you're good enough, and you're not going to get any real definitive answer after one month. You won't find out if you come home. Maybe you're not quite as good as you were in Kingsport, but maybe not quite as bad as you are in Dubuque. Hang in there, and see what happens."

So I finished out the rest of the season, came home, and began the first of two jobs that off-season working for Berkshire Homes building trusses. That was the beginning of a theme of having a job every off-season.

One afternoon that fall, a bunch of us at Berkshire were listening to Game 7 of the 1960 World Series on the radio while we worked. To add a little spice to the game, we each threw in a buck on the half inning when the game's winning run would be scored. I wound up with the bottom of the ninth. After Bill Mazeroski hit it out, I was $18 richer. So I guess even before we knew each other, Maz was paying dividends in my life.

Later that off-season, I got a carpenters' job working for the father of a high school teammate and one of my best friends, Ken Harring. Ken's dad was a contractor from Sweden, and I worked for him that winter pounding nails in the cold Connecticut weather to help him build a house. I thought, *Boy, I really want to be a major league pitcher because this ain't much fun pounding nails at 8:30 in the morning when it's about 34 degrees out.*

So between my father's tough-love words of wisdom and the sting of the occasional hammering of a finger in freezing temperatures, I was inspired to improve on my Dubuque experience.

Getting invited to the world champion Pirates' 1961 spring training camp at Fort Myers, Florida, was one of the greatest thrills of my life. Despite having separate locker rooms and hotels from the big leaguers, it was my first true taste of what it felt like to be a part of the major leagues. It allowed me to dream about possibilities.

While staying at the Franklin Arms hotel with the other minor league invites, Karen's cousin and future big leaguer Tom Parsons and I roomed together. We would sometimes spend late afternoons after workouts practicing our autographs in case we ever made it.

The organization kept me at Class D that spring, but my venue changed to Batavia, New York, where I had a big year and began living a utopian existence. I was on my own, money in my pocket, drinking beers and chasing girls, all while living my dream of playing professional baseball. Most important, I went 13–6 and struck out a ton of batters.

That season at Batavia was also special in that I was a witness to history. Midway through that 1961 season, Gene Baker replaced Jim Adlam as our manager and became the first black man to manage an affiliated team in the minor leagues. Everybody may know that Frank Robinson became the first African American to get a manager's job at the major league level when he was hired by the Cleveland Indians in 1975, but few trivia buffs may know that Baker, for two innings in September 1963, was the first black manager in the big leagues after Danny Murtaugh got kicked out of a game.

Baker had played with the Pirates in 1960 on the world championship team, got into managing, and was one of the nicest and neatest guys I had ever met. He was as cool as a cucumber and had a good handle on everything. As a 19-year-old kid, I just thoroughly enjoyed playing for Gene. He could not have created a better atmosphere.

Gene not only managed our team, but he also played some infield and hit .387 in the second half of that season.

Despite all of the success I had on the field and the joy off of it, I did learn a valuable lesson that season. I learned to never leave tickets for two girlfriends at the same game. It happened one night when my dad and future wife Karen drove over from Connecticut to watch me play. I made the mistake of leaving a ticket for a girl I was dating in Batavia while also reserving two tickets for Karen and my Dad. As it turned out, the seats were near each other and, before long, a relationship was being tested. Karen has never let me forget it. I have not forgotten it. Lesson learned, and we all survived it.

Even still, that was probably the only downer of the season.

After doing well in the Arizona Instructional League in the off-season and proving to the organization that I could thrive against Triple A hitters, the Bucs promoted me from Class D ball all the way up to Class A in Asheville, North Carolina. I proceeded to get my face ripped off again. I went a very quick 1–4 at Asheville, called Dad again, and he said, "I still want you to hang in there like I told you before. There are going to be bumps, but you proved last year at Batavia that you could play pro ball. This is just another challenge. Hang in there. It'll come. It'll come."

I got demoted to the Class B Kinston, North Carolina, affiliate in the renowned Carolina League. This was the same Carolina League that the movie *Bull Durham* was based on. I could have easily added four more hours of stories to that film. Susan Sarandon was not there the year I played for Kinston and, trust me, I looked for her.

Every bus ride we would torture Joe Gibbon. Like the Crash Davis character from the movie made famous by Kevin Costner, Joe was in The Show but was down playing in Kinston while rehabbing from an injury. We peppered him with every question we could imagine to get a better idea of the big-league life. Joe was also a former All-American basketball player at Mississippi who became a good left-handed pitcher for the Pirates and stayed around a long time.

I was back in a good place with Kinston and just tore it up, going 17–3, striking out 209 batters, and sporting an ERA of 1.97. Plus, a buddy of mine, a left-handed pitcher named Frank Bork, went 19–7 with a 2.00 ERA. So we were just kicking ass and taking names. After each game I pitched, I recorded my stats in a little yellow legal tablet. Each page had a month. It was a pretty impressive little yellow tablet by the end of that season.

That was also the season I met Gene "Stick" Michael, who remains one of my great friends to this day. Stick would have a phenomenal career with the New York Yankees, first as their longtime shortstop, then as a coach, manager, general manager, and scouting director. I always thought Stick embodied a lot of the qualities that I admired and wished I had more of. He was a straight shooter, never a "yes man," and never took the easy way out. I think that's what endeared him to Yankee owner George Steinbrenner and why he had so many different jobs with George.

Gene embodied the integrity that you would like all your really good friends to have. I know Stick went to Steinbrenner with the names of various former players who needed jobs. And Gene persuaded George to hire some of those players to help them out because he trusted Stick's judgment. A lot of people benefited from Steinbrenner's generosity, and Stick had a hand in a lot of those situations. He had George's ear, and George respected Gene. George was tough to get respect from, but, over many years, Stick had earned it.

Gene's best work was done during the time of Steinbrenner's suspension in the early 1990s. When George was forced to give up the day-to-day operations of the Yankees in 1990, the Bombers were the worst team in baseball due, in part, to his irrational signings, ill-advised trades, and a revolving door in front of the manager's office.

By the time George came back to the team in 1993, the Yankees were relevant again, had a strong farm system, and were on the verge of a run that is still going strong today. Gene made astute trades and developed prospects like Bernie Williams and Mariano Rivera instead of trading them. Gene will say that he taught George patience, while Steinbrenner gave Stick a work ethic.

At Kinston, however, Stick was a just a skinny kid like I was, and we had a lot of fun together. Stick couldn't sleep on buses, but our manager, Harding "Pete" Peterson, had this enviable ability to fall asleep right away. Pete, who had caught for the Pirates and later became general manager when the Bucs won the World Series in 1979, had this wonderful head of thick black hair, beautifully combed. When we arrived at the towns of our road games, Pete would check us into the motels we stayed in. The problem was, the minute he'd go to sleep on the bus, Stick went to work with a can of shaving cream. By the time Pete went to check us in, he looked like a unicorn. Stick would put this wonderful tassel of shaving cream on Pete while he was sleeping in the bus, so when he would go into the motel very business-like to check us in, we all just tried to imagine what the desk clerk must have been thinking. We had a busload of these amped-up young ballplayers with a manager who comes in with black hair and a nice white crown. So that became a kind of ritual.

Another great memory of Stick from that 1962 season was a night we had in Durham. We were all beered up and found out what room a honeymoon couple was staying in on their wedding night. Back in those days, old hotels like this one had transoms above the doors that opened up a little bit to improve air flow. So I hoisted Stick up on my shoulders so he could take a peek at what was going on in there. To this day, I just wonder why he didn't hold me up so I could to take a look! After all, he was taller than I was.

He and I have come so far since then. Most important, we no longer stay in hotels that have transoms above the doors. My friendship with Gene was cemented for good near the end of the 1965 season at Columbus. Stick's car was in the repair shop when his wife called and said she was getting ready to deliver their first child. He didn't have a ride, and I just dropped everything I was doing and immediately drove him up to his home somewhere north of Columbus in time for the delivery. It helped him out, and he never forgot that.

I capped off that great 1962 season with my best catch of the year. Late in the season, Karen and my dad made another one of their trips together to come and watch me pitch. I went down to Kay Jewelers and got this little silver metal box with an engagement ring in it, and I proposed to Karen. She said, "Yes," and it's been all good ever since. So it was a very good season both on the field and off.

There's this funny trivia question in Pittsburgh that's been around for years. Who's the only person who has ever played for the Pirates and Steelers? Many would say, with a wink, Benny Benack, the bandleader. But actually there is an athlete who played for both teams. Rex Johnston, a standout running back from USC, ran back kicks for the Steelers in 1960 and later became an outfielder for the Bucs in 1964. Rex and I roomed together with Tommie Sisk in the Arizona Instructional League in the fall of 1962.

Parlaying my success at Class B Kinston with good stints in Arizona and at spring training, I made the big jump to Triple A Columbus. Rex was beginning his second season at Columbus, and we rented a house there with teammates Frank Bork and Bob Priddy. One night, Priddy was over-served at a few bars we went to up in Buffalo. The next day, he begged us to hide him from our manager, Larry Shepard, so he could sleep things off. During the ballgame—which was played at War Memorial Stadium, made famous in the movie *The Natural*—Bob hid inside the tube of the tarp used to cover the infield from rain. It was so skanky inside the tube, which was made downright decrepit from years of moss and dirt inside of it.

Around the sixth inning or so, Larry was looking everywhere for Bob because he wants to put him in the game to pitch. I went to get Bob and started hollering inside the tube to wake him up, but he was sound asleep, looking every bit like a bear in hibernation. I stood over the top of the tube and started beating it with a fungo bat while in my baseball uniform. They could have arrested me or taken me to a mental hospital for that! By beating on the tube, it shook all the shit down on Bob. He came out of the tube and headed straight to the mound, covered in sweat, dirt, and all kinds of nasty shit all over his uniform. Every time he threw a pitch, big puffs of dust jumped off the back of his jersey.

I ended up having a good season, going 11–8 and averaging better than eight strikeouts per nine innings. I felt as if it might be good enough to possibly get a shot at making the jump to the Pirates the next spring. After the season ended, I bought my first car, a 1963 Pontiac Catalina. I was getting ready to drive home to Connecticut to get married when Priddy asked if I could drop him off in Pittsburgh on the way. Bob was born and raised there. I said, "Sure."

As we are driving near the end of the Fort Pitt Tunnel, we saw the beautiful vista that is the downtown Pittsburgh skyline. It's a wonderful and well-known sight, unique in that immediately after the tunnel ends, the bridge starts, and this truly breathtaking scene explodes on you. But I had never driven through that area. I did remember coming through it as a high school kid on the way to the Pirates' tryout, but I was on the gong show that day and didn't notice anything.

Now, all of a sudden, I've got Bob Priddy and his luggage in the car and right at the end of the tunnel it's a four-lane deal going one way into Pittsburgh. To my amazement, right at the end of the tunnel he calmly turns and says to me, "Stop. This is good right here." I thought, *My God. I'm on a four-lane road at the end of the tunnel, looking at downtown Pittsburgh, and he says, "Stop. I'll get off right here!"*

I thought he was a troll! I thought he lived under the bridge, because at this point we were at the end of the tunnel on the Fort Pitt Bridge, stopping traffic, when he got out of the car, took his luggage, and went down this stairway and I never saw him again. I didn't know what the hell was going on. He just got out and walked home. A bit frazzled, to say the least, I continued driving and had no idea where I was. I got lost three times driving through Pittsburgh before finally getting on the right road en route to Falls Village.

Karen and I got married on October 5, 1963, a spectacular early autumn day. It was great. That was certainly the good news. A little young and naïve, I had my wedding suit on but forgot to get any formal shoes. I had to borrow the shoes I got married in from a guy named Joe Hamzy, who owned the only grocery store in Falls Village. Then, after the reception, I took my new bride to this motel on the mountain for our first night as husband and wife. Of course, I didn't make any reservations, but I was a big professional ballplayer and didn't think I had to do that. So we got to the motel, and the front desk clerk said, "I'm sorry sir, we're sold out."

So we ended up spending our wedding night at the Howard Johnson's motel on the New Jersey Turnpike, which is not exactly how we had planned it. The reason we were on the New Jersey Turnpike in the first place was because we were en route to dropping off my car near the Pirates' spring training facility and taking a flight to the Dominican Republic to play winter ball. The owners of the Aguilas Cibaenas offered me $1,350 cash, no taxes, per month, just to go down there and play during the winter. I couldn't turn that kind of money down, but in hindsight, maybe I should have.

Here Karen and I were, on our honeymoon, in a country in complete disarray. It was about two years after its dictator, Rafaël Trujillo, was killed. The U.S. had severed political ties. It didn't even have a consulate down there. We were so naïve to go down there as 21-year-olds, married two days before. I mean, you talk about walking into a shit storm! We wouldn't have gone now if we had thought about it.

Plus, we were not even staying in Santo Domingo, which was the country's kind of garden spot. We went into the interior of the country to Santiago, which was a mess politically. Worse still, the Aguilas put us in the Matum Hotel, which sat by itself on a hill overlooking the city. It was a dark, dirty, and evil-looking place, something you might picture in a Stephen King novel. It had a swimming pool with no water in it but plenty of algae and mold. It was just god-awful.

Eventually, the team got us a room with a family, and that kind of saved us. But even that transition wasn't without a level of confusion for a kid from Falls Village. The first time I walked into their bathroom, I saw a bidet. The only thing I knew was that it was not a drinking fountain. I didn't know what it was, but I *knew* it was not a drinking fountain. The family eventually showed me a brochure of what a bidet does.

They also made sure we slept under a mosquito net because when we woke up in the morning, there were insects crawling all over the place. Thank God the Dominicans loved baseball so much that they kind of looked after and protected us to a certain degree. After much stress those first couple of weeks, Karen and I went out one night and did what most couples would do to relax. We went out on the town to see a movie. Our only option, however, was a movie called *The Ugly American*. You can't make this stuff up!

And we actually went into the theatre and watched it! It was stupid enough for us as Americans to see that film in a foreign country but much more so during that period of time in the Dominican Republic. To add to the drama, during the film the lights suddenly came on, and there were military police running down each aisle with their guns out, looking for a fugitive. Because the outside door was locked, nobody could get out, and there was real panic in the theater.

Karen turned to me and said, "Let's leave quickly."

I told her, "No, why don't we just sit here until everything settles down."

And that's what we did.

Another unexpected twist occurred on November 22, 1963. Karen and I were in a taxi in Santo Domingo and kept hearing on the radio, in Spanish, President Kennedy's name over and over again. We're in the backseat assuming that perhaps Kennedy was going to be making some kind of trip to the Dominican before we realized he had been shot. You talk about feeling disenfranchised. Not only is your President killed, which is bad enough in your own country, but we're outside our country feeling very isolated. We're thinking, *What's going to happen in the world now?*

We didn't know if that was the end of the tragedy or if there was more bad news coming. We didn't even know what the details were, because we couldn't understand what they were saying on the radio. That was a very strange feeling.

The Aguilas were one of four teams in the Dominican Winter League. Two played in Santo Domingo, one in Santiago, and the other in San Pedro. Willie Stargell was also playing down there that winter, as the Pirates had a working relationship with the league to send their good prospects down there to get some off-season work and conditioning in.

The games were a circus atmosphere. With all the turmoil in the country, even at the ballpark, they had white uniformed military policemen with machine guns at both ends of each dugout. Real live action! Not movie action but machine gun action! The military policemen just kind of stood around while we played ball, and before long we got used to it.

That didn't mean there weren't some exciting and tense moments. One night, the lights went out at our ballpark and we literally crawled off the field because we didn't know what the hell was happening. It turned out to be just a power failure, but by staying close to the ground we were hedging our bets that no gunfire would ensue.

Another time, there was a guy who leaned over our dugout in the seventh inning of a game and said to me, "You win, I got money for you." I could see this guy had a gun. I don't know how he got by security, but at the end of the game, he handed me five American $100 bills. At first I thought, *Gee, this is really great!* But then I started thinking, *There's got to be somebody over on the other side who lost this and he's probably got a gun, too. Damn!*

I was a hothead back then, and that personality deficiency led me to making one of the worst decisions I have ever made. One of the opposing hitters I faced one night, a Yankees infielder named Pedro Gonzalez, kept trying to bunt on me again and again. Finally, he got a bunt down, and instead of going after the ball, I went and tackled him. It turned out he was a native of the Dominican Republic.

Now there's a brawl. Everybody on both teams comes out. It was a typical baseball brawl in that nobody got hurt, but Gonzalez got to go home after the game while I was sent to jail. In my uniform!

I called Karen, my new bride, and told her, "Honey, I'm going to be a little late tonight. But don't worry. I'm not in a bar. I'm just in jail." I didn't stay there long, maybe an hour or two, but they made their point because I started some shit with a native son.

A week or so before Christmas, I had to deal with a far more serious issue back home that made everything I had experienced in the Dominican Republic seem small in comparison. I received a phone call from my Aunt Skip, my dad's sister, that my mother had left my father in Connecticut and went to Florida to be with another man.

I didn't want to go. I wanted to honor the fact that the Aguilas wanted me down there and were paying good money. Plus, I was well aware of all the guys who went down to play winter ball in various countries but didn't fulfill their commitments by staying the entire season. I wanted to honor my deal with the Aguilas, but my dad was a mess and I had no other choice than to leave.

So we flew home to Connecticut and got the story of what was going on. Aunt Skip told me exactly where my mother was staying, and I turned to Karen and told her to stay with her parents while I flew down to Florida. She agreed, so the next day, after just having arrived from the Dominican, I went back to the airport and flew from Hartford to Tampa, got on a bus, and traveled to Fort Myers where we had left our car.

I drove up to Sarasota and didn't know what I was going to confront, because I knew they were in a motel. To this day, there is nobody who knew how frightened I was to confront this situation. Terrified, I went to the local police station, explained the situation, and asked an officer to come with me. I wanted backup.

He agreed, so I followed his squad car over to the motel. While he stayed in his car, I knocked on my mom's door. She barely said a word before I said, "Mom, we're going home." I didn't ask her for any details.

I just told her, "I'm not going in there. You pack up right away. I've got a policeman out here; he's going to watch us as I take you back to my car." I never saw the other man involved, but I know who he was.

We packed my car with her things, got a room to stay in overnight, and I drove her back to Connecticut on US-301. There was no I-95 or any of that stuff in those days. We got back home and I don't know the details of how she patched things up with Dad, because I left right away and went back to the Dominican Republic to honor my commitment of finishing out the season.

My return made me a real hero down there because not only had I been pitching well, but I simply came back. Returning to winter ball after going back to the United States was not all that common. I convinced Karen I had to return, but she had had enough and remained in Connecticut.

With Karen still in Connecticut with her parents, I spent my first Christmas as a husband by myself. I still remember being outside in the heat listening to Frank Sinatra singing "Have Yourself A Merry Little Christmas," one of the saddest Christmas songs ever written. Feeling very blue at that moment, I called Karen and said, "You've got to get back down here. I miss you and can't be down here without you."

"But you only have a little bit more time left there," she replied. I told her to think about it.

After we were off the phone, her mother told her, "Your husband wants you there. You need to go back." She did and, unbeknownst to us at the time, was pregnant with our first son, David.

After everything Karen and I had been through both in the Dominican Republic and back home, we found some perspective by way of the Aguilas' eight-year-old little batboy. He was so proud to be my friend that he would hang outside of the house we were staying in and walked me to the ballpark every day. After a couple of weeks, he took me by the hand and walked Karen and I to this dirt street in a poverty-stricken area of Santiago where he lived. He wanted me to see his house, and his family was kind enough to invite us in for a meal.

The timing of the experience truly was inspirational. It was a tough overall period for us in the Dominican Republic. We were newly married, in a strange country, our president was dead, and now there was a family crisis at home. But the one constant was the craziness that was Dominican baseball. Pretty much everybody gambled on the games down there, so emotions ran very high. After losing the last four games of our playoff series after winning the first three, the Aguilas' fans tipped our bus over outside the ballpark. It was just wild stuff.

I finished out the winter league season strong with a record of 9–2. Despite the brawl, the fans loved me down there.

But most important, I developed a slider down there that became the main reason why I became a successful major league pitcher. I experimented with the slider out of necessity. Although my curveball was good, it was also too inconsistent to be effective in the big leagues.

The slider is an easier pitch to learn and be consistent with than a curveball. In fact, a slider, according to Ted Williams, was the pitch that changed baseball because it doesn't give away the fact that it's a breaking ball the way that a curveball does by the spin. A slider is basically a fastball that quickly cuts across maybe 8 to 10 inches sideways. It's easier to develop and master a slider than a curveball because the latter requires a lot of timing and release over the top, in addition to a lot of spin and wrist action.

A lot of pitchers who couldn't be consistent with the curveball went to the slider. That being said, it doesn't have the speed of a fastball or the break of a curveball, being a hybrid, so the critical thing with the slider is location. When you throw a slider located properly, it is a very difficult pitch for the hitter because he doesn't see a break or a spin like a curveball. He instead sees what he thinks is a fastball that, all of a sudden, darts away from him. So that's the beauty of the slider.

The negative of the slider is that if you don't get it in the right spot, Ted Williams said, it gets hit farther than any other pitch. So a slider is a breaking ball that you can master, but it's all about location and throwing it exactly where you want.

I got to the point in the Dominican Republic where I felt like I had mastered the slider to a degree. I could throw it when I was behind in the count, which is a huge advantage, because every hitter lives on looking for a fastball when he's ahead in the count 2–0 or 3–1. So, if you can throw batters a breaking ball for a strike when it is a hitter's count, then you've got a winner because they sit on the fastball. Hitters get to the big leagues by waiting for the fastball when the count is in their favor.

I mastered my slider on my own without the help of any coaches. One of the positives of the Dominican League was the fact there was so much flexibility to experiment on pitches. I had all the time and latitude to work on the slider, so I just threw it constantly to try to get the feel of it. And that created my success in the big leagues.

The other thing about the Dominican League was how superior it was to the off-season instructional leagues which I had previously taken part in. The Dominican Winter League was a very high grade of baseball. All three Alou brothers were on one of the teams. Juan Marichal was on another team. It was the equivalent of probably Triple A to Quad A level baseball, and that made for competition that wasn't against kids who had just signed. These were all either major leaguers or high-profile minor leaguers.

The level of competition was important. Because I was learning a slider while throwing against the Alou brothers, who were in their prime, as well as other really good players, it gave me a true sense whether the pitch was going to work or not. So, in spite of all the political upheaval and working on a new marriage, I found my best pitch, the slider, in the Dominican Republic.

Karen and I flew straight from the Dominican to Fort Myers for the start of spring training and, another one of my favorite pastimes, the dog track races. Enter Tom Butters. Tom is one of my heroes because he was always remarkably consistent with his principles, and I was always a little bit lacking in some of mine. I was drawn to him much the same way as I was with Stick and Maz.

During that spring of 1964, Tom and I loved going to the dog tracks. I was out of control with my betting, but Tom, for whatever reason, would only bet the 1–7 quinella. That was enough for him, and he liked doing it. I, on the other hand, bet everything I had, and Tom just loved it because I would get so excited that I had to take a piss before every race. He was just fascinated by the fact I was that much out of control. We went on a regular basis and were both fairly recently married. Our wives hated the fact that we were obsessed with the dog track to the point they eventually forbade us from going any longer.

Shortly after getting that directive from the wives, Tom and I were shagging balls during batting practice at Fort Myers. Tom was in right-center field and I was in left-center. I started walking toward him, and he said, "Don't come near me. My marriage is on the line. Don't come near me. I know what you want!"

I said calmly, "Tom, I need to talk to you. I have the best financial offer you will ever have the rest of your life. No matter what happens to you the rest of your life, you will never have a better opportunity financially. Here's the deal. There are 12 races at the dog track. We put in a dollar for each race. That buys us a $2 quinella for each one. If we don't win, I will give you your $12 back."

He instantly said, "I'll pick you up at 6:45."

Our wives have never forgiven us for that. And the results didn't even matter.

To this day, almost 50 years later, he says it's the best financial opportunity he has ever had in his life. And he's made a ton of money. But he has never had a better, more secure offer for his finances than he had that afternoon in right-center field at Terry Park in Fort Myers.

The next spring, he was back in spring training as a valuable Pirates prospect after having some success with the big club the previous year. Tragically, a car accident really messed up his neck to the point that whenever he would try to throw, he would get violently ill. I guess the technology was not the same back then. But it caused him great pain and distress, and as a result of that accident, late in spring training the Pirates released him.

A lot of us were staying at duplexes at Cape Coral, just outside of Fort Myers, when they released him. As he was getting ready to go home, I went over to his duplex and spent some time with him. He was crushed because his dream of playing big-league baseball since the age of eight was now over before it had hardly begun. The ending of "the dream" is the most devastating that will ever happen to an athlete. My visit meant a great deal to him, and he has never forgotten it. That cemented our relationship.

Tom is a study in perseverance. After a few months of coming to grips with his baseball career ending, he realized that he was still a young man that, thankfully, was not paralyzed by the accident. Tom would go on to great things. He became the baseball coach at Duke University, replacing the great Enos Slaughter. He then moved up the ranks to be named director of the Iron Dukes, the fundraising arm of the University. His success there put him on the road to becoming athletic director, where he wound up hiring Steve Spurrier as the football coach and Mike Krzyzewski, better known as Coach K, as the basketball coach.

The fans and boosters wanted to run Tom out of Durham during Coach K's first few rebuilding years with Duke. But Tom stuck by his choice because he believed that Coach K's emphasis on defense would win championships and, 11 Final Four appearances and four NCAA championships later, one could say that Tom was certainly rewarded for his convictions.

There is now a building named after Butters at Duke, and a bust of him on the first tee at the University's golf course, and he's in the North Carolina Hall of Fame. So he is somewhat of a legend at Duke University.

Tom and I still have the absolute best relationship. He invites me to stay with him and attend his member-guest golf tournament each year at Treyburn Country Club in Durham, North Carolina. Sadly, his health has suffered in recent years, but he puts up a thousand bucks and has me come down as a guest and has me paired up with a member and club champion named Charles Woody. We finish last every year, but Butters laughs at us because he is financing this failure. He gets enough mileage out of making fun of us that it's worthwhile to him.

So as the 1964 spring training was wrapping up, I felt very good about my chances of making the major league team. I was receiving positive feedback from the coaches and had certainly put in my time in the minor leagues and winter ball. I was so close to fulfilling my boyhood dream, I could taste it.

In fact, just three days before the team broke spring training for Pittsburgh, I went up to Joe Brown and said, "I've got a wife who is pregnant, and Joe, I need to know if I'm going to make the club because I don't know where to tell her to go. She's going to drive the car, and I have to travel with whichever ballclub I am going to be playing for."

He said, "You're on. You've made it."

So Karen took off for Pittsburgh, but two days later, Joe did a 180 and told me that the Pirates were sending me to Columbus. So, in essence, Karen made the team and I didn't. She got to the major leagues before I did. But it certainly wasn't a big-league situation for her.

Here she was, 21 years old, newly married, and pregnant. She drove to Pittsburgh, a city she didn't know anything about, completely alone. Now she gets a call from her husband, saying, "Change of plans. I'm not going to Pittsburgh but to Columbus, instead."

Now she had to pack everything she had in Pittsburgh and drive to Columbus, another city completely new to her. And, not knowing anyone, she wound up staying at the YWCA. On top of that, she had to find an apartment before her husband arrived. So you think being a ballplayer's wife is glamorous, huh? Think again! Dream on, teenage queen!

When I think back now, I wish I could have helped her more during that time. And it reminds me of how oblivious I was to so many things around me during my baseball career.

I was very disappointed about not going north with the club but kept a positive attitude, reminding myself that I was just 21 years old and still refining my craft. So when I eventually got the call, I believed I would be more prepared than ever.

After starting the season at Columbus with two strong starts, I had a sense that getting my ticket to Pittsburgh was just a matter of time.

CHAPTER 4

A Wake-Up Call to the "University of Baseball"

"I'd like to talk to Steve Blass," a gentleman on the phone said to Karen the morning after an all-night bus ride back to Columbus following a game in Syracuse.

"Well, I'm sorry, but Steve was up all night, and he's sleeping now. Can you call back later?" But the man was persistent.

"No, I really need to talk to him. I really do need to talk to him." Now Karen was starting to become impatient.

"Didn't you hear what I said? He was up all night. He's sleeping now, and I don't want to bother him."

"Mrs. Blass, this is Joe Brown," the Pirates' general manager said. "I want to tell him we're calling him up to the big leagues."

All Joe could hear after that was Karen shouting, "Get your ass out of bed! Get your ass out of bed! We're going to the big leagues!"

It's the call that everybody waits for and everyone can tell you chapter and verse what the circumstances were. I thought mine, on that Thursday morning of May 7, 1964, was a little bit unique. A lot of times a guy will be playing in a minor league game and the manager will take him out of the game, which is standard procedure so he doesn't get hurt when they get the notice from above.

The player will ask, "Why did you take me out?"

"Well you're just not getting the job done," the manager will tell him. "You're not hitting. You're not pitching well. I just want to get you out of the game." Then, the manager will wait a minute, hesitate a bit, and tell the confused player, "Well, you're going to the big leagues!"

After getting my call-up to the Pirates from Joe, Karen and I scrambled to get everything together. There is so little time to prepare for something like this. You've got to gather your belongings, get out of your apartment, and transform yourself from minor league apartment to the big leagues.

We drove in a pouring rain from Columbus, Ohio, to Pittsburgh that same day. There was a hotel called the Webster Hall in Oakland, walking distance to Forbes Field, which visiting teams and rookie call-ups regularly stayed in. We checked in, and I left Karen there and headed straight to Forbes Field.

It was still hours before the scheduled night game, and the rain was still coming down hard. I walked through the clubhouse door, and the equipment manager, John Hallahan (who, by the way, could have written his own colorful book), was there to greet me. "Congratulations, Steve," John said. "Come on in. I'll show you where your locker is."

In my mind, I was just on the "gong show" at this point, completely starry-eyed. John walked me over to my locker, where I saw, in bold type, "Steve Blass," positioned along the top of it. Next to all the names in the clubhouse lockers was the Iron City Beer logo, a team sponsor. I just stared at that locker until John broke the silence and asked, "Well, aren't you going to put on the uniform and go out on the field, check it out?"

I said, "Well, I would, but it's raining cats and dogs out there."

He said, "Steve, look in there, you can put it on. If it gets wet, there are three more just like it. That's one of the reasons they call it the big leagues."

I was in heaven.

The next day, perhaps in my excitement over spending my first full day as a member of the Pittsburgh Pirates, I forgot to leave a ticket for Karen at the will call window. When Karen informed the ticket agent that she was my wife, he asked her, "Who the hell is Steve

Blass?" I am not sure how the issue was resolved, but Karen and I are still married today.

I would have to wait until Sunday, May 10, in the second game of a doubleheader with the Milwaukee Braves, to make my first appearance in the big leagues. It should have been a completely euphoric experience for me. Instead, it turned into a most uncomfortable one.

Enter Tommie Sisk. Tommie was a big right-handed pitcher whom I came up with through the minor leagues. We competed against each other in a friendly way to see who might get to the big leagues first. Tommie won that contest, getting called up in 1962. He started his third season in 1964 on the big-league team. After my call-up, he and his wife, Donice, were kind enough to invite Karen and me to stay with them until we found a place of our own. That was great, because staying in a hotel was expensive for us at that point in my career.

Tommie started the game of my first appearance and got crushed, facing six Braves in the top of the first inning without retiring any of them. Danny Murtaugh brought me in to relieve Tommie, and I went on to pitch five shutout innings. We would battle back from a 5–0 deficit to win the game with three runs in the bottom of the ninth 6–5.

After the game, in the clubhouse, Tommie and I were getting ready to drive home when Murtaugh told Tommie that the club was sending him down to Columbus. So while I was on Cloud Nine because I had just made my major league debut and pitched five scoreless innings against Henry Aaron and the Braves, my house host was getting sent down to the minors.

I thought, *Talk about mixed emotions. My God, how are we going to handle this?* We drove home describing to our wives the elation of my first appearance and Tommie's devastation over just learning about his demotion to Columbus. The Sisks were very gracious about it all and allowed us stay to stay in their home while they packed up and left for Columbus. That was probably one of the most awkward rides I'd ever experienced, like a rollercoaster at an amusement park. The good news for Tommie was that he was back up with us the next year and had four more productive seasons before being traded to the San Diego Padres.

My first big-league start would come eight days later in Hollywood style. Literally. The scene was Dodger Stadium. The night before my debut, Doris Day, my fantasy movie starlet, who stole my heart in her role in *Calamity Jane* when she sang "Secret Love," was sitting in the front row. Even today at age 70, it is on my bucket list to meet her. Meanwhile, the Dodgers were the defending World Champions, having dethroned the mighty Yankees in four straight games the previous October. The opposing pitcher was future Hall of Famer Don Drysdale. It would have been a daunting task for any pitcher, much less a kid starting his first major league game.

I called everyone I knew back in Falls Village. It took only about three quarters. It's a small town. When calling my parents, I said, "Listen, Mom and Dad, I'm starting against Drysdale on Monday night. Tune in early because I don't know how long I'm going to be around."

Teams typically gave their starting pitchers a brand-new baseball to warm up with, putting it in their lockers. I remember picking up my baseball and thinking, *My God, it feels like a shot put.*

At Dodger Stadium, the visitor's clubhouse is a fairly good walk behind the first-base dugout. I walked down that tunnel by myself and, upon entering the dugout, looked out at their big JumboTron in center field that read:

STARTING PITCHERS TONIGHT:

Steve Blass for the Pirates
0 Wins 0 Losses

Don Drysdale for the Dodgers
5 Wins 1 Loss
ERA: 2.19
NL Total Wins: First
NL Total Innings: Second

It probably listed how Drysdale ranked with the National League leaders in several other pitching categories, but that was all I needed to see. I went out to the bullpen to warm up and threw for about 15 minutes. The adrenaline in my body was going up as I threw as hard as I could. I tried to look over to see where Drysdale was warming up but couldn't find him.

I walked back into the dugout and really got a sense of how tough it was going to be to pitch in the major leagues after Bill Mazeroski tapped me on the shoulder, pointed over to Drysdale, and said, "Pitch a shutout, kid, and we'll play for a tie." That was vintage Maz. He didn't say much, but he had some great one-liners.

Between Drysdale and Sandy Koufax, the Dodgers likely had the best one-two punch of any starting staff in baseball. But to sweep the Yankees in the World Series, they needed a great lineup as well. The Dodgers had a very balanced attack, a good mix of speed and power. Frank Howard was so damn big that I thought his bat was going to hit my hand on my follow-through. I weighed about 160 pounds and had to face that monster. But he was hitless in four trips, and I struck him out twice.

The running game was just starting to come into vogue around that time. The Dodgers had tremendous speed with Maury Wills, Tommy Davis, and Willie Davis, so they were kind of the pioneers of using the stolen base as an offensive weapon.

Smoky Burgess was my catcher that night and kept calling for the fastball to give himself a better chance to catch them running. In the fourth inning, I went up to him and said, "Smoky, I do have a breaking ball. Keep that in mind."

Leo Durocher was coaching third base for the Dodgers and certainly earned his nickname of "Leo the Lip" that entire game. In an effort to rattle me, make me nervous, and make me pay more attention to him and less on the opposing hitters, he called me everything one could imagine. I got a formal education on every profanity known to man, most of which was in English.

Against all odds and distractions, I wound up going the distance, a complete game victory, as I gave up seven hits while also striking out seven. When people ask which game was most significant to me, the five shutout innings in my first appearance or the complete game in my first start, I tell them there is no contest. Winning your first major league start, a complete game at Dodger Stadium, and beating Drysdale in front of a crowd like that, wins easily.

Years later, I interviewed Drysdale for "Greats of the Game," a series that I did, and my first question to him was, "Don, does May 18, 1964, have any significance to you?"

He went, "No, not that I can think of."

I said, "It was my first major league win, and it was against you."

Drysdale said, "Ah, shit, not another one."

It was like he was a gunslinger and everyone was coming into town to beat the fastest gun. Despite reveling in the victory and doing a number of interviews, I did remember to call home. I waited until the next morning after that game to call my dad first and then my high school coach, Ed Kirby.

I told Ed I didn't call after the game because it would have been 2:00 AM back in Falls Village. Ed told me, "Well, I was still drinking beer at 2 o'clock in the morning, so you could have called. We were still up from listening to the game."

Back in the day, when we were on KDKA radio in Pittsburgh, my folks back in Connecticut could pick up the station at night. To give a perspective of how small Falls Village is, whenever I pitched, my dad would get a six pack, get in his car, and just drive around town until the reception came in well. He would just stop there and listen to the game. God only knows what people must have thought driving by and seeing this guy sitting there in his car with the radio on with a six pack. He probably should have been arrested three or four times.

At the end of each season, he would send our radio announcer, Bob Prince, an invoice for two car batteries and 16 cases of beer. Prince loved that story and ended up using it on the banquet circuit. My dad jokingly would say, "The sonofabitch never paid my invoices."

Getting off to a great start to my baseball career was a relief. There were nerves for sure, but I knew I had a job to do and was thankful I got on a roll. Besides all of the obvious perks I began to enjoy as a major leaguer, I felt even more fortunate than other young players because I was not just a player, but also a huge fan of the game. Time after time I had the chance to pitch against my heroes.

The first time I faced Willie Mays, I thought, *My God, I think I may still have his bubble gum card in my wallet.* In that at-bat, Mays chopped a ball to first base and, in my delight that he didn't hit it out of the park, I was a step late in covering the bag. Mays beat it out for an infield single.

The next day, one of the coaches came over to me and said that Murtaugh wanted to see me. I figured Danny just wanted to have a father-son kind of chat. But, instead, Danny looked me right in the eye and said, "That Mays can really get down the line, can't he?"

"Yeah, Danny," I replied. "He sure can."

"Well, it cost you $100," Murtaugh said. "See if you can beat him there next time."

It was one of the great eras of major league baseball. Guys like Aaron, Mays, McCovey, Koufax, Marichal, Seaver, Carlton, Billy Williams, and so many others made it special. They played the game *so* well, were *so* accomplished, and were all just *so* immersed with what they were trying to do. To this day, I am so proud to have played in that era. I look back and say, "Damn, I was good, but I was good against the best, and that makes it times 10."

I became a serious fan at 10 years old, back in 1952, a terrific era for baseball. I was knee deep in the middle of it. There was a movie made about Jackie Robinson back in the early 1950s that I remember going to see at a drive-in theater in Canaan, Connecticut. My grandmother used to put six of us in the car and try to hide us so we wouldn't have to pay for everybody. I had Jackie's bubblegum card. I wish I had it now, as it's probably worth a fortune. I guess I'm like every other kid in America whose mother took the shoebox full of cards, put them in the attic, and had some ghost come along and take them.

The era I played in versus today was very different. There are great athletes now, for sure. In fact, if you compressed the major leagues right now into eight teams in each league, you would have phenomenal talent on each club. So whereas I can't say my era was a better one than today, it was certainly just as good.

As far as talent and character were concerned, the Pirates of the 1960s had as much of each as I could have hoped for as a young player. I simply could not have walked into a more professional scenario than the 1964 Pirates. I would not just learn to improve my game as a pitcher but also as a major leaguer. I refer to that team and experience back then as "The University of Baseball," and the guys on that team were my professors.

I had a feel for the team from being around them during spring training, but now I needed to validate to them that I was good enough to be a teammate and not just another kid in the back room in spring training. During spring training, I was more of an observer. Now, I had to put it up there. It was a stimulating thought that I was obsessed with.

Unbeknownst to me at the time, during spring training in 1964, Murtaugh did me one of the biggest favors he could have imagined when he approached one of our veteran pitchers, Bob Friend. As Friend tells it, Murtaugh said to him, "Say, Bob, I want you to get a hold of Blass."

Bob said, "Who in the hell is Blass?"

Murtaugh said, "He's No. 54 running out there in the outfield. I'd like you to get a hold of him and room with him."

Bob said, "Well, that's fine with me."

That was the beginning of a longstanding friendship with Bob that is still going strong today.

Bob and his wife, Pat, really helped Karen and I get our feet wet at the major league level. Pat helped Karen a great deal in how to handle being a baseball wife and with getting to know the city of Pittsburgh better.

As a roommate and mentor, I could not have asked for anyone better than Bob. It was a big deal to have your first roommate take you under his wing like he did with me. Bob helped show me what I should take on a road trip, how I should dress, what restaurants to go to, what to invest my money in, and how to deal with the media. He was very influential to me.

We didn't talk too much about actual pitching because, despite his being such a star back then, we didn't have that much in common in terms of style. Besides being one of the best pitchers in baseball, Bob was knee deep with everything in the city, which included a membership with the high-end Pittsburgh Athletic Association.

During a trip to San Francisco during the season, we had an off-day and Bob said to me, "C'mon kid, I want to show you something."

We went to a really nice club that had a reciprocal agreement with the PAA in Pittsburgh. He said, "We're going inside to go get a steam." I didn't know what the hell he was talking about. My father was a plumber, and his business was the only thing I could relate to with steam. I weighed only 160 pounds and didn't want to sweat anything off. But I went along with it because everything was very luxurious.

As we sat in the steam room, all of a sudden the door opened up, and in walked a waiter wearing a tuxedo with a tray of six ice-cold draft beers. I said, "What the hell is that?"

Bob said, "Well, kid, we're going to break even today."

I said, "Damn, is this another reason they call it the big leagues? Life is good!"

Our early friendship was reciprocal to an extent. I learned life lessons from him and how to act like a major leaguer. And he genuinely enjoyed my sense of humor, particularly my imitations of famous people. He liked my John F. Kennedy and Frank Fontaine's Crazy Guggenheim impressions, but he loved a bit I did of character actor Walter Brennan so much that he would introduce me to his friends as the three-time Oscar winner. It sometimes felt like I was a jukebox around him, like he could push a button and go, "Alright, give me a little Walter Brennan here."

The funny thing was that they were terrible imitations, but Bob loved them and made me say them all the time until his friends would go, "Bob, enough, you have to let it go."

In fact, my impressions were so bad, one time I did Frank Fontaine's Crazy Guggenheim on a postgame show with Prince, and Maz's wife, Milene, thought I was making fun of people who didn't speak well. She asked Maz, "What is he doing?" And she was right, because it was so bad it didn't sound anything like the character.

But being a rookie, I was going to go along with practically whatever Bob wanted. Another thing he had me do was walk to the ballparks with him from whatever hotel we were staying at. He considered it good exercise for himself because as a starter, he pitched only every fourth or fifth day. So he introduced me to his program, which he was obviously used to and I was not. And there were no exceptions, even if the walk was quite far.

For example, we would walk from the Warwick Hotel in Philadelphia to Connie Mack Stadium. It had to be five or six miles through a very tough neighborhood. It would take so long, I remember we even stopped for sandwiches along the way a few times. We did the same thing in St. Louis, where we walked from the Chase Park Plaza Hotel to Sportsman's Park, another long, extended walk where we ventured through another rather difficult area.

During one of these trips, he turned to me and said, "Keep it moving. We're not sightseeing here. These are rough neighborhoods." Bob was used to it, but I was usually exhausted by the time we got to the ballpark. Again, the rookie didn't question the vet. Those walks created a very sincere appreciation of the team bus for me.

Dick Groat was another influential teammate who caught my attention in terms of what it takes to become a major leaguer. Dick proved that you don't have to have a massive frame to become a star in baseball, but rather you need to have an understanding of how you can use your body *and* your head to succeed.

Dick was a guy who was never out of position. I watched him, and he looked like a guy who knew exactly where to be, and what to do, and he looked like he was always in total control with his game at shortstop. He looked like a guy who maxed out everything he had, never leaving anything on the table. He was, in a word, a grinder.

I saw a little bit of myself in him. I was never a flame thrower. I thought maybe I could make it in the same style as Dick Groat, someone who maybe can't dominate physically but can find other ways to beat you. I was built a little bit like Dick. We were living proof that you don't have to be a monster to succeed in this game.

Another teammate who had a tremendous influence over me during my early years in the bigs was Mazeroski. He helped instill in me the notion that there are no excuses in baseball. Just go out there and get the job done. He conveyed to me stuff like, "This is the big leagues. People want to know why you did, not why you didn't."

In a postgame interview, when a reporter asked on the rare occasion he made an error at second base, "What happened there, Maz, what happened there?"

"Well, shoot, I just kicked it," he said. "There's no excuse. I just booted it."

For Maz, the ball never hit a pebble. Never took a bad bounce. It was always a play he felt he should have made. It was as simple as that. I admired his taking responsibility for his rare miscues all the more when considering where we played our home games.

The infield at Forbes Field was, perhaps, the worst in baseball. It was a bad surface to begin with, but when we would go on 10- or 14-day road trips, the Pirates' ground crew would put the tarp on the whole infield and bake it, making it even harder. It reached the point where that surface got so bad that a lot of visiting infielders would come into Forbes Field and not take infield practice for fear of getting into bad habits or having a ball bounce up and whack them in the head.

The most famous example of an infielder getting injured on a bad hop at Forbes Field happened in the 1960 World Series, coincidentally in the seventh game that made Maz a household name. Yankee shortstop Tony Kubek was struck in the throat on a sharp grounder hit by Bill Virdon and had to be carried off the field. It bothers me to watch many of Maz's fielding records made on the Forbes Field infield be broken by guys playing on a carpet. It's sad. To this day, I think Maz's fielding records should be acknowledged more because of where he played second base.

Plus, you have to add to the fact he shared the right side of the infield for years with first baseman Dick Stuart, nicknamed "Dr. Strangeglove" for his fielding problems. On any pop up to that side of the infield the first thing you would hear at Forbes Field was, "Maz, plenty of room! You got it Maz!"

Along with Roberto Clemente, Maz was another guy I thought I had to win over. I had put Maz on a pedestal because he didn't like to throw compliments around. Compliments were like manhole covers to him. You had to earn his respect, and I knew that. I badly wanted to impress Maz. I wanted to know he felt it was okay for me to be on the same ballclub with him. So, for me, he was in the same category as Clemente.

I had the good fortune to be roommates with Maz in 1969. His birthday that year fell on the same day as my only home run as a big leaguer, so we went out after the game together to celebrate. To be honest, I really don't recall much about the details surrounding the only home run of my career. My memory of the event is pretty vague, but I do remember it happened on September 5, 1969, at 2:04 in the afternoon. The humidity was 43 percent. The winds were moving out to left at five mph at Wrigley Field under slightly overcast skies. Ken Holtzman was the pitcher. I went 4-for-5 that day.

The great thing about it was, after I hit the ball and started running toward first, our first-base coach, Don Leppert, yelled to me, "Take a left!"

I had always taken a right back to the dugout.

But other than that, everything is really quite sketchy.

Chicago allowed ballplayers the ideal place and time to celebrate such days that Maz and I shared together. Because they played only day games at Wrigley back then, we were on the street in Chicago by 2:04 PM.

Looking back at that day, perhaps because Maz and I probably were thinking it might never happen again, which it didn't, we completely maxed out celebrating my home run and his birthday. My gift to Maz was that he had to play the next day.

I said, "Maz, you get to play in a major league game tomorrow. Good luck!"

Maz was so great about it. He was hurt during much of the season that we roomed together in 1969, and I remember seeing on his face how much it broke his heart that he couldn't play. He got into only 67 games that season and, despite the injuries, felt that if he was on a big-league team, he should be playing no matter what the circumstances. That told me a lot about Maz. All he wanted to do was play ball. I have as much regard for him as a professional as anybody I have ever been around.

Getting continually honored by the Pirates means a lot to him, but in my mind it's probably not the most comfortable thing he does. But his loyalty to the team has never been questioned, and he always does the right thing. His work representing the Pirates Alumni Association has made it one of the strongest in the major leagues.

When he got a statue dedicated to him by the Pirates outside of PNC Park in 2010, Maz told the gathering of people there, "How could anybody ever dream of something like this? All I wanted to be was a ballplayer. I didn't need all of this." Make no mistake; he is proud of his World Series home run in 1960, but because it has been brought up to him so many times, sometimes volume takes the luster off of some things.

I know he'd rather talk about that entire championship team because he says, "If I hadn't done it, someone else would have done it."

That home run also takes a little bit away from the body of work he did as a major league ballplayer, in terms of his defense and his hitting ability. He was a pretty damned good major league hitter, all things considered. So there is a degree of discomfort but at the same time still a lot of pride. He might say he is more proud of his career than that World Series game–winning home run, but it was still a pretty damn special moment to have.

A few years ago at spring training, he told some players, "Just don't forget, guys, the name on the front of your uniform is more important than the name on the back." That has always been his message. Your ballclub is bigger than you are as an individual, and that goes back to how he feels about his home run.

I find myself still trying to impress Maz, make him laugh, or get his attention. I still kind of have Bill Mazeroski on a pedestal after all these years. And I love it. I absolutely love it.

Later in my career, another Pirate who factored greatly in my development as a pitcher was Hall of Famer Jim Bunning. Jim came over to us after years with Detroit and Philadelphia. He was a no-nonsense pitcher, a kind of baseball businessman. Jim pitched for us only in 1968 and part of 1969 but played a major role in teaching me to deal with the highs and lows of pitching. In short, he helped me develop a mental toughness to my game.

When he came over to the Pirates that first spring, my family shared a duplex with his on Anna Maria Island. This gave me some valuable time to spend with him away from the field. I went on to have a great year, going 18–6, in part because of the guidance he provided me.

We again shared the duplex during spring training in 1969, and one of the first things he reminded me of was to keep my balance. He told me, "The highs in the big picture are too high, and the lows are devastating. The more you can stay in the middle, the better off you're going to be." And he was right, of course.

Jim's first year with us was uncharacteristic for him, as he went 4–14. The reason was simple. He was pitching hurt. He could have said, "I'm hurt, I can't pitch." But he took the ball every time. He was the second pitcher I was around like that. Friend took the ball all the time, too.

Jim was also angry out on the mound, and observing him pitch helped me get a little edge. I was having the time of my life, and I think just watching him helped me apply myself a little bit better. I always thought it was a great experience for me to be around a guy like Jim Bunning. I loved the approach that he had. He was a tough-ass major league pitcher, and any part of that that rubbed off on me is still appreciated.

Rounding out my short list of the Pirates who helped shape me as a big leaguer was Jerry Lynch. "The Sweeper," as Prince called him, was a teammate of mine during my first three seasons and was one of the great pinch-hitters of all time. Jerry was a good guy to be around, but that wouldn't stop him from getting into a teammate's face if the situation merited it.

During my rookie year, while I was still learning to get things right and avoid making some mistakes along the way, we had batting practice one day at Forbes Field. I will never forget it because, for whatever reason, I was in the clubhouse while the rest of the Pirates were on the field. Jerry walked in, saw me, and said sternly, "Listen, kid, don't ever, *ever* let me catch you in the clubhouse when your team is out on the field! That's your team. You should be out there with them."

I stood there, looking at him, speechless.

Jerry continued, "And I don't just mean batting practice, I mean fielding practice. You catch up with people hitting fly balls out to the outfielders. Be a member of this team. Now get your ass out there!"

I never forgot that. He ripped my ass real good, and I appreciated that. It helped make me a better team player.

While many call baseball a team sport, it is also my belief that it is a game of individual efforts that create a team result. It's a very naked sport. There's no pulling guard. There's no moving pick. Rather, it's the shortstop against the baseball, the center fielder against the fly ball, or the pitcher against the hitter—individual matchups.

I guess it was how I handled and learned from my experiences around the Pirates' clubhouse that would help mold me into a good teammate, a better player, and one who knew how to enjoy the major league experience. It was like I had graduated from the "University of Baseball."

CHAPTER 5

A Lesson in Perseverance

The year 1965 may have ended well for me, but it certainly had a start that was both unexpected and disappointing.

First, let me start off by noting that I was only "just okay" with the Pirates' new manager, Harry Walker, who replaced Danny Murtaugh after the 1964 season.

After a rookie campaign in which I showed so much promise by out-dueling Don Drysdale for my first win, pitching a four-hit shutout over a very good Philadelphia Phillies team, and having an ERA a hair over four runs per game, I felt sure that after I broke camp with the club to play an exhibition game in the new Houston Astrodome that I would then head north with the Pirates to start my second big-league season.

But Walker didn't really have a high regard for what I was all about with my pitching. He told me, "We're going to send you down. Maybe you need to come up with a kind of trick pitch or some other extra pitch, because your stuff is a little short." So he sent me down without pitching an inning in 1965.

Walker was just addicted to hitting. He had strong convictions with his hitting philosophies, and I give him a lot of credit for his work with guys like Matty Alou, who won the batting title his first year with the Bucs

in 1966 after coming over to us from the Giants, where he had batted just
.231 the previous season.

I went back down to Columbus with a good attitude, and that was
the key for me in eventually getting back to the majors the following year.
Murtaugh had a great philosophy. When he sent me and other players
down to the minors during spring training in previous years, he would
always call whoever he was demoting to his office and would tell them
basically the same thing.

"I have never gone through an entire major league season as a manager
with the same 25 guys," Danny would say. "There *will be* players called
up from Triple A. If you go down there with your head up your ass, you
might not be one of them. But if you go down there and work your ass off,
you might be one of them. So we will be looking down there. It depends
on you what you want to do with this opportunity."

Murtaugh projected that he cared about me. And I believe he did.
But I want to be clear. He did not inspire me to pitch better. My entire
philosophy on being a professional athlete is that you inspire yourself.
With that being said, when we take baseball out of the equation, what
do we all want as human beings? We want to be cared about. And that's
why Danny meant so much to me. Years later, he would tell me that he
never would have sent me back down the minors if he still had been the
manager in 1965.

Joe Brown cared about me, too. He arranged it so when I later bought a
home, the $25,000 I borrowed from the Pirates was interest free. I paid them
back by having them take money out of my paychecks. There were other
times when I would borrow $5,000 from the Bucs to get me through spring
training into the season. The world was different then. Joe Brown didn't have
to do any of that stuff, but he did. Between those two guys, they made me
feel as if we had a relationship and I was not just a player to an organization.

In spite of the strong rapport I had with Danny and Joe, I was still
very discouraged when Harry sent me back to Columbus. But on the plus
side, I was still high up in the system and doing exactly what I wanted to.
Plus, getting sent down also gave me another year under the tutelage of
Columbus manager Larry Shepard.

In my two-plus years in Triple A, Larry helped me enormously in becoming a major league pitcher. On the field, Shepard was constantly on my ass and didn't give me any slack. He was almost a continuation of my high school coach, Ed Kirby, in that respect. He felt like I had the abilities to succeed in baseball, but he wasn't going to let up on me because he knew what I was going to face in the majors. I thank him to this day for being tough on me, because I know in my heart what his intent was. He was great for me during that period as a pitcher, because I wasn't particularly disciplined, structured, or focused all the time.

In fact, I was kind of full of myself, and he kept me grounded and gave me guidelines that I remember being very positive toward my development. You can go through the minors, dominate, and throw the ball by people. But when you get through Triple A and go to the big leagues, it is an enormous step. In helping me make that leap to the big-league level, Larry was absolutely terrific.

A lot of people don't realize how far it is from Triple A to the big leagues. In Triple A, you've got maybe two to four guys in the opposing lineup who can hurt you. But when you get to the big leagues, you're looking at six to eight guys who can just kill you when you make a mistake. You can't throw fastballs when you're behind in the count, so you better have something else in your bag. That's why developing a slider was so important to my career.

The 1965 season at Columbus was also an opportunity to play on what turned out to be a dominant team in the International League with a cast of characters who knew how to have fun.

We played a lot of poker both to pass the time and to keep us out of the bars. At Columbus, it became like therapy for the group of guys I played cards with. Guys like Gene "Stick" Michael, Tom Butters, "Sad Sam" Jones, George Spriggs, Tony Bartirome, and I were the guts of the ballclub.

But when a couple of our pitchers didn't see it that way and complained to Shepard that we weren't as sharp on the field because we sometimes played cards half the night, it fell on deaf ears. Larry told them, "I don't want to hear about this, because these are the guys that are having the best years on the club." Larry knew we would always be ready to play, and we were.

"Sad Sam" was a good card player, but, as we would discover, there was a good reason why. He cheated. One night, we realized we were missing an ace. Everyone stood up, and Sam looked like a point guard because he was moving the rest of his body around but kept his left foot firmly planted and wouldn't move it. It looked like he didn't want to be called for traveling! Eventually, he came clean that the ace of clubs was under that foot.

"Sad Sam" was a true character of the game. He pitched a no-hitter for the Cubs against the Pirates in 1955. His career was winding down, but he was with us at Columbus as a reliever. Sam had one of the biggest roundhouse, side-to-side curves I have ever seen, as good a side-to-side curve as Bert Blyleven had up and down.

Sam would come out with a pint of vodka in his back pocket and sit in the bullpen until he was called upon to pitch. But he would talk to me out there, and he kind of took me under his wing. He was down in the Dominican Republic to pitch when Karen and I went down there in 1963, and it was interesting because "Sam Jones" to the Spanish-speaking fans sounded like "Saint John." Well, he was anything but a saint.

But he talked to me about the philosophy of pitching, and when we won our division title in 1965 at Columbus, Sam took a bunch of us to this black nightclub, similar to the one shown in *Animal House*, and delivered me back to my apartment where I was staying with Karen at 4:00 AM and rang the bell. Karen opened the door, and all Sam asked her was, "Where do you want him?"

She said, "Right there. Leave him right there in the entry way." So it was obviously a very good celebration.

So another year honing my skills with Larry, an International League title, a good year on the mound, and the birth of our first child would be impossible to classify as anything other than a success. I was looking forward to 1966 and getting back into the big leagues for good. That's exactly what happened. I made the team in the spring and had a good season with the major league club, going 11–7 with a 3.87 ERA and helping the Pirates to a 92-win season. I felt like I had validated myself enough as a pitcher to finally be considered one of the guys.

Enter the Blue Max group. The Blue Max group was a spinoff I created from the World War I movie starring George Peppard that had just come out. Our group included me as the ringleader, Jim Pagliaroni, Pete Mikkelsen, ElRoy Face, and Luke Walker. We were in Chicago, on an off-day, and I went to see the movie about the German Fighter Aces. On my way back to the hotel, I was just screwing around, fruit flies in my head, and stopped by this gift shop and bought some white scarves, little trinkets, and some of these non-religious, little iron crosses—just a bunch of junk. The leather aviator helmets and goggles would come later on, because they were expensive.

I brought everything I bought to the clubhouse the next day and came up with the idea of the "You can't do it every day," "Hang in there," and "Get 'em tomorrow" trophies. In the beginning, the trinkets went to someone who may have gone 0-for-5 or got knocked out in the first inning. The presentations always happened the day after it happened, of course, because had we done it the same day, someone would have gotten pissed. I quickly turned around and started making the presentations after good performances. It worked better that way and we had more fun with it.

So the Blue Max group took on a life of its own. Our group started wearing the scarves and the leather helmets and other World War I German military paraphernalia. The group started gaining attention because we were having a good year. It finally got to the point where United Artists or somebody flew one of the old aces over to Toots Shor's where there was a luncheon. That's where Dick Young, a columnist from the *New York Daily News*, took exception and wrote a column skewering me, saying I was making fun of our boys who died over in Europe. What Young didn't realize was that it was all in fun and, damn it, my father fought in World War II and my grandfather in World War I. In fact, my grandfather modeled for a dough boy statue that still stands in Canaan, Connecticut. So, hell, what Young wrote was so far from what this whole thing was about.

My mother, who was like an agent to me, a personal representative times 50, sent a scathing letter to Dick Young and just aired him out. I don't recall exactly what she wrote in it, but I know it was just laced with profanities and she laid him out.

The irreverence that was attached to the Blue Max trophies was not worth some of the aggravation it caused, so we ended up changing it so it wouldn't have an association with a German fighter pilot. It wound up being the Black Max, and there was a picture of Pagliaroni in *Time Magazine* in 1966 with a little blurb about us.

We had a lot of fun with it. It was intended to be just that and nothing more. One of the best things about the Blue Max group was it really got me engaged with the guys and helped keep the team loose.

I was now with the Pirates to stay.

CHAPTER 6

The Year of the Pitcher

M ajor League Baseball had never seen anything like it in the modern era. Pitching so dominated the game in 1968, the so-called "Year of the Pitcher," that the results were awe-inspiring. The American League's ERA was 2.98. It had never sunk under 3.00 since 1918. The National League had an ERA of just 2.99, the first time it had gone below three runs a game since the dead-ball era in 1919.

The year 1919 was also when the Chicago White Sox threw the World Series in the Black Sox scandal. Babe Ruth and the long ball, of course, would save the game from "the fix" throughout the 1920s and, by 1936, the American League ERA had reached a modern-day era high of 5.04. And that was decades *before* the designated hitter rule came into effect. The National League would hit an ERA peak of 4.97 in 1930, never approaching that number again.

So 1968 was truly extraordinary. But nobody was more so than Bob Gibson and Denny McLain. Gibson went 22–9 with a miniscule, modern-day record-low ERA of 1.12 with 28 complete games! The really interesting stat for Gibson was that he somehow lost nine freaking games.

How does that happen? He was shut out only three times by the opposing pitcher, so there must have been a whole lot of unearned runs in those nine games he lost. To have a 1.12 ERA is the most phenomenal thing I have ever seen in baseball. Baseball people talk about Cy Young winning 511 games and how that total wins record will never be broken, but no one is ever going to have a 1.12 ERA again, either. *Ever.*

McLain won an astounding 31 games against just six losses with a 1.96 ERA to go along with 280 strikeouts. You want more stats? I had an ERA of 2.12, and there were *four* pitchers in the National League with lower earned-run averages. In the American League, *five* pitchers had ERAs of fewer than two runs a game. Luis Tiant had an ERA of 1.60 with an American League–leading nine shutouts and didn't have the credentials to beat McLain for the Cy Young Award.

Twelve pitchers in the major leagues totaled 200 or more strikeouts. The American League had only one .300 hitter in Carl Yastrzemski, and the National League's only hitter with more than 100 RBIs was Willie McCovey. The American League would hit, as a league, only a .230 batting average, while the National League could muster just .243.

I could go on, but you get the point. The pitching was so tremendous that it was revolutionary. In fact, it was a game changer.

The following season, in an effort to produce more runs and increase offense, the major leagues lowered the mound to just 10 inches high. In 1968, the mound was "officially" 16 inches but as high as 20 inches in places like Connie Mack Stadium in Philadelphia. God knows what it was at Dodger Stadium. In fact, after games in 1969 either the ground crew or the umpires would take a string and they would run it from home plate out to the top of the mound, just to make sure everything was within Major League Baseball guidelines. God knows what happened after they turned the lights out, but the Dodgers' mound was always the best in baseball. I'm not sure if they brought more hard clay out than they should have, but that stuff would never give, and as a result there was never any slipping or concern over one's footing. For a team that lived off its pitching, it was a classic case of a club building its field around its greatest strength.

The year 1969 also saw the major leagues add four new expansion teams with the Seattle Pilots and the Kansas City Royals in the American League and the San Diego Padres and the Montreal Expos in the National League. Although this was done mostly because of the popularity of the game and not to add offense, it diluted both the pitching and the hitting, thus creating a net opportunity for more runs to be scored.

I never considered either the lowering of the mound or expansion to have been big deals with respect to how pitchers performed. I never used that as an excuse (remember Maz's philosophy about excuses?). In fact, I considered expansion to be a helper for me because now the teams had to have more pitchers and hitters who were rookies and possibly not ready for the big leagues. So I figured it was just as much an advantage for me than anything else.

In any event, 1968 was both my breakout season and the best campaign I had ever pitched in. For as great as Gibson was that year, I had the National League's best winning percentage at .750, posting an 18–6 record. It was a huge improvement over my 1967 season, when I was 6–8 with a 3.55 ERA.

Of some significance was the Pirates changing managers before the 1968 season, promoting my old skipper at Columbus, Larry Shepard. We were a good match. I can get into all of his managerial attributes but, for me personally, he was a positive change from Harry Walker, who was never a big fan of mine. Shepard had helped me with my approach and attitude in the minor leagues, so when he was hired, in the Year of the Pitcher, it was a feel-good relationship that he got the managerial job. Psychologically, to have a pitchers' manager instead of a hitters' guy like Walker was a major benefit to me. Now I had a guy who knew me and how to press my buttons to get the most out of my abilities.

Case in point was an instance during that season when we were staying at the Sheraton Palace in San Francisco. One Sunday morning before we went to Candlestick, I bought my first $5 cigar at the gift shop. That was a big deal to me. You could smoke in the hotels then, and I had the cigar going pretty good. Sensing that I was feeling great about myself, Shepard, who went to Mass every morning, walked down to the lobby and said, "Put that thing out. We're going to church."

He had doubled down on me. He took away my cigar to bring me down a notch and had me go to church. That's not how I usually started my Sundays. I was feeling pretty good about myself until my cigar was taken away, and then he got my Catholic guilt going because I rarely went to church. He had taken control of me, and we hadn't even gone to the ballpark yet. That's how well he knew me.

Despite having an ally like Larry in my corner now, I didn't start until the 15th game of the season, when I defeated the Cubs and Fergie Jenkins. The simple reason was the Pirates didn't need me until then. Guys like Bob Veale, Jim Bunning, and Al McBean pitched extremely well, even in losing efforts. I hadn't had the opportunity to show the Bucs what I was capable of until I began starting games regularly.

After the victory over the Cubs, I pitched well but had a slew of no-decisions. In fact, on the morning of June 7, I still had only one win. But that would change with a 5–0 shutout over the Astros and my old friend, Dave Giusti. The victory was something I could build on, and all of a sudden my pitching took on a life of its own. The momentum became like a rock rolling down a hill.

The win over Houston would start a seven-game personal winning streak that included wins over All-Stars such as Mike Cuellar, Don Sutton, Nolan Ryan, Jerry Koosman, and Milt Pappas. For the first time in my career, I was, as they say in baseball circles, "getting it."

Some pitchers have a lot of talent, but they can't win. A lot of pitchers who have talent and don't succeed lack gut instincts. They don't know how to pitch. They've got great arms and can throw hard, but that instinct of how to pitch, what pitch to throw next and where to throw it, is something I don't think can be learned. Rather, I think a lot of that is either inside of a pitcher or it is not.

I began saying to myself, *I'm going to throw this pitch to this guy now, and I'm going to throw it here. I don't know why, but it's the right thing to do. And then here's what I'm gonna do next.* That's pitching on instinct and feel and what they mean when they say a guy "gets it." It may take years for that to come out of a pitcher, kind of like breaking scar tissue. That's what happened to me in 1968.

There was nothing mechanical about it. It was just a momentum of confidence. I now went out expecting to pitch well and win. It's a simple statement, but "expecting, not hoping, to win" is huge. It's what it's all about. It was an absolute lark, and the great thing about that run was that I didn't lose track of how much fun it was. It was just a joy. You don't want to say it was easy, but for that year and that roll I was on, pitching for me in the big leagues really was.

There were nights, of course, when success didn't come. But I still felt when I was going out there that I had confidence not unlike that of some of the most dominating pitchers in the game. And I had it for that one season more so than any other year in my career.

It was so good, in fact, that I would extend the postgame interviews if the writers had not asked me about something I wanted to tell them about. I couldn't wait to wake up in the morning and go out and get the newspaper. I would often ask myself, *What are they going to write about that performance?* Because if it was a great game or I pitched a two-hit shutout or something, I was like, *Oh my God, let's go out and read about it.* So it wasn't only a good year, it was a fun year to be able to pitch like that.

Another factor was the chemistry I had with Jerry May, our primary catcher. Back in those days, a pitcher typically couldn't request his own personal catcher like Steve Carlton could with Tim McCarver. With Jerry, though, I was fortunate because we came up through the minor leagues together, and he had caught me throughout the years. He was familiar with what I was often trying to throw.

The reality of a pitcher's relationship with his catcher is that if he's on a roll, he is almost his own decision maker. By throwing a pitch that the catcher calls for, you endorse his sign. But it you don't like it, you can change it. He can put down anything, and as long as you keep shaking your head, you're going to get to the pitch that you want to throw. I don't know if baseball people sometimes overdo the pitcher-catcher relationship I had with Manny Sanguillen in later years, because it involved a World Series. But Sangy knew me just as much psychologically as the nuts and bolts of the actual pitch calling. And that's huge. And that comes with time.

When a pitcher is on a roll, even if the catcher puts down something you're not thinking about, you're so confident that you often think, *Okay, you want that one? I can get him out with that one, too.* That's when you're really cooking.

After I validated myself as the ace of the Bucs' pitching staff, I was starting regularly on just three and four days' rest. This naturally is a far cry from many of today's pitchers who go out there on five days' rest, pitch six innings, and turn the ball over to a middle relief specialist. I loved pitching as many innings as I could. Pitchers then were developed to think that when the manager gave you the ball, you pitched a ballgame. That was it. You didn't think about quality starts. You didn't think about being programmed, developed, and trained for five or six innings. An old theory was that the more you pitched, the more you built up arm strength. And the more arm strength you built up, the more that helped you resist injury. It was all good. You could pitch longer, you could win, you could build up your arm, and your arm got stronger.

A stronger arm can also equate to fewer injuries. Everybody's arm tolerance is different, and the economics of the game have colored everything. But I had the kind of arm where I could pitch all the time. And that's an accident of birth. That's kind of the way my arm, my shoulder, and my elbow are wired genetically.

I never did anything particular to pamper or baby my arm, except for the advice given to me by my high school coach, Ed Kirby. He said, "You want to take care of your arm? Keep your jacket on all the time when you're not pitching. When you're done throwing and you're in the shower, hold your arm straight up and pound hot water on your elbow. New blood will come and circulate through your body, and old blood will go back to your heart." I followed Ed's advice all throughout my career after each time I pitched. It may have done absolutely nothing, but who knows?

Or maybe I was just lucky. I had the perfect body. I was skinny. I had a strong arm because I pitched all the time. And when I was pitching well, I wanted the ball on the fourth day. And why not? I was young, strong, and on a roll. The longer I waited between starts, the more I forgot about how good that previous one was. I wanted the ball, and I wanted the ball quickly. I didn't do much sideline throwing. All I would do the day after I pitched was play long toss just to stretch my arm out after working the night before. And then I'd leave it alone unless I was working on a specific problem.

It was a different philosophy than today, but the investment the major league teams financially put into these kids creates the need to be more cautious with them. If I were an owner, I would probably be more careful with them, too. It's almost like a Catch-22. Perhaps the more careful teams are with them, the more injury-prone they become. I see more kids on the disabled list now than ever. I wonder sometimes if their arms are really hurting or if they are just being protected by their respective teams.

We live in an age where a pitcher will go on the disabled list for a tired arm. It ranks right up there with another one, flu-like symptoms. He might say, "My God, I feel great now, but who knows? I might have a bug that's going to bother me in two days. I may be on the verge of a colossal cold." Or one of my new favorites that's closing fast on all the other stuff—*discomfort*. It's ludicrous.

The irony of it all is that in addition to pitchers of my era throwing all the time and hardly ever going on the disabled list, neither did we take care of ourselves like the players do today. First of all, we never did shit in the off-season. Most of us had jobs. And we were forbidden to go near weights. Now the training rooms are better than Bally Total Fitness.

I am not around the current players much, but I know they watch what they eat and drink more than we did. Plus, their training regimens are obviously better and performed year-round. While many of today's players are drinking vegetable juices and smoothies, we were out drinking beer every night. There was no SportsCenter, so you wouldn't go back to the room and see if you made Plays of the Day.

We worked hard and played hard. It was out of control in the 1960s, and some of us continue to do everything we can to carry the torch today. It's not as easy as it was because we're not in as good of shape. So it's getting harder to go back to back on back-to-back nights.

One of the reasons players are more careful today is because there are cameras and microphones everywhere. Everybody has a cell phone that takes pictures. So if a player has a beer in his hand, a picture or video showing that could be on SportsCenter, Twitter, or someone's blog tomorrow. Another reason is the money, which has changed everybody's viewpoint. One scandal can cost a player millions of dollars in salary or advertising revenue.

Despite having a lot of talent on our ballclub in 1968 and proving that by winning nine straight in June, we faltered terribly in July with a 10-game losing streak that dropped us to a season-high 17 games out. We pitched and hit pretty well but were second to last in the National League in one-run games that season. That was perhaps the biggest reason for our troubles.

On August 15, I pitched a 2–0 shutout over the Giants in what would be the start of another personal long winning streak, this time nine games. In the middle of that winning streak, in a game against the Braves, I actually got to start, relieve, and play a bit of left field all in the same contest. I was called into Larry's office the night before the game, and he said, "We're going to trade ElRoy [Face] to the Tigers. It's a done deal, but he needs another appearance to tie the all-time [Pirates] record for lifetime pitching appearances. So here's the deal. You're going to start the game, because we want you to pitch against the Braves. ElRoy is going to come in after you get the first out, and you're going to go to left field. After he gets an out, we are going to bring you back in to pitch. And that's the way it's going to be."

Larry was the boss, so I said, "Okay, if that's what you want, we'll do it that way." In fact, with my personality, I thought, *Goddamn, this is going to be fun.* As it turned out, when the switch happened and ElRoy was able to make his 802nd lifetime appearance, it wasn't particularly dramatic. And I had no way of realizing at the time that this maneuver was going to keep me from tying the single-season shutout record for Pirates right-handers. We won the game 8–0, but because I recorded only 26 outs, it didn't qualify as a shutout on my career record.

But I liked ElRoy and was glad to help him out. Plus, it was payback for sleeping on his lawn. I'll explain. I went to a charity golf event that summer, and ElRoy lived down the street from Churchill Country Club, the site of the tournament. I got just ripped up from all the boozing. At 4:00 AM, I knew I couldn't drive home, so I just rolled the car down to his driveway, and not wanting to wake him up, I just went and slept on his lawn. At 6:00 in the morning, the phone rang at ElRoy's house and this lady said, "I don't want to alarm you, Mr. Face, but I think there's a dead person on your lawn." So giving up my complete game shutout for ElRoy was the least I could do.

That game represented the third time of the season I had put up nothing but goose eggs against Atlanta. Coincidence? I'm not so sure. I never approached a start against the Braves that year thinking, *Oh, this is going to be easy. I'm going to do well.* I felt confident as a result of my previous starts against them, but I wasn't thinking like, *Oh, these are the Braves. Here's my secret against Atlanta.* I just happened to pitch well against them.

Before a game at Forbes Field, Henry Aaron once told me he felt I had the best slider in the National League. Wow, talk about making me feel like a million bucks! I don't write that to sound self-serving but to rather show how if I could often neutralize their best hitter, it adds credence to why I had success against the Braves. Even when I hit rock bottom in a dreadful start when I was hitting guys and throwing behind others in 1973, Henry was 0-for-2 against me.

Sometimes a pitcher feels like he can pitch well against a given team because, at the beginning of his career or a season, he has a good game. Then he has another one. Now his confidence level is rising. He thinks, *Gee, I've gone out there and done well, so I feel comfortable. I feel confident as a result of what's happened.* Not that he has a specific gimmick or key. He's just building on previous results more than anything else.

On the flip side, a pitcher can also go out to the mound with, say, a 4–0 mark against a team, and then in August they light him up and rip his face off. He thinks, *What happened there? I pitched well against them all year.* And that's the wonderful thing about baseball. You can't predict anything. You can't assume just because of what happened previously that it's going to continue. It's one of the charms of the game.

Just as this can occur with a particular team, it can also happen against a particular batter. For example, a pitcher can dominate a Willie Mays or a Henry Aaron. Meanwhile, a "Joe Smith" lights him up. So, who knows?

All I know is that in that particular year, when I got going I could throw my slider and use just a third of the strike zone. And I could do it whether ahead or behind in the count. I had such confidence in that particular pitch that I pitched almost backward. I used the fastball to set up a slider rather than the slider to set up the fastball.

My winning streak would last through a 2–0 win over the Reds on September 24, my third shutout in a row. By putting up zeros in the first two innings of my next start, I had pitched 29 straight innings of shutout ball. The feat was good enough to help me earn the National League's Pitcher of the Month honors for September. It was a great way to end the season.

I suppose it's a coincidence, but, just like I did in my best minor league season at Kinston, I kept a written journal of each of my games throughout my finest major league season in 1968. Those were the only two years I ever kept a journal in my 15 professional seasons. Those two seasons got going so good that I kind of got fascinated with following it on paper to chronicle it. I have no idea why I didn't do it in 1971 or '72, my other big years.

I was still young enough in 1968 where I was still fascinated by pitching that well. Perhaps I reached the point where I felt like I had proven to myself that I belonged and writing about it became less fascinating. It was still a good exercise to do, but it was no longer as great. Maybe I should have kept a journal each year. If I had pitched as well as I did in the two years I kept one, I'd be in Cooperstown.

As a result of my 18–6 season, the Pirates doubled my salary to a whopping $30,000. Although the extra $15,000 a year was huge and greatly appreciated by the Blass clan, consider what that kind of year would earn a pitcher now. I would think any agent worth his salt could get their client a deal of around $9.6 million per year for four years.

I told my parents several years back, "If you would have waited 20 years to have me, instead of the socks I'm sending you now, I would have bought you Nebraska, a rather nice state for you to have."

Karen and I were scratching around then and staying in a modest apartment during the season with our two very young boys, but $30,000 in 1969 wasn't all that bad. The raise was a far cry from the major league salary of $7,000 I had made in my rookie year. We were doing okay.

I still worked every winter for three reasons. I wanted to keep busy. I liked the people I worked for. And I could use that money. After all, I had to pay $130 a month for our house! For several years, I worked for Stadium Systems Athletic Reconditioning in Canaan, Connecticut, where I lived. I had a wonderful relationship with the owner, a man named Arthur Schopp, and I am still dear friends with his entire family. I went to work every morning, drove the company's truck, and delivered equipment primarily to prep schools throughout the northwest corner of Connecticut.

Because I dealt with the schools' athletic departments, it would take forever to complete my rounds. While I was supposed to make seven stops a day, I might make just two or three. I would talk to the coaches, and many times they would bring the kids in to join in the discussions. My God, it was so flattering.

At the end of a given day, I would go back to the office and Artie would ask if I made all seven of my stops and I would say, "No, I made two."

He'd shout, with a twinkle in his eyes, "What?!" Artie understood that, as a professional athlete, the time I spent at these schools was terrific public relations.

I would always answer back, "We are locked! You will never lose their business."

I loved returning to that small-town feel of Falls Village to tell everybody about my latest big-league season. The people were great. And after the winter was over and it was time to drive down to Florida, they would give me terrific send-off parties before we left. There was one great one from a VFW that displayed a large banner that read, "Steve, 20 wins in 1969!" They also gave me a license plate, SRB-28. It may have been hard to hide in that small town before 1968, but now it was impossible.

So baseball's answer to the dominant pitching of 1968 was to lower the mound. Was this the most profound rule change in baseball? Yes and no. In the National League, I would say it was. Despite my own opinion of it not having a profound effect on pitching performance, it very well might have and I was just oblivious to it. Proof positive is how the National League ERA went from 2.99 in 1968 to 3.59 in '69 and then jumped to 4.05 in 1970.

However, in the American League, the designated hitter rule (ugh, puke), which was introduced at the start of the 1973 season, was the biggest change baseball ever made to goose offensive numbers. It was so obvious and right out there for everyone to see. It's not a hidden stat. It's not a number you have to go and research. The DH rule is just in your face every day. I think the DH is ludicrous and completely unnecessary. It is just another example of us trying to over-glamorize a game that doesn't need that kind of cheap shit. It also dramatically affects the strategy of the game, which is part of its appeal.

For example, say I was going through the Reds' tough lineup and I think, *I've got a problem. There are no outs and I'm in a jam. I've got the No. 6 hitter, Tony Perez up. How can I work through this situation with the least amount of damage?* Right away, in my mind, I can write a script where I get down to the pitcher's spot, where he represents either the second or third out of the inning. That's part of the fabric of the game and how a pitcher works an opposing lineup.

But the American League threw a wrench into this kind of strategic thinking with the bullshit of a designated hitter, which intrudes on the integrity of the game.

Anyway, looking back now at 1968 and the Year of the Pitcher, maybe the stars were just aligned. Perhaps it was just one of those crazy years that is not so easy to pin down for answers. After all, the mound was the same height for all those years leading up to 1968, so why wasn't there another year like that after 1919?

There are some things in baseball you can't explain, in spite of the barrage of stats.

CHAPTER 7

The Clemente Mystique

I t was 3:00 AM when the phone rang. Our PR director, Bill Guilfoile, was on the line with some horrifying news.

"Steve, there is an unconfirmed report that there was a plane that went down in Puerto Rico and Clemente was on it. Unconfirmed."

We had been hosting a New Year's Eve party at our house. It was back in the day when we had epic parties in our neighborhood, the kind where people crawled home and forgot which house they lived in. The Giustis, despite living just four houses away, decided to crash with us that evening. The sobering call came shortly after we had all gone to bed. Now, of course, it would be a sleepless night.

Dave and I got dressed and, without knowing exactly what to do, went to Joe Brown's house in Mt. Lebanon. Joe was up and we had coffee, sitting around and trying to get information. Back then, you couldn't get information readily from the Internet or the 24-hour news networks.

Around dawn, Dave and I drove over to Willie Stargell's house and spent most of the morning over there, talking about Roberto and hoping we had gotten a report that was wrong. The three of us then drove over to Bob Prince's home for his annual New Year's Day party. The party had now become a wake. The news was all over the radio, confirming our worst fears. Roberto was on that plane and presumed dead.

The evolution of my relationship with Roberto was unlike any other I had in baseball. It began in my first spring training as an 18-year-old neophyte in Fort Myers in 1961. The Pirates had just won the World Series over the Yankees the previous October. As a minor league invitee, I joined the other minor leaguers in a back room of the clubhouse, separated by a door from the major league guys.

We didn't dare mingle with the major leaguers at all in the locker room, but I would occasionally sneak a look around the door and see Maz, Face, Law, Friend, Clemente, and the rest of the World Champions. They were all on a pedestal, but Clemente was more so because he was very stern and businesslike. The other guys would screw around and holler, but Clemente was different even then. He carried himself with grace, pride, and dignity.

I was just in awe of him. He was so gifted and a thrill to watch play. I wasn't really sure about wanting to reach out to the other guys, but I was positive I couldn't with Clemente. He just carried himself differently than the average major league player. He was a man of great pride who never let his guard down. He didn't want to be misquoted in the papers or have anyone be critical of his accent. He was a very bright guy. Spanish was obviously his native tongue with English being a secondary language, but I always had the feeling that he was wary about using words in English that wouldn't convey what he really meant in Spanish. He didn't want to be ridiculed and made light of it because English was his second tongue. Roberto never wanted to be embarrassed or humiliated.

Early on in his career, some of the media, like Dick Young, would quote him by using pidgin English. And I'm not so sure some of the writers in Pittsburgh didn't do that, as well. I know that he couldn't have liked that very much.

Later, Roberto would help young Latin players on the Pirates and around baseball adjust to playing in the major leagues. On the Pirates, guys like Sangy, Rennie Stennett, Jose Pagan, and Jackie Hernandez were given valuable advice from him on everything from dealing with the media to ordering off a menu.

Hernandez, in particular, credits Clemente with helping him get on the Pirates' roster. A Puerto Rican team he played on had success against one that Roberto was a part of during winter ball one year. Clemente in turn put in a good word with the Pirates' brass about Jackie, and the rest is history.

Roberto was also a leader to our Latin players and kept their confidence up when needed. In Jackie's first game with the Pirates, for example, our new shortstop made an error that cost us the contest. Roberto put his arm around Jackie afterward and told him to forget about it, that he was an important part of the Pirates. The gesture made all the difference in the world to Jackie.

The media also got on Roberto for perceived hypochondria. I remember him screaming at a writer one time, "A hypochondriac cannot produce!" I always remembered that line.

He dealt with a double-dose of prejudice being black and Latin. He was very aware of the environment he walked into in Pittsburgh. I can't address it too much because I wasn't around when he came up in the 1950s, but in him I saw a person who had an awareness and emphasis on the common man. I remember him saying to a writer, "I like people who suffer. I deal with people who suffer. I relate to the people who suffer." He was for the underdog, for the less privileged, and I don't know to what extent, but when you heard him get serious, that was his theme. That made a difference, too, because none of the rest of us had our own campaigns. We would do what we could for charity and try to do the right thing, but it was almost like a crusade for him.

I considered him a high-ranking officer, while the rest of us were just enlisted guys. It was intimidating to me because I was afraid that if I went up to him, he would bite my head off. He wouldn't have, but like most minor leaguers, he probably wasn't sure if I was a decent ballplayer or not. I always felt I had to validate my abilities to play on a team with him. That carried on through my first two or three years in the big leagues.

It probably wasn't until around 1967 or so that Roberto began to loosen up a little bit around the guys. By winning the 1966 National League MVP Award during the off-season, Roberto perhaps finally felt like he had been validated in the eyes of the writers. For more than a decade, he had been overshadowed by the likes of fellow outfielders Henry Aaron, Willie Mays, and Mickey Mantle. Two of those guys played their best years in New York, a major media market. We were out in the hinterlands. Plus, those three were home run guys. It's not just the chicks; everybody digs the long ball.

Clemente didn't hit a lot of home runs, and his RBI total was not staggering. But Roberto played with such passion and flair that if you didn't see him every day, the numbers wouldn't dazzle you. But we saw him every day, and we couldn't take our eyes off of him. People around the baseball world knew of his talent, but the world was different then. If there had been ESPN, MLB Network, and all that stuff they have now, you would have seen Clemente every night.

Roberto also saw the clubhouse begin to flip over. That 1960 team started to fade away into history. Dick Groat was traded to St. Louis. Bob Friend went to the Yankees. And the rest of the heart of that old guard kind of fell away or departed. Clemente was left with a lot of the kids who came up through the minor league system whom he hadn't grown up with. We were a bunch of very irreverent people, and eventually there was no way he could not be absorbed in that atmosphere.

Roberto still had Maz and Stargell, but the ballclub was being infiltrated by the likes of a Dock Ellis, who marched to the beat of his own drummer, once claiming to have pitched a no-hitter while on LSD. Let me tell you something about that story. Right after Dock told the LSD story to the writers, one of them came to me for a comment. I told the reporter, "I don't believe a word of it. But I'm going to hedge my bet and go out and buy some just in case." Then, after a pause, I said, "If you write this, I will hunt you down and slay you." Then there were Robertson, Oliver, Giusti, and myself, among others. Basically, the Bucs had actually evolved into a bunch of drummers, a group of individual percussion departments. So, Clemente couldn't avoid it, and he came to enjoy it.

The change in the clubhouse, combined with the fact I was validated by pitching well, enabled me to bond with Clemente. By pitching well, it gave me the confidence to use my personality around Roberto and the other guys. Roberto started referring to me as "Little Loquito," after I became good enough of a player to horse around with him. One time, I broached the subject with Roberto of how I would get him out if I ever faced him in a game.

"If I ever get traded," I told him. "I'm going to pitch you inside, because every National League pitcher pitches you away and you hit .350 every year."

"Blass, I'm going to tell you this," responded Clemente. "You pitch me inside; I will hit the freaking ball to Harrisburg."

Still knowing my place, I said, "Okay, we're good. That squares that up. Let's move on with our lives."

I did have one of those special bonding moments at the start of spring training in 1968 with Roberto that involved a pelican off the coast of Panama. Joe Brown had a belief that because we had been active in the Caribbean, he liked to go down to one of those countries each year in spring training to thank the fans there and keep the relationships going. So it was normal for him and a few of the Pirates to go and visit places like Puerto Rico, the Dominican Republic, and Mexico. In this particular year, we went to Panama.

While we were there, the Panamanian army folks who policed the canal got wind that we were there and invited whoever wanted from the Pirates to go on a fishing trip. The only three people who signed up were Joe Brown, Clemente, and I.

We were on a military craft, staffed by their personnel, so it was one of those situations where it was a complete luxury. We got there at around 8:30 AM, and all we had to do was sit and relax near the back of the boat, while they had cold beer on ice for us. They even had our fishing poles ready, with the bait already on the hooks! None of the three of us knew one damn thing about fishing. But it sounded like a good idea.

So we're going along and damned if Clemente doesn't hook a pelican in the water. Now it became great theater. For the delight and benefit of all, Clemente was going to give us all a clinic on how he was going to rescue the pelican and save its life. Standing on the deck, he announces, "Here's how we're going to rescue the pelican."

He goes through like four or five minutes of philosophy and theory of pelican rescue. But as he tries to reel in the pelican, it becomes more and more tangled in the line. At one particular point, Roberto was able to get the pelican up on to the boat, still wrapped in the line. While gently holding the frightened pelican in his arms, it starts to shit like the world is going to end.

Merely students of the great pelican rescue, Joe Brown and I move away as the pelican shit is flying everywhere. But Clemente, a true champion of pelican rescue, hung right in there, the only victim of being hit several times with pelican shit.

So here was Roberto, one of the greatest baseball players in the land, with a tangled, panicked pelican on a military craft in the Panama Canal. It was an even funnier site if you throw in the three or four rounds of beer we had imbibed by that point. It all ended nicely. The pelican got released unharmed. Clemente's clothes got cleaned. The military people were very appreciative of not only us joining them, but the lesson learned in the art of pelican rescue.

We all went on with our lives, including the pelican.

Roberto could go into great discourse on anything from pelican rescue to hitting against Sandy Koufax to how you might order breakfast. It was always lengthy and entertaining. I had always known that he had certain regimens that he followed while in the clubhouse. One of them was getting his arthritic neck worked on every day up until three minutes before each game. He had it down where he would get off the trainer's table after Tony Bartirome worked on his neck, get into his uniform, and be ready in two and a half minutes, dashing on to the field just in time for the national anthem. He learned how to get undressed and dressed in less than three minutes during his six months in the Marine Corps Reserves.

This one time, he was face down on the table and I crawled under it. It was like an episode of *Mission Impossible*, and I made Roberto like the Peter Graves character in the phone booth when he's getting his assignment.

I said, "Alright, Mr. Clemente, this is your neck. Your assignment today is to hit three doubles off Jack Billingham, throw two guys out at third base, and knock in four runs. If you or any of these assholes you work with get caught, I will disavow any knowledge of you and your neck. This tape will self-destruct in five seconds."

I could see the table shaking. I'm under the table like a mental patient, imitating this *Mission Impossible* shit. And he's up there laughing like a maniac.

So another night, he's on the table and, as always, he has it timed down to when he's got to get up from there and get his uniform on. I had taken his uniform out of his locker, so now he runs off the table without a stitch of clothing on, and he's got no uniform. It was the first time in major league baseball history that they played the anthem and a team had eight guys on the field and no right fielder. He mother-fucked me for three days after that.

Like every position player, Roberto always thought that because he had an incredibly strong arm that he could have been a pitcher. He'd say, "Watch this curveball, Blass."

It was terrible. I would say, "Keep your day job."

His interaction with the rest of the team was becoming more prevalent as well. He did something down in the Astrodome that I'll never forget. Sangy was a runaway train on the bases. Sangy would not stop until somebody tagged him out. So after one particularly crazy display of base running, Clemente called all of us into the trainer's room.

He had gotten a cardboard box and got Sangy up there in front. He had put slits in the box and put tongue depressors in it to act like the steering mechanism on a Caterpillar tractor. Clemente's fictitious tractor had levers to push it back and forth to steer with. He started imitating Sangy running the bases and said, "Here's Sangy pulling into second base," and he pulled the tongue depressor along the slit.

"Okay, there's second base," he continued.

"And here he goes to third," as the other tongue depressor would go up the other slit. It was hilarious. We were all howling, including Sangy. It was a 15-minute monologue by Roberto on Sangy running the bases.

Like a lot of teams from that era, long before iPods and laptops, some of us entertained ourselves when we traveled by playing poker on the airplanes. We were once flying from Pittsburgh to Los Angeles and there were Sangy, Clemente, Bartirome, Giusti, and whomever else I could trap into trying to take their meal money. But the problem was, from Pittsburgh to L.A., we would play only four hands because Clemente would give Sangy a clinic after each one of them.

"Sangy," Roberto would say, "you have two clubs, and one heart, and there's only two cards left. You can't make a straight! You can't make a flush with this!"

Clemente would then deal off practice hands before he'd let us play again. We thought we had hooked some fish that didn't really understand poker that well and, meanwhile, we couldn't make any money because Roberto would act like the professor of poker.

The greatest poker game occurred when Larry Shepard was the manager. In one instance, he came back to our poker game, and there was lots of cash. There must have been $400 or $500 on the table. Shepard said, "That's it. No more poker. I don't want some guy getting pissed off because he's losing money to a teammate."

So the next trip, we got 15 matchbooks, ripped all the matches out, and made every match worth five bucks. Shepard came over to us and said, "Oh great, you're playing for fun."

Meanwhile, our "pot" of matchsticks got so high it was like that scene from *Close Encounters of the Third Kind* when the Richard Dreyfuss character makes the model of Devil's Tower. While Shepard is standing there watching us, we hit some turbulence. The matchsticks went all over the floor, creating a mad scramble. It was elbows and assholes going down to pick up as many matchsticks as we could. There must have been 6,000 fucking matchsticks. All you could see were these major leaguers down on the floor like four-year-olds playing jacks, grabbing as many matchsticks as we could as fast as we could. We had burns on the tips of our fingers from the carpeting. Roberto was in the middle of all of that with us. He was having fun.

One guy whom Roberto developed a great friendship with was our clubhouse guy, John Hallahan, but anyone who didn't know better would have thought they hated each other. The racial slurs and the filthy, profane indictments that went back and forth between them were unrelenting.

At Forbes Field and later at Three Rivers Stadium, we would often have a night game on a Friday followed by a Saturday day game. Hallahan would go out after the Friday night game, drink a lot of beers, and either spend the night in the clubhouse or get home real late.

On Saturday mornings, Clemente would stand by the clubhouse door and wait for Hallahan to come to the ballpark. John would be all messed up and hung over, and Clemente would start screaming at him, "The shane!" because he couldn't pronounce the "m." "The shane of the uniform is on you, you shit maggot!"

Hallahan would shout back, "Fuck you! Go back to Puerto Rico! Get away from me! I've got to work! You're going to go 0-for-4 today! I don't give a shit what you do!"

And they would go back and forth. And they were the best of friends!

By 1970 or so, the idea was that all bets were off in that clubhouse. While Clemente was screaming at Hallahan, you'd see Robertson screaming at Ellis and Ellis would be screaming at Giusti and Giusti would be screaming at Clemente to leave Hallahan alone. It was a circle-jerk. Totally insane. I would try to prompt it by asking somebody some stupid question or tell them what somebody said about them, and then I would walk into the trainer's room and leave them all alone. It was like a house fire. They tried to explore how it got started, but the accelerant was gone, hiding in the trainer's room with Tony.

Anyway, Clemente was right in the middle of that, too. It was great fun. And it was great fun because we were good. None of that shit would have been fun if we weren't, because when you're not good, nothing's funny, as I proved to myself later.

Clemente was more aware than anybody I've ever been around of the clubhouse door and who was coming in and out of it. When people came in whom he wasn't aware of or sure of, there was very little byplay. He felt they would not understand our clubhouse atmosphere. It may have created the possibility of his being embarrassed, misunderstood, or made fun of when someone went into the clubhouse he didn't know. When it happened, he wasn't the same guy. When it was just us, it was great. And that's not entirely different from most clubhouses.

Clemente wore a suit most days on road trips. The rest of us were more casual, but he was always extremely well dressed. Soon after making McKechnie Field in Bradenton our spring training home in 1969, the team had a golf outing. Instead of getting a pair of golf shoes, Roberto wore a pair of alligator boots with the zipper on the sides, a fashionable look for those days. Back then, they must have cost $150.

And like when he helped Sangy at poker on the planes, he gave a "clinic" after every putt, too. Roberto would get into a stance that was almost exactly the same as the one he used when he hit, putting his right foot five or six inches from the ball, saying that was the proper way to putt. It was all just hilarious to watch. Roberto and I will always have a special link because of our success in the 1971 World Series. Despite Roberto winning the MVP Award and my being an established pitcher, this was the first time we were really able to display our talents on a national stage.

The Baltimore Orioles were a juggernaut, and they took the first two games of the Series in convincing fashion. One reporter jokingly wondered if the Orioles would take the best-of-seven series in three games. Back in Pittsburgh, I was to pitch the third game. I was hyper, nervous, and antsy.

To calm myself down, my ritual was to study some heavy-duty porn magazines, real heavy-duty, like *Penthouse*.

The trainer's room we had at Three Rivers Stadium had a small little side area with a whirlpool bath. Clemente, as usual, came in to have his neck worked on before the game. I'm in there in my skivvies, sitting on the floor by the whirlpool with this *Gynecologist Monthly*–type of magazine, just passing the time, waiting for the game to start. Bartirome took Clemente by the hand, stood him by the door of the whirlpool room and said, "Look, Roberto, look at who we have our money on today. A pervert!"

Clemente said, "Blass, you piece of shit maggot, the 'shane' of the uniform is on you. Kiss my nasty black ass when I shit no wipe."

To be clear, Roberto and I weren't the best of friends. We both had friends we were closer to, but it was a good feeling to have won him over by not just being funny but by also being a good ballplayer.

Clemente did it all in that Series, showing off all of his tools. I had pitched complete game victories in both the critical Game 3 to get us back in the Series and then in Game 7 to finish off the Orioles. People ask me to this day, "Don't you think you had a legitimate chance to be the World Series MVP in '71?"

I say, "Yeah, I do. But that was Roberto Clemente's World Series, and I had no qualms about him winning it. That was his show, and I was thrilled that everyone else could see what we had been seeing for all those years."

It sounds like a cliché and condescending and self-deprecating, but he was so special in that Series. The power, the throws, the base running. It was fun to watch him run because he galloped, but he got around the bases quickly. Most people who would have that kind of gallop wouldn't get around that quickly, but he was an absolute baseball machine.

After winning the Series, Roberto and I were being interviewed in the visitors' clubhouse on NBC by Bob "Gunner" Prince. Standing on the podium, I was in a state of euphoria. Clemente was far more reserved. In Spanish, he said something along the lines of giving blessings to his sons and his parents. Not understanding what he said, I interrupted and said, "Mr. and Mrs. Clemente, we love him, too!"

What I blurted out, in the thrill of the moment, didn't apply to what he was saying. Arghh! If I could cut my arm off now to not have said that, I would. It had nothing to do with his message to his parents. I just wanted to relate that we loved him, too. Maybe it wasn't as bad as I thought.

I still look back at that moment on the podium with Roberto and get the chills, thinking, *Look at me, that skinny kid from Falls Village, Connecticut, and sharing that spotlight with one of the best players in the world. How cool is that?* The extent of that realization never occurred to me until years and years later. I have more and more appreciation of that moment as time goes on.

After the World Series trophy presentation on the podium, we got separated. He was with writers; I was with writers. Then we finally got on the plane to return to Pittsburgh. Karen and I were seated right about the middle of the plane, and Clemente was a couple of rows in back of us. I had the window seat, reflecting on the day's events, when Roberto walked up to my aisle and said, "Blass, come here. Let me embrace you."

I would have trampled six buffalos or walked over glass and fire to get out into that aisle. Here was Clemente, he had his suit on, we'd won it all, and he wanted to acknowledge my contribution. All Roberto did was give me a hug. Didn't say a word. Just a hug. I didn't say a word, either. All I did was hang on. The embrace spoke volumes.

That beautiful memory, as well as so many others, cascaded through my head at Gunner's house on that terribly sad New Year's Day, 1973.

The next day, Dave and I went into the Pirates' offices and began calling our teammates to get them to Pittsburgh to take the charter down to the memorial service in Puerto Rico. Dave and I were there when owner Dan Galbreath called and said President Richard Nixon wanted to meet the three of us at the White House. The next day, Dan picked Dave and me up in Pittsburgh, and we took his private plane down to Washington.

Nixon wanted to see Dan about making a contribution from HUD, as well as a personal donation from him and wife Pat Nixon, to Roberto's "Sports City" project in Puerto Rico.

It was all very exciting. We were in radio contact with the White House as we got closer to its airspace and were picked up by a military limo, which drove us to an anteroom there. Secretary of State William Rogers said we were scheduled to have 18 minutes with Nixon.

While in the Oval Office, we found Nixon to be very knowledgeable about the World Series and the Pirates. I didn't know how much he was briefed on that, but he made us feel very comfortable. When we came out, Secretary Rogers said, "Well, he must have had a good time with you, because you were well over your allotted time."

We ended up spending 29 minutes with Nixon, and I jokingly tell friends that our meeting may have been part of the 18½ minutes of missing tape that Rose Mary Woods, Nixon's loyal secretary, claims to have inadvertently erased. Of course, the Watergate break-in and Nixon's crucial conversation about it three days later had occurred six months earlier, but I never let the truth get in the way of a great story.

Above: Signing my first pro contract on June 27, 1960. Wow! $250 a month.

Right: With my dad in the army my first three years, it was me and mom against the world. All day, every day.

In 1962, I went 17–3 with the Kinston Eagles and also got engaged to Karen. What a year!

Above: Signing an autograph for a young fan. I'm still flattered to be asked for my signature.

Left: Firing away. I did not possess a technically correct set of pitching mechanics, but it worked for a lot of years and never resulted in a sore arm.

Roberto Clemente. The perfect baseball specimen.

Above: With my baseball dad, Danny Murtaugh, who was always in my corner.

Left: Bill Mazeroski, the best second baseman in major league history, turns the double play. Bill was and remains the consummate professional. (Getty Images)

Joy! That's the only way to describe the incredible release when Bob Robertson caught me after the last out of the 1971 World Series.

Above: Sneaking your Dad into the clubhouse after winning the World Series? Priceless! He and I are joined by Dave Giusti and Nellie Briles.

Below: This iconic photo by Rusty Kennedy highlights two 12-year-old kids in adult bodies.

Above: After Clemente died, Pirates owner Dan Galbreath (far right), teammate Dave Giusti (second from right) and I spent time in the Oval Office with President Nixon, who wanted to be involved with Roberto's Sports City.

Below: One of the greatest days of my life, October 22, 1971, was Steve Blass Day at the North Canaan train station with two of my favorite people—high school coach Ed Kirby and my dad.

By the time we got back to Pittsburgh, much of the arrangements for our charter flight to Puerto Rico were complete. The charter was filled up with not only baseball people, but also local politicians and other sports figures.

It was also on that day that Bill Guilfoile came to me and relayed a request from Joe Brown that he wanted me to give the eulogy at the memorial. I was blown away.

During the flight down, I kept thinking, *Jesus, Holy God. I have to speak at a church from the pulpit and deliver the eulogy for Roberto Clemente.*

What I read was inspired by a poem done for Lou Gehrig, given to me by Guilfoile. Guilfoile had previously worked for the Yankees and received permission from them to paraphrase it to fit Clemente. I was never more nervous in my entire life. No contest. I may have pitched in some huge games, but that was part of my craft. When I pitched, I could trick people, play little mind games. But this was absolutely straight.

Speaking at Clemente's memorial service was the most serious thing I have ever approached in my life. I kept thinking thoughts like, *I can't make a mistake. I've got to do it right with the correct inflection. I've got to get through it without getting too emotional.* This was not something I did for a living. This was completely out of my comfort zone.

I choked up several times throughout the speech but was able to clearly articulate the poem that Guilfoile gave me to read, which went as follows:

> *We've been to the wars together*
> *We took our foes as they came*
> *And always you were the leader*
> *And ever you played the game.*
>
> *Idol of cheering millions*
> *Records are yours by sheaves*
> *Iron of frame they hailed you*
> *Decked you with laurel leaves.*
>
> *But higher than that we hold you*
> *We who have known you best*

Knowing the way you came through
Every human test.

Let this be a silent token
Of lasting friendships gleam
And all that we've left unspoken—
Your friends on the Pirate team.

I don't believe there was a dry eye at the San Fernando Roman Catholic Church.

I did get through it, though. I don't know if I did a good job, but I got through it. I was so proud to have done it. It was something I will remember the rest of my life.

You look back on a life, and certain things jump out at you. I was so proud that I was able to become a friend of Clemente's and kind of win him over after coming such a long way from being a kid who had been afraid to approach him. All of us rookies were like that, but I am glad I got to the point where I was on such good terms with him. I will go to my grave feeling good about that.

CHAPTER 8

That Championship Season

"What's the big deal?" manager Danny Murtaugh asked a group of reporters that gathered in his office after a late-season game. "I just sent my nine best players out there tonight."

What Danny did was not by design, but in a September 1, 1971, victory over the Phillies, he made baseball history by fielding nine minority players to start a game. It was the philosophy of Joe Brown to just go out and get the best players, whether organically through the farm system or via the astute trade. The philosophy just so happened to produce the first multiracial, multinational team in sports.

I liked to kid around and say we had blacks, Latinos, and white trash. The diversity not only helped create a close, rowdy, fun-loving, politically incorrect clubhouse, but also a *damn good* team.

And we knew it.

The Pirates were pioneers in scouting Puerto Rico, the Dominican Republic, and the rest of the Caribbean leagues for talent. Joe Brown had a super scout named Howie Haak who was able to mine that field of prospects for almost four decades. Haak's biggest claim to fame was his primary role in the Bucs' selection of Roberto Clemente in the 1954 Rule Five draft.

Besides Haak, Joe had a helluva scouting department with guys who were truly gifted. Even today, when you have personnel who can evaluate talent, it becomes the cornerstone of your organization. You can write all the checks you want, but if you don't write them for the right talent, it doesn't matter.

During the mid- to late-1960s, we had a farm system that I would put up against anybody else's in the major leagues. We were loaded. That's why it took some of us so long to move up to the Pirates. In a two- or three-year period around the turn of the decade, we watched the maturation of farmhands Robertson, Oliver, Hebner, Sanguillen, Moose, Dock, Kison, Gene Clines, Dave Cash, and Milt May. It was like "Katie bar the door" when that young talent joined the Stargells, the Clementes, the Mazeroskis, and the Bob Veales of the club. It was like a perfect storm of talent.

It came to a head in 1970 when we won the National League East and earned a date with the Reds in the National League Championship Series. We ended up getting swept in three straight that series, but our pitching staff gave up only three runs in each game to the Big Red Machine.

Personally, I have always felt that the playoffs are a crapshoot, anyway, and that a team's true value is what it does over 162 games, not a best-of-five or best-of-seven series.

You win the most regular-season games, you're the best major league team. Period. Congratulations to the World Series winner, but personally that's how I feel. We all felt we had proven that we belonged in the conversation with the elite teams in the big leagues, and we expected to win it all in 1971.

Besides our talent and style of play, what made us most intriguing to the baseball world at that time was the diversity on our ballclub. Years later, we were the subject of a book titled *The Team That Changed Baseball* because of it.

We were equal parts Latino, black, and white and had figureheads within those groups in Clemente, Willie, and Maz, respectively. The three were almost like benevolent and patient uncles to those wild nephews of theirs who made up the rest of the club. They would just kind of oversee us.

We were all products of the system, and they were all veterans at that particular time. I don't like to call them "leaders" because I think you lead yourself. But they were *great* examples of how to practice your craft. All we had to do was listen and watch them; they really didn't need to say much.

Maz never said much, but I watched him play and thought, *That's the kind of ballplayer I want to be.*

With Clemente, I was just so fascinated by his talent and style of play that I couldn't take my eyes off of him. As such, I would be embarrassed if I didn't give every ounce of effort to show him what I was capable of doing on the field. I knew I would probably never be as good as he was, but shame on me if I didn't show him that I was going to work hard enough to earn the right to be on the same ballclub as somebody like him.

Stargell, who was younger than the other two, was a slightly different case in that some of us had come up through the system with him. He was kind of an in-between guy to veterans like Maz and Clemente and led more by example. Of the three, he was likely the one playing in the prime of his career in 1971. He would go on to put up stratospheric numbers that season with 48 home runs and 125 RBIs. He finished second in the MVP balloting to Joe Torre and, as much as I respect Joe's .363 average that year, I railed against the Baseball Writers Association of America's decision. In fact, I still rail against it.

But those three "uncles" we had were wonderful. It was almost like at times they would sit back and watch us play in the clubhouse. It was our playpen, and they let us get out of hand. We loved to impress them, even more so when they had time to join in the fun, which they did.

The giving of one's time, in my opinion, is the only real gift we have as human beings. It says a lot about how we are going to be judged. If somebody gives you his time, don't ever take it for granted because he only has so much of it. It's not negotiable. I think more about that philosophy as I get older, but at that time we were practicing that phrase and living it on that team.

You hear the phrase "we're like brothers" an awful lot today. We didn't use that to describe our clubhouse back then, but we genuinely liked each other. It was like a family. We could fight; we could damn near kill each other, but we didn't let anyone come inside of our circle because that belonged just to us.

We also were good, and we respected one another's abilities and the way our teammates approached their craft. You respect effort. It's a big thing, because you can have guys who aren't great major leaguers, but you respect their effort no matter what their level of talent may be. That's the cornerstone of any kind of business.

It was a different era, before the term "political correctness" became a big part of the American lexicon. So everyone took it in stride and in the correct spirit of clubhouse banter when one guy was calling the other a "redneck" and someone else was yelling out "nigga," or "dago," or "spic." Nothing was sacred, and we all got along great. When you have a mutual respect with somebody, you can call him whatever you want because there's an underlying foundation of affection at work. And now, more than 40 years later, we're all still good friends. If we had lost all the time, we'd still be buddies and it would be fun to get together, but it would be different.

A fan might wonder how some of the best baseball players in the world can have the time and energy to clown around as much as we did. But if you're an established player, there's a good deal of downtime at the ballpark. You go out, take your batting practice, the other team hits, and it's almost a way to blow off steam. It's a good thing, because if you've got your game face on from 4:00 until first pitch three hours later, my God, the stress and the intensity will eat you up. As long as you are ready when the bell rings and they start playing the anthem, you're in good shape. You gain the ability to compress the intensity into two hours by sometimes staying away from the awareness of it all.

One of the pranks we loved to do to keep the levity was to start rumors. We used to send a rumor out to either someone on the grounds crew, an usher, or a ticket-taker on a given day. Basically, one of us would go up to some guy and saying something like, "You can't believe what happened in the clubhouse today! Dock Ellis took a knife to Hebner and was going to cut him. But Richie had some kind of sawed-off bat and they just started beating the shit out of each other. Now, promise you won't tell anybody. This stuff should never get out of the clubhouse."

We would wait around and see the flame that it took, the life it took on. Before long, the news was all over the place. We've got writers storming in and asking, "Did Hebner and Ellis get into a fight again?" We'd just start shit and see how far it would go.

Don Leppert brought some balance to our frivolity by being a very stern coach. I was a little wary of Don because he was a tough guy. Besides coaching first base, Don was in charge of the baseballs. It was like a sacred trust to him. With Don around, nobody fucked around with the ball bag. I don't know if it was an economical thing or if the club told him he'd better not lose any baseballs.

Dock saw this as a challenge and would always try to get the baseballs. I don't know what he did with them. Maybe he threw them up in the stands or just did it to provoke Lep. Lep knew this and kept a closer eye on Dock than any other player on that ballclub. As keeper of the baseballs, *nobody* was going to screw around with his responsibility.

Every once in a while I tried to get one or two balls and Lep would say, "What's that?"

"I'm getting them for Dock," I'd reply.

He'd shout, "Put them back!"

So we kept Lep sharp.

Nothing went by. Everything was challenged and screamed at. Dave Giusti would argue with Clemente, and he's pulling up as much Italian as he can, while Clemente is just blistering back at him in Spanish. Then they would just look at each other, turn around, and go back to their lockers. It was hilarious to see, but it was just the way we were.

And it was okay because it was all on the surface. The lines were completely open. It's like you never had clogged arteries in your heart. If it was on your lung, it was on your tongue, loud enough so everybody could hear it. The good part of that was there weren't any undercurrents where someone would go over to another guy's locker and start whispering stuff. Right away, someone would walk over and say to them, "Well, what the hell is this all about? We've got secrets?"

Nobody could hide. If you went into the trainer's room to tell Tony Bartirome you had an issue, he might shout back, "Go see your family doctor. I'm working on real players. Rub your own arm."

Meanwhile, we had Dave Ricketts and Jose Pagan working the clubhouse, screaming to everybody in no uncertain terms, "Are you scared? Are you scared tonight? Because if you are, go home!"

Around the start of the season, I got a hold of a set of 8-by-10 headshots of the players. I quickly transformed them into police mug shots by putting horribly labeled captions underneath their pictures and started taping them to the bathroom wall. For Hebner, he was wanted for "Breaking and Entering." Under Nellie Briles, "Acts of Perversion." For another guy, "Incest." The fun was continual and unrelenting.

One of the Pirates clubhouse's more entertaining inhabitants was Sangy. Everybody saw on the field how Manny was such a gifted athlete. But we also came to understand how "gifted" he was when we saw him showering. It reached the point where we wouldn't shower with him, because you don't want to be on a major league baseball team with an inferiority complex. Willie referred to Manny's "gift" as a roll of tar paper. Then there was the danger factor. Someone might be showering with his eyes closed and face the risk of injury.

Sangy used to powder every night in front of his locker. I would look over, and it was like a Category 4 blizzard. It looked to me to be in the range of 8 to 10 inches of accumulation (get your mind out of the gutter; I'm talking about the powder). So Sangy was a baseball hero in just *so many* ways. Maybe that's why he is always smiling.

Charlie Sands was one of Sangy's two backup catchers. He had spent a little time with the Yankees, so we enjoyed listening to some of his Mickey Mantle stories. We nicknamed him "muncle" because, after we asked him about what his family did for work, he answered in his Virginian accent, "Well, m'uncle owns a car dealership." So he became "muncle." Charlie liked the nickname because it made him feel included.

We all like Charlie to this day. He has that fun-loving, jovial sense about himself. But during the championship season, he had a little "back door" problem, some butt issues. So he went into Dr. Joe Finegold's office one day and said, "Doc, got to get up on the table. We've got a problem back here."

Stark naked, Charlie, who was not a small person, got up on all fours onto the table, so the visual was not exactly a pretty site. After Finegold took a look in there, he walked into the clubhouse and, for whatever reason, said to Clemente, "Robbie, my boy, come in here." So Clemente's got this little shit-eating grin on his face because Doc always amused him.

Clemente, a Puerto Rican, would imitate the phrasing and accent of Finegold, a short, Jewish doctor. They were dear friends, and Roberto would imitate him when Finegold would ask for some promotional item. Finegold might say something like, "Hey Robbie, how about a glove for my boy? My boy would like a glove from you." Clemente would hold his nose, and get that phrasing just right.

So Roberto walked in, and there was Charlie Sands in a perfect pose on the table. Finegold says, "Robbie, my boy, come over here and hold this man's asshole open." Now we're fascinated. A bunch of us are hanging around the door like the Dead End Kids looking into a candy store.

We looked around the corner to see the greatest right fielder in the land, in full uniform, going up to Charlie and, like the Jaws of Life trying to get a crash victim out of a car, grabbing his cheeks open.

Doc does what he has to do to handle this hemorrhoid or whatever it was, but not before Charlie had a little reaction and shit started flying everywhere. Clemente was laughing so hard. He looked back at us because he didn't want to face forward. We were all stunned this vignette was happening.

It's just one of those things that could never happen these days. For one, I would hope there would be more sanitary conditions and this would not be done on a trainer's table. And two, I don't think you're going to get A-Rod or Ichiro or somebody like that to come in and hold a big fat catcher's ass open. I just don't think it's going to happen now. And if it does, it had better make the Top 10 Plays of the Week.

After Hebner joined the Phillies as a free agent to start the 1977 season, he turned to Mike Schmidt and asked him, "Doesn't anybody have any fun around here? The place is like a morgue." After working as a gravedigger during the off-season, Hebner would know.

Hebner and I knew how to have fun. One time during the dog days of spring training, I came in just as a joke to horse around with one of those styrofoam pith helmets. And Hebner, possibly because he had had an unsuccessful night the night before, immediately took the pith helmet, broke it over his knee, and had a good old laugh. That was fine. After he went out to play the game, I was going to leave early to go home because I had my work done. Instead, I took his sock out of his shoe in his locker, proceeded to the toilet, and was able to position the sock in such a way that I was able to pinch off a seven-inch "steamer" right down into the sock. Very proud of myself, I stuffed it back in his shoe and went home. Richie never messed with me after that. And we've always had a good laugh about it. He always told me, "That's what you call getting even."

He would say years later, "We were all crazy on the Pirates, but we played every October." Richie was absolutely correct. You looked forward to going to the ballpark not just for the game, but also for all the bullshit, because it was so much fun and we were so good.

Major league baseball is serious stuff. People pay good money to see you play, and some think you're so perfect. But many times you have your glove over your face to keep from showing how much fun it all is.

With 1970 being a kind of forerunner to our championship year because we were learning how good we were, 1971 became the apex of the culmination of all of that because now we knew. Murtaugh would say it was a tougher managerial challenge for him in '71, despite winning the National League East by seven games, because we were no longer the dark horse to win the division title.

We would christen our first full season at Three Rivers Stadium with a World Championship. I get asked often about the theory of what it is about new ballparks that often breeds successful teams. I actually discount that logic and list it as an excuse for why a player and team can experience success in the big leagues. A major league winner doesn't want to be motivated by perimeter shit. You want to be motivated by yourself. A new stadium plays by the same rules as any other park, whether home or away. It's still 60'6" from the mound to home. It's still 90 feet between the bases. Home field advantage, my ass. It comes under the heading of just another excuse.

That being said, we were excited about the move from Forbes Field to Three Rivers because it was new. Three Rivers had carpeting and air conditioning in the clubhouse. That was a big deal for us. As for getting down to the real nuts and bolts on how it might affect our game, I was wondering if the artificial turf surface would be strictly a positive for the offense.

I knew ground balls would tend to get through the infield quicker and gap shots would go to the wall faster. Outfielders had to contend with little, looping flares that would take these phenomenally high bounces, turning singles into doubles. Infielders had to deal with over-spin on a ground ball's second bounce, which often ate them up. As a pitcher, I was concerned about those factors.

The reality was that they would not be as big a factor as I thought, because they would be counterbalanced by several positives. Ground balls hit right at infielders would create easier double plays. Infielders suddenly had the ability, because of the hard, even surface, to make long throws more easily across the diamond. Shortstops, for example, could go into the hole, backhand the ball, and instead of trying to reach all the way over to first base with their throw, could one-hop it instead. Five-time Gold Glove shortstop Dave Concepcion, whose Reds also played on turf at Riverfront Stadium, became the poster child for the turf bounce throw. Lastly, balls would get to the outfielders faster so, in a given situation, a guy at second base might not score as easily on a base hit to left field. One of the problems for pitchers, we soon realized, was their safety. Some of those bullet one-hoppers back to the mound would just eat your lunch. You could really get tattooed by a sharply hit comebacker.

So the game, with the balance of the positives and negatives, was generally little changed on turf. I always liked Tug McGraw's answer when asked about the difference between natural and artificial grass. He said, "I don't know. I never smoked artificial grass."

My answer to the same question was a little more conventional. I used to say, "I don't see any difference. I'm still pitching off the dirt on the mound."

Not all of us were completely excited about the move. Pirates management told Maz, "Bill, we're going over to this beautiful AstroTurf and we know you chew tobacco. Would you please not spit on the turf?" All Bill did was look at them like they had three heads.

The evolution of AstroTurf was, in my opinion, a net negative for Maz's legacy. Bill set a lot of fielding records on that rough, uneven Forbes Field infield. Because of turf, a lot of his records were either diminished or broken by infielders who didn't have anywhere close to his abilities because they played on ideal turf conditions without having to worry about bad hops. It bothers me to this day that his records are viewed equally with more modern-day second basemen who have played in far superior conditions.

The consistency of our success in 1971 was like none other that I had experienced as a Pirate. During the entire 162-game season, we never lost more than four straight games. After a relatively average start in April in which we finished the month a couple of games over .500, we really started to turn it on in May and never looked back.

We went 17–9 in May, 20–10 in June, and 18–10 in July. By July 24, our first-place lead in the National League East stood at 11 games. After slumping a bit during the dog days of August, we turned it back on again and on September 24 hit our high-water mark for the season by being 34 games over .500.

They may have called the 1979 Pirates "The Pittsburgh Lumber Company," but damned if we didn't have some big bats of our own. In fact, the power numbers between those two Pirates championship teams are eerily similar. The '71 Pirates actually had a slight edge over the '79 edition in home runs (154–148) and runs scored (788–775), while sharing exactly the same slugging percentage of .416. We led the National League in home runs, runs scored, and RBIs and came within a single percentage point of taking the Triple Crown by finishing at a batting average of .274 versus the Cardinals' .275.

Runs scored determine if you win or not. Everything else is just details. A team can have a great batting average, but runs are what determine the standings in the paper the next day. And leading the league in runs like we did was huge. We were not just winning but often blowing away our opponents. In blowout games, which are defined as winning margins of five runs or more, we had a record of 32–9. It was the result of what happens in the best of times for a ballclub, when pitching and hitting come together.

Our pitching was often overshadowed by our hitting while in fact we started to emerge with a very good non-headline staff. Giusti came into his own as our closer, and we wound up with a starting rotation of myself, Ellis, Moose, Bob Johnson, Luke Walker, and newcomer Nellie Briles. We got Nellie along with Vic Davilillo in a trade with the Cardinals right before spring training started.

We had to give up Matty Alou, a very productive Pirate for several years, to obtain Briles. Matty was a base hit machine. So in those terms he was very good for us. I thought the world of him personally. This was before free agency and trades were a part of life. It was a trade that made sense because it gave us another established starting pitcher, and you can never have too many of them.

And I knew what we had in center field. Despite hitting for a high average, Matty was a slap-hitting center fielder without a lot of speed. We had Oliver, who was a gap-shot, power guy who was really coming into his own and beginning what would be a possible Hall of Fame career. We also had Gene Clines. Clines had tremendous speed and would have started on a lot of ballclubs.

So Joe Brown knew he already had speed and production at the center-field position in his back pocket. It gave him the flexibility to make that kind of move knowing he had those two guys. As it turned out, it was a trade that worked well for both teams. Matty would continue to register big offensive numbers for the Cardinals by hitting .315, while Briles went 8–4 with a 3.04 ERA. Vic batted a solid .285 and really helped us coming off the bench late in games as a pinch-hitter.

Our bench was phenomenal. We had Milt May, a rock-solid catcher who hit .278 that season and was our most underrated player. May easily could have started on a lot of teams. We also had Rennie Stennett, Jose Pagan, and, of course, Vic, who, in spite of some other issues around him, had a great major league career.

Basically, Vic had a little Chicago problem that season. He liked to have a cordial or 12 after each game. Or sometimes during a game. Or sometimes before a game. Chicago was a problem because back then the Cubs played only day games at Wrigley Field and Vic would be out on the street around 4:00 in the afternoon. That was entirely too much time for Vic. On July 5, I was going to pitch and the bus was going to leave our hotel at around 8:30 AM for a typical Wrigley Field day game. As usual for me, I went out to the bus at 8:00 because I was an early riser and typically anxious on days I pitched.

The door was open, so I boarded the bus and it appeared as if nobody else was around. So I went up the steps and, slumped in the very last row is Vic, who'd had a very, very difficult full shift the night before. Vic didn't even bother going back to the hotel to sleep because he thought he would miss the bus. So there he was, half asleep, half still-smoked, gazing out the window and probably pondering the nebular hypotheses of the origin of the planet Earth.

And at that very moment, while Vic was looking out the window, Colonel Harland Sanders, also known as Colonel Chicken, comes out of the front door of our hotel and he's looking good. He's in the white suit, he's got the string tie, he's got his cane, and he's got a big white hat. The vision is just all too much for Vic to handle. I don't know what possessed him, but Vic hollered out the window, "Hey, F-you!" Then he shoots the Colonel the finger!

The Colonel, to his credit, turned toward the bus, dropped his cane, and hollered right back at Vic, "F-me?! F-you!" Then the Colonel gave Vic the finger right back! So I had this great visual of a hungover Venezuelan going back and forth with Colonel Sanders at 8:00 AM to help relax me.

All I could do was sit back on the bus, laugh out loud, and feel less anxious about having to face Billy Williams four times that afternoon. I probably should have thanked Vic, because I went out and pitched a complete game despite Williams going 2-for-5 with a double off of me.

Earlier in the season in Chicago, on June 9, Vic was also pretty smoked. We tried to protect him from Murtaugh to the point where we hid him in this huge industrial dryer where they took care of the laundry for the players. Vic was only about 5'6", so he fit in there with no problem. For Vic's protection, we had another member of the team stand by the dryer so no one would hit the button and start a cycle with him in there. The last thing we wanted was to look in the window and see Vic tumbling around in a circle.

The game started with Vic resting comfortably in the dryer. Everything was going according to plan until the ninth inning with two outs when Murtaugh turned to me in the dugout and said, "I need Vic to hit. Get Vic." It is a long trip from the dugout at Wrigley to the visiting clubhouse. You have to go through a tunnel and up a flight of stairs.

I turned to Danny and said, "No, no, Danny, you don't want Vic today."

He looks at me and says, "Of course I want him. I want him. Get him out here."

A few of us ran up the tunnel into the clubhouse to get Vic, who was now sleeping on the trainer's table. Vic quickly woke up, ran to the dugout, grabbed a bat, and started taking warm-up swings in the on-deck circle, still very wobbly. "John Barleycorn" still had a choke hold on him.

Worst of all for Vic, future Hall of Famer Fergie Jenkins was pitching for the Cubs. Fergie always had a great change-up, while Vic had a hitting style like Ty Cobb where, as a left-handed hitter, he would raise that right leg high for timing and stride. Because his leg was raised so high, it was critical that he start his stride somewhat before the pitch or during the early part of the pitcher's delivery. Fergie wound up and Vic lifted that right leg and, zip, a fastball blew by Vic for strike one.

Vic, obviously a little late, and still a little sluggish, decided that he was going to start his stride even earlier on the next pitch and would be ready should Fergie throw another fastball. Fergie wound up again, but this time Vic, with his right leg elevated early, had to keep it hovering in the air for what seemed like an eternity because Fergie had pulled the string and threw him a change-up. It was simply too much time for Vic's leg to be suspended that long, and all we could see from the dugout was the ball floating in, Vic losing his balance, and him falling back into the Cubs' catcher's arms.

So what you have here was a packed Wrigley Field crowd paying good money to watch a tipsy Venezuelan in a major league catcher's arms. And nobody knew where the damn ball was. So that didn't work out so well, but I've never seen 50 major leaguers laugh so hard.

But, in spite of all the drama, Vic was a good teammate and was an important part of the ballclub. With our depth in every department, it was not surprising to me that we were so consistently good throughout the course of the season. You have to be good when your longest losing streak is only four games. Over 162 games, if balanced, a team's hitting will carry the club when the pitchers aren't pitching well, and when they're not hitting, its pitching will have to carry them. We had that kind of ballclub.

I finished the regular season with good numbers: 15–8, a 2.85 ERA, and I tied Bob Gibson, Milt Pappas, and Al Downing for most shutouts with five. At that point in my career, only my 1968 numbers were better. In a sense, my '71 performance mirrored the club's with respect to how well I consistently pitched from start to finish.

As satisfied as I was with my pitching from a personal standpoint, I was so proud of our ballclub. I could hardly wait for the NLCS to begin. Danny was giving me the ball in Game 1, and I anxiously awaited making the first postseason appearance of my career. Having clinched the National League East more than a week before the regular season ended, we had to wait for the last game of the year to find out who our opponent from the National League West would be. It would turn out to be the Giants, who rode the broad shoulders of Juan Marichal in their final contest to stave off the second-place Dodgers by one game.

For the fans and the media, the Giants were a tough team to handicap before our series with them. They struggled mightily in September, finishing the season's final month with an 11–16 mark. Plus, because they were forced to use Marichal in the last game of the season, their ace would not be available until at least Game 3.

However, they played extremely well against us that season, going 9–3. And they had a phenomenal lineup. It started with Bobby Bonds, their leadoff hitter. Hell, because of Bonds, if you were pitching against the Giants at home you could be down 1–0 and still hear the last three notes of the national anthem. He could nail you that quickly. He was just an unbelievable leadoff man with power and speed. A truly gifted player.

Then they had McCovey, Mays, Jim Ray Hart, and the whole bunch of them. We knew they were good, and that was without factoring in how they had struggled in September or how well they'd played against us in the regular season.

All we were thinking about going into the series was how we were playing the Giants, and whether they were hot or cold, whether they played well against us or not, all that stuff was off the books. In the postseason, all you need are a couple of hot pitchers or a couple of hot bats, and you can beat anybody.

We didn't have any doubts that we were good enough to play with them. Our September record was great, and we were on a roll. They may have had four future Hall of Famers in Mays, McCovey, Marichal, and Gaylord Perry, but we had three of our own. We weren't thinking about anything other than that we were a very good team that had to make a statement early in the series. We learned a valuable lesson the year before against the Reds. By getting swept in three games, we understood the significance of each game and the sense of urgency you had to play with. Things can unravel very quickly if you get into a hole in a best-of-five series.

With this way of thinking, Murtaugh didn't make any adjustments despite our poor regular season won-lost record against the Giants. Back then, there may have been six or seven guys on the team who could have told you what our season record was against the Giants. Now, that type of information is documented everywhere because of the media age we live in.

I didn't get a start in the '70 NLCS, so I was pretty pumped up to start Game 1 in San Francisco. Maybe too pumped up, because I remember thinking, *Okay, postseason is more important than regular season, so maybe I've got to be better than I was in the regular season.*

That was a trap, because you've got to stay with what has given you the degree of success that you've had. I was outside myself. I thought that I had to throw harder and make better pitches. I went out and had nine strikeouts in five innings, which was not me. I wasn't a power pitcher and certainly not a strikeout machine. I just tried to do more than I was capable of doing. Eventually, it caught up with me my third time through the Giants' lineup.

I was actually very close to getting through five innings with just one run allowed and the chance to pick up a win. But with two outs in the fifth and a man on, Tito Fuentes took me deep, depositing an out-of-the–strike zone slider into the right-field stands just above a leaping Clemente to give the Giants a 3–2 lead. After walking Mays on four pitches, McCovey followed with a two-run blast off a fastball to make it 5–2. Just like that, two swings of the bat, and the Giants suddenly had control of the all-important first game of a short series and held on to win 5–4.

By overthrowing, I wasn't as consistent or accurate with my fastball. It took me out of my natural rhythm. With my slider, I was trying to be too fine. Attempting to be perfect with pitches is a tough business. Instead, you have to trust your ability.

We bounced back in Game 2 thanks to a monster game from Bob Robertson, who hit three home runs and a double and drove in five runs to lead us to a 9–5 victory. It was vintage Pirates as we slugged 15 hits, played solid defense, and got decent starting pitching from Ellis while Giusti slammed the door in the ninth. I think it also helped the team for Dock to pick up the win following some controversy that involved him and Pirates' management before the Series. Dock didn't like our hotel accommodations in San Francisco or the fact we seldom flew first class.

Dock referred to the front office as "The Establishment" to the media, which couldn't have been any farther from the truth. Lep, who had his share of run-ins with Dock, said it best, that "everybody in the organization was treated equally, from the guy that swept the clubhouse floor, to partial owner Bing Crosby." I had the same sense of that as Lep. Dock could pitch his ass off, but 75 percent of the shit he started was to provoke a reaction. Most of us just reacted to his comments about the front office as "Dock just being Dock." It certainly did not distract us from what we were trying to accomplish on the field. I never had a problem with him, because I never took him too seriously. I thought his issues with racism or the ballclub were things that, unless I was approached directly, were none of my business.

There is no discounting the fact Dock won 19 games for us that year, and we needed him to excel in that game. And to a degree he came through. We had evened things up at one apiece and were going back to Three Rivers in what was now a best-of-three series.

The pivotal Game 3 could have been extra challenging for us if not for the effort of spot starter Bob Johnson. Briles was supposed to pitch that game against Marichal but came up with a physical issue shortly before the game. Murtaugh had no other choice than to go with Bob, and he pitched the game of his life. After Johnson held the tough Giants lineup to just one unearned run through the top of the eighth inning, Hebner connected with a two-out solo shot off Marichal in the bottom of the frame to break a 1–1 tie. Giusti closed it out with a perfect ninth, and we were one win away from a trip to the World Series.

Danny gave me the nod to pitch in Game 4. My approach was the same as in Game 1. I wasn't going to change or make any adjustments. The Giants weren't going to trick me. I still believed I had to throw my fastball harder than usual and be extra fine with my slider because of the magnitude of the game.

It still hadn't occurred to me that I had fallen into a trap. I was still trying to do more than I was capable of on the mound. The result was no different. Chris Speier and McCovey went yard against me in the second inning, and we were quickly down 5–2. My day was done, as Danny went to the pen to bring in Kison to start the third. Bruce, a 21-year-old rookie at the time, was stellar. He pitched two-hit shutout ball over the next 4⅔ innings while we rallied behind three-run homers from Hebner and Oliver to open up a 9–5 lead after six innings.

Giusti continued his postseason dominance by throwing hitless ball over the final 2⅓ innings to give us the National League championship. My teammates had picked me up. I was disappointed personally, but we had found a way to win it. Even though we were not pitching great, we had a good offense that could bail us out.

I was more delighted and preoccupied with winning the pennant and going to the World Series than I was with my performance. I don't remember exactly where I was mentally. I knew I'd get a chance to start but didn't know what Murtaugh had in mind for the World Series and how he was going to use me.

What we all knew for sure was that we would be playing the Orioles, managed by the brilliant yet irrepressible Earl Weaver. The so-called Earl of Baltimore had been kind enough to give us all the bulletin board material that we would ever need. At the start of the playoffs, he told reporters that "a team could not win a World Series with Jackie Hernandez at shortstop."

He would, of course, live to eat those words.

CHAPTER 9

A World Series Date
with the Mighty O's

I can't get caught up in the enormity of the occasion, I kept reminding myself after the playoffs ended. *I don't have to be better than I normally am just because it's the World Series. Just go back and be yourself. I'm not a power guy. I'm not a strikeout guy. I'm a slider pitcher, damn it. Just try to be who you are and remember how you got here.*

Not only did I have to shake off my two horseshit starts against the Giants in the NLCS, but I now faced the daunting task of stopping a steamrolling Baltimore Orioles team with our club already down 2–0 in the Series.

A headline in a Baltimore paper screamed out, "It May Be Baltimore In Three!"

Legendary sportswriter Jim Murray wrote, "The Pirates are going back to Pittsburgh now. It's like the elephants are coming home to die."

And why wouldn't they think those things? The list of accolades for the Orioles was a mile long. The Birds of Baltimore were winners of three straight American League pennants and had won 100 or more games in each of those seasons. They had a four-leaf clover of 20-game winners in Jim Palmer, Dave McNally, Mike Cuellar, and Pat Dobson. They had a powerful lineup featuring sluggers Frank Robinson and Boog Powell.

Their defense ranked among the all-time best with Brooks Robinson, Mark Belanger, and Paul Blair, a trio that would combine to earn a total of 32 Gold Gloves over the course of their careers. Vegas had them pinned as 5-to-3 favorites *before* the World Series began.

Now, after winning the last 11 games of the regular season, sweeping the A's in three straight in the ALCS, and winning the first two games of the Series, they were coming into Game 3 riding a 16-game winning streak. Not only were the Orioles winning every day, but they were doing so in a variety of ways. This World Series would be no different. The first two games were played in Baltimore, where the field conditions at Memorial Stadium were simply terrible.

I'm not complaining about it; both teams had to compete under the same set of circumstances. But it had a surface more suitable for a pickup game than for a World Series. It doubled as a football field, a common practice in those days. The Colts had just played there the week before, so the outfield was chewed up to the point where they spray-painted it green. In fact, after batting practice, we picked up about three dozen green baseballs. The lines weren't cut very sharply either. I actually didn't notice that until I watched a tape of the Series a year or so later. But Roberto Clemente's feelings about the field were made loud and clear after the first game when he declared it the worst major league field he had ever played on.

Bad conditions or not, we jumped ahead 3–0 in the top of the second inning in Game 1 thanks in part to some uncharacteristically shoddy pitching and defense by the Orioles. McNally walked Bob Robertson and wild-pitched him to second to start the inning. Sangy followed with a ground ball to Belanger, whose throw to third deflected off Robertson's helmet into the Orioles' dugout, allowing Bob to score and Manny to move to second.

With one out and Sangy now at third, Hernandez put down a squeeze bunt that McNally picked up and threw a bit wide to the right of catcher Elrod Hendricks to allow Manny to score and Jackie to move up to second base. Dave Cash then hit a two-out single to drive home Hernandez and give us a three-run lead.

It may not have been the prettiest inning, but we were off to a great start. We had our 19-game winner, Dock Ellis, on the mound, and they had just handed us three runs. It was a good feeling, although we all understood we didn't have this thing locked up. As a major leaguer, you never think you've got enough runs when you're up 3–0 in the second inning.

As it turned out, this game was certainly not over, as Dock didn't have his good fastball and the Orioles took full advantage. In the bottom of the inning, Frank Robinson led off with a long home run to deep left field to cut the lead to 3–1. The following inning, Merv Rettenmund belted a three-run homer just out of the reach of a completely outstretched Willie Stargell in left-center field to give the O's a 4–3 lead. On the play, Willie made one of the greatest leaps for a big man imaginable. Somehow, he got his left hand on a railing and elevated himself tremendously as he went up high with his glove hand. He came so damn close to making an incredible catch of that home run ball.

After walking the next batter, Dock's afternoon was over. Ellis had complained that the beds at our hotel were too short, so maybe his bad outing could be blamed on a bad night's sleep. Dock, of course, was just looking for a reaction with his lodging complaints. The real reason for his ineffectiveness came after the game when Dock would say, "I knew my arm was gone, but I'll be back."

We wish he would have been that forthright with us when he declared himself fine after long-tossing from second to home with Sangy the previous day. Maybe by saying his arm felt good, he was trying to give himself a psychological lift, a mind-over-matter kind of thing. I'm sure he didn't want to give himself an excuse beforehand if things didn't go well. You never want to say, "Hey, my arm isn't right," because you don't want that getting in your head.

I'm sure his arm was hurting, perhaps for longer than we all knew. What might give a more accurate reading is how Dock pitched in the second half of the season. He was 14–3 with a 2.11 ERA at the All-Star break and was the starting pitcher for the National League in the Midsummer Classic. After Dock's big first half, he went only 5–6 the rest of the regular season. By bouncing back in 1972 with a 15–7 record and a 2.70 ERA, it leads me to believe Dock almost certainly had some arm issues throughout the second half of 1971.

Baltimore continued to flex its muscles in the fifth inning when Don Buford crushed a home run off Bob Moose deep to right field to give the Orioles a 5–3 lead. All of the Orioles' runs had come by way of the long ball. And McNally was superb the rest of the way, giving up just one hit in the final seven innings to go the distance for the win. It was just one victory, but the Orioles, except for some blunders in the second inning, looked as good as advertised in every phase of the game.

We just didn't hit. And the expected second-guessing from the media was starting up in full force. Two of our best hitters, Oliver and Hebner, didn't start the game against the southpaw McNally, replaced by Clines and Pagan, respectively. Oliver, a guy who I always thought should get more Hall of Fame consideration, was particularly disappointed over the move. Al thought he could hit a pitcher whether he was left-handed, right-handed, or if the ball came out of his forehead. He was as confident a hitter as any I have ever been around. *Ever.* And that includes Clemente and Stargell.

But Murtaugh never paid much attention to what the media or his own players thought he should or shouldn't do. I always felt like Danny had kind of a gut feel about managing and seldom went with the percentages. Danny never explained much of that to us. He never sat us down and said, "Boys, I'm playing so-and-so because of this and that." He just wrote out the lineup card, and we went out and played. The simplicity of his approach with his players is still with me. Danny absolutely believed in all 25 of his players and we absolutely believed in him.

When I earned my 15th win that season, I did it without Willie, because Danny started a September call-up named Richie Zisk in his place against Mets lefty Ray Sadecki. It's a little hard to imagine that a rookie, even one that would go on to a degree of stardom like Zisk did, could be inserted into the lineup to replace a guy who would hit 48 home runs, but that was Murtaugh. And Willie didn't complain one bit. As it turned out, Zisk hit a two-run homer in the game to help me earn a 4–0 shutout. Nice move, Danny!

The other big question milling about was what was going on with Stargell, who was now 0-for-17 in the postseason. Willie was, of course, an MVP candidate and one of the most feared sluggers in the game. All we could do was offer him encouragement. Lighthearted stuff like, "You've spoiled everybody. Now they expect you to hit home runs every day." Stargell, it would later be revealed, would need off-season surgery for cartilage damage in one of his legs.

Danny tabbed Bob Johnson to pitch in Game 2. Despite being the third or fourth starter in our rotation during the regular season, the move didn't surprise me at all because of how tremendously well he had pitched in that pivotal playoff game against Marichal. I had no problem with it, because I had been lit up in the playoffs. In fact, I didn't think I particularly deserved any consideration to pitch in Games 1 or 2. I didn't care where I pitched in the World Series rotation. I was just hoping to get my opportunity and, in games I didn't pitch, root like hell for everybody else.

We had to wait an extra day to start Game 2 because of a rainout, and the game was moved to a Monday afternoon. The Orioles wanted to play a night game, but commissioner Bowie Kuhn wanted to keep the pomp and circumstance of the historic first World Series contest under the lights to stay intact for Game 4 back in Pittsburgh. Like I did in the first game, I kept my own scouting report of the Orioles in a notepad during Game 2. The purpose was to write down what I could find out about their hitters. The Orioles made that very difficult, as they looked like a totally different team than they did in Game 1. As opposed to hitting home runs, they scored 11 runs on 14 singles, a completely different approach. They would win the game going away 11–3.

The only thing we could really take away from Game 2 would be two of the best throws I've ever seen from the outfield. The first took place in the bottom of the fourth inning, which at that point kept us in the ballgame. With the Orioles leading 4–0, Buford hit a fly ball to Stargell in left. Davey Johnson tagged from third, and Willie threw a rocket toward the plate. It took a slightly high bounce, and Sangy had to reach above his head for it, making him extremely exposed and vulnerable. Davey hit him hard with a forearm right in the upper chest under the chin that sent Sangy flying and damn near tore his head off. Sangy, with no mask on, held on to the ball and Johnson was out. I've never seen a catcher take a shot like that.

We all know about Clemente's arm, but seldom has the strength of Stargell's come up in baseball lore. Maybe it's because Willie was better known for being a first baseman, but Stargell had a gun for an arm in the years he played left field. In fact, when he came up to the majors, Willie's arm may have been as strong as Clemente's or even a bit stronger from a pure strength standpoint. Maybe his throws weren't as consistently accurate as Roberto's, but Willie had a cannon.

The second throw, this time by Clemente, would be shown countless times in highlight reels. Frank Robinson hit a ball deep to right field which sliced away from Roberto toward the foul line. Clemente reached out, caught it, and did a 360-degree turn before firing a strike to Richie Hebner at third to barely miss getting Rettenmund, who had tagged up from second. It was such a wonderful play that it is shown again and again despite the fact that an out wasn't even made.

But the plays still didn't take away from the sting of losing our second straight game. I unintentionally ended up leaving my scouting report notes on top of my locker in Baltimore, to which Manny said good riddance because we didn't know what kind of team the Orioles would run out there next. Would we face power hitters or the "swinging singles"?

We knew we were in a hole. It was a short Series. We certainly weren't happy about where we were. But we still felt like we could compete. You win one game in a Series like this and you're back in it. So we knew we were in trouble, but we weren't devastated. It wasn't like we sat down and said, "Boy, we've got to go out and win this one." There wasn't a lot of talking or dialogue because we had a pretty professional bunch who realized how you play is more important than how you talk.

Though now mentally prepared, I was still nervous as shit to pitch, because you can't take away the importance and meaning of a Game 3 when you are already down two games. It may not have been the seventh game, but it was certainly critical for us to win to stay in the Series. Danny attempted to calm down Pirate Nation by telling the media hordes, "You haven't seen the real Pirates yet." That quote would later be inscribed on the boxes that held our World Series rings.

Despite Earl Weaver trying to neutralize Oliver by throwing another southpaw, Danny started Al anyway, probably because Mike Cuellar was a screwball pitcher. Because the screwball actually moves away from right-handed batters, the pitch would actually come toward a left-handed hitter like Oliver. That neutralizes the effectiveness of the pitch. So Danny took that into consideration and decided to start Al over Gene Clines.

Cuellar loved throwing the screwball and was very successful with it. Years later, you would see the same thinking by opposing managers when facing the great Tom Glavine, because his best pitch was the change-up. That pitch is going to fade into the lefty hitter like a screwball. A change-up from a lefty like Glavine was much more effective running away from the right-handed hitter.

Danny also decided to go with Gene Alley over Jackie Hernandez at shortstop in Game 3. Jackie had been playing well, especially in light of Earl's comments, but Gene was still our regular shortstop. There was no mistaking that. When Alley was healthy, he played, and Jackie was his backup. Before a sellout at Three Rivers, we got the crowd into Game 3 early when Cash led off the bottom of the first with a double down the left-field line. Clemente would score him later in the inning on a groundout to second, and I had a 1–0 cushion to work with.

On the mound, I was dealing. In fact, I didn't give up a hit until Brooks Robinson singled with one out in the fifth inning. I was able to transfer my thought process and just stay within myself. I had gotten past the approach of "trying too much." That had buried me in the playoffs. I was able to stay within that frame of mind to the point where I was basically using half the plate with my slider. And the few times I got behind in the count, I could throw my slider for a strike. I was throwing the ball where I wanted it and the way I wanted to, which is a tough combination to beat. I was in a zone, a perfect rhythm, and I couldn't wait to get the ball back from Sangy after each pitch. My mentality was,

Give me the damn ball. I was in total command. When Sangy put down his fingers with the sign, I was going to let him know if it was the right one. I would shake him off if it wasn't.

Actually, though, Sangy was working right there with me. As soon as I got the ball back from him and before I could start waiting, he had the fingers down with exactly what I wanted to throw, so we were on the same wavelength. I don't remember shaking him off a lot, which was probably the result of a bunch of years pitching and catching together. He knew what I wanted to do and knew when I was cooking. We had a great rhythm.

We added another run in the bottom of the sixth when Sangy led off the frame with a double up the right-center-field gap. Jose Pagan followed with a single to left field that scored Manny, and we now led 2–0. The O's would make me pay for my only bad pitch of the day. I hung a slider to Frank Robinson to start the top of the seventh, and before it even reached him, I knew it was a bad pitch and shouted, "No!" I wished I had had a string to pull it back, because Frank absolutely crushed it for a long home run to deep left field to make it a 2–1 game.

But I settled right back down to strike out both Ellie Hendricks and Brooks Robinson, and I got Davey Johnson to ground out to short to end the inning. That set the stage for our bottom half of the seventh, and what remains is one of the great Pittsburgh mysteries that may never be solved. Clemente led off and hit a comebacker to Cuellar that he booted but kept in front of him for a throw to first. Roberto, who busted his ass up the line, may have caused Cuellar to hurry his throw, which pulled Boog off the base and allowed him to reach first base safely.

Stargell followed and walked on four straight pitches. That would bring up Bob Robertson and the play of this World Series. With nobody out and runners on first and second in a 2–1 game, Robertson looked down to our third-base coach, Frank Oceak, for the sign. Robertson, to this day, goes back and forth on whether there was actually a bunt sign given and, if so, did he miss it? Because he had never bunted before, he very well might not have known what the sign was.

In the World Series highlight film produced by Major League Baseball Promotion Corp., it says that Oceak flashed the bunt sign not just once but twice. However, the same film also shows Clemente, while on second base, trying to call time because, as he was quoted as saying, "I was trying to tell Stargell to be alert for the line drive. The only thing I was concerned about was the hit-and-run." Clemente never mentioned anything about a bunt.

So, to me, that doesn't play out to the bunt sign because, if you're on second base like Clemente was, you're watching the third-base coach too. Because Robertson had never bunted and was swinging a hot bat the entire month, a hit-and-run might have made more sense. On the other hand, with Sangy on deck, a bunt sign was conceivable because he was a great contact hitter.

Bob would make it a moot point when he swung and launched a rocket into the right-center-field seats for a three-run homer to give us a 5–1 lead. In the film, as Robertson is coming across home plate, he is quoted as saying that Stargell greeted him facetiously with the words, "That a way to bunt the ball, Hoss!" I was fairly near Danny on the bench and, after the home run, I went over to him and said, "If he missed the bunt sign, whatever you fine him, I'll pay it!"

With Oceak, Clemente, Stargell, and Murtaugh having passed away, Robertson is the only one who might tell the truth about the sign after three or four beers. The one thing that is certain is that there was a lot of confusion. And, of course, no fine.

We breezed through the eighth and ninth innings and, after Hendricks grounded out to Cash to end the game, in my jubilation I ran over to Robertson and embraced him. What followed was one of the finest moments I ever had in my life.

As I was being interviewed by NBC's Tony Kubek, my dad dodged stadium security, jumped off the top of our dugout onto the field, and ran over to me to bask in the moment. The look on his face was one of absolute joy. It looked like he had won the damn game!

We all have had fathers. And we all have had shining moments with our dads that we hold dear. When he ran out on that field, it was one of the singular moments not just with him but of my entire life. And I carry that image with me all the time. I hear people say, "Oh, my dad's my best friend." I respect the thought, but for me, they are two different categories. I have a lot of friends but only had one dad. So I don't subscribe to that theory. A father is in a different category than a friend.

That moment I will never, ever, ever forget. He gave me a hug, someone took a picture, and it wound up in *Sports Illustrated*. Tony Kubek sent Dad an 8-by-10 of that picture with the inscription, "To Bob, thanks for one of the warmest moments I've ever seen in the game of baseball. Best Regards, Tony Kubek." Kubek proved again why he is one of the classiest guys you can run into.

With the World Series now at two games to one, our clubhouse was buzzing. We were all thinking, *Okay, we're back in this.* The guys were not elated, not going crazy, but hey, the mighty O's 16-game winning streak was over, and we proved that we could compete against them.

The best days in a starting pitcher's season are always the days after he pitches a good game and wins. Before Game 4, it was a classic Indian summer day, and I was on the top of the world, relaxed, and shagging flies in the outfield. It couldn't get any better than this, I thought, until it was time to come off the field, and Sandy Koufax approached me.

"Hey Steve, I didn't want to bother you," said Koufax, who was working the pregame show for NBC during the Series. "But could you give me five or 10 minutes for an interview?" I immediately thought to myself, *Are you insane? Do you need a month? I can give you a month. No more than a month. Okay, okay, maybe two months at the most! Sandy Koufax is asking me for my time!* If Sandy had said "shit" to me, I would ask him how much and what color.

It truly was a wonderful day as we got ready and pumped up to start the first night game in World Series history. Looking back now, I'm so embarrassed that we started that crap. If I was commissioner, World Series night games would be the first thing I would eliminate. We're trying to sell our game to kids, and now we're telling them we're going to start the game at 8:30 or 9:00. The games now go until it's after midnight, and most kids probably are not allowed to watch the whole thing.

Growing up in the 1950s, World Series day games were part of our autumn. That's how we grew up. We all ran home from elementary school and tried to catch the last two or three innings on TV or a radio. The teacher might put the score up on the blackboard if she was great, or someone would have a transistor radio. It was like a Norman Rockwell kind of setting back when I was growing up.

But I guess the networks knew what they were doing. Game 4 gave NBC the largest national television audience in American history, with 61 million people watching some or all of the game. Consider that in 1971, the U.S. Census determined that there were 203 million residents in the country; it meant that almost one-third of the country was tuning in. It also didn't hurt the gate, as it produced the largest crowd ever to see a major league game in Pittsburgh.

None of us were thinking about or were even aware of the record-setting television audience while the game was going on. All we were focused on was the chance to get even that night and how exciting it was going to be. In fact, you can never think about the millions of viewers watching you play in any game. If you do, you'll go insane. A major leaguer is trained, developed, and focused to perform at the highest level. If you let the enormity of the game bleed in, you're done.

Danny sent Luke Walker out there to start, deservedly so, because he'd had a great September. Luke had great stuff and was one of those left-handed guys who could not throw a ball straight if his life depended on it. If his pitch went over the middle of the plate, it got there from somewhere else. It certainly didn't start there. He was a guy that could throw 20 minutes of batting practice against his teammates where he was trying to throw it down the middle, and he would throw a batting practice two-hitter. Few guys could make solid contact. His ball moved that much.

Unfortunately, it just wasn't there for him that night. He started the game by giving up consecutive singles to Blair, Belanger, and Rettenmund. A passed ball followed to allow the first Orioles' run to score. That set up an intentional walk to Frank Robinson to reload the bases. After sacrifice flies by Brooks Robinson and Boog Powell, Walker was already down 3–0 with two outs in the first. With the dangerous Davey Johnson coming up, Danny had seen enough and called on 21-year-old right-hander Bruce Kison to relieve him.

Kison looked about 15 years old and weighed, oh, maybe 35 or 40 pounds. If he'd had a varsity sweater, he could have been only from a school like Indiana or Iowa, because there wouldn't be room for any other letter except "I." His physical appearance aside, Bruce was a giant for us on the mound in Game 4. He gave up just one hit over 6⅓ shutout innings, though he did set a dubious record by hitting three batters in a single World Series game. One of his victims was Frank Robinson, who got plunked in an area that put into question whether he would ever be able to father a child again.

Aside from his outstanding pitching, Kison was hell on wheels on the base paths, pummeling Davey Johnson with a rolling block on a double-play ball in the bottom of the fourth. So jarring was the takeout on Johnson that after getting up off the ground, Bruce mistakenly put on Davey's Orioles cap instead of his own.

While Bruce held Baltimore in check, we battled back and tied it with two runs in the first and another in the third. We could have taken the lead had right-field umpire John Rice called a laser down the line by Clemente fair for a two-run home run, but he indicated that the ball just missed the white line by *that much* as he held two fingers an inch or so apart. Our bullpen guys gave the home run signal, certain that is was fair, and Murtaugh came out to argue.

When Rice explained to Murtaugh that it was so close to being a home run, that "if I called it the other way, I would have had an argument from the other team," Danny became enraged.

Murtaugh shouted, "Well, that's idiotic! In other words, you don't want them to argue!" It's entirely possible Rice preferred to argue with Danny instead of Earl Weaver. And who could blame him for that?

In any event, we felt good about our chances, as Orioles pitcher Pat Dobson proved hittable on this night, giving up 10 hits and three walks in 5⅓ innings. But we just couldn't truly cash in against him. Missed opportunities were our theme in the middle innings, as we loaded the bases twice in the fifth and sixth innings but came up empty.

We finally broke through in the seventh with the go-ahead run when 21-year-old Milt May, pinch-hitting for Kison, came through with a two-out single to right-center field to score Robertson. It proved to be the game-winning hit in our 4–3 victory. It was kind of neat that it was Milt, looking every bit like Ronnie Howard back then, who delivered the big hit in this game because he and Bruce were best buddies and had come up through the minor league system together. They have remained friends all these years and still live near one another.

But it was Bruce's night, and his effort stifled Baltimore's attempt to put a choke hold on the Series. Although I took pride in mentoring Kison and some of our other young pitchers, I didn't utter a word to him during this game while we were on the bench together. When a guy's out there working, and cooking, you leave him alone. In fact, it was kind of a rule of thumb that we never said much to each other while a game was taking place. Whatever I helped him with between starts, he internalized it and made it work for himself.

But I was drawn to Bruce as a young player because he was absolutely fearless. I liked his style of pitching hitters inside. And, of course, I liked the fact that he laughed at my crappy jokes. He probably felt like he had to be polite, just like I had to be when I was a rookie. What I tried to help Bruce and the other young pitchers out with the most was how to handle the media and be polite, because there are some subjects the press will try to get out of you that are best avoided. I did that for Bruce, in part, because guys helped me when I was starting out. That's the way it's supposed to work. You pass it on. You help them become a major leaguer in every sense. That kind of stuff makes a difference.

It was great to even the Series, especially the way we battled back in Game 4 after trailing 3–0. I think we owed the Orioles one because in Game 1 we were the ones who went ahead 3–0 and lost. Our clubhouse was brimming with confidence. Now the goal went from trying to take two out of three at home to seeing if we could do what just three days earlier seemed impossible to the baseball world, sweep the Orioles in Pittsburgh.

Murtaugh went with Nellie Briles, a pitcher who had to work hard to alter his delivery after Major League Baseball lowered the mound following the Year of the Pitcher in 1968. His follow-through would take so much out of him that he sometimes would fall flat on his face. Briles was not a string bean. He had a thick, heavy body but was one of the most limber people I've ever seen. We'd do calisthenics in spring training, and he was like the rubber-band man without the kind of body you would associate with that. He not only could touch his toes, but he could put his hands flat down on the ground while keeping his knees straight. I'm fairly certain that had something to do with the way he followed through and how far he could get down on the ground. After watching his ERA soar from a 2.81 in 1968 to 6.24 in 1970, he bounced back to have a very good first season with us. He gave the Pirates' organization and the fans much of the credit for supporting him throughout the season and helping him turn his career around.

Nellie was positively brilliant in Game 5, pitching a two-hit shutout. He didn't allow an Oriole to reach second base in a 4–0 victory. It was easily the greatest game he ever pitched. And for good measure, he singled home a run in the bottom of the second to put us up 2–0.

I wasn't aware of it at the time, but when Nellie came to the plate in the eighth inning to a standing ovation, tears rolled down his face because he was so touched by the gesture. He was able to put his feelings into words after that game and following the Series about the people in Pittsburgh, his teammates, the whole package. It meant a great deal to him, and he was able to express it very well.

Nellie went on to get involved in the Pirates' Alumni Association and quickly became its point man. He was one of the big reasons that our organization is so well-done, well-planned, and well-respected around Major League Baseball. Nellie was fabulous in establishing and maintaining our alumni group and helping it prosper. He was the perfect guy to be our alumni ambassador.

Nellie also championed a campaign to get Maz into the Hall of Fame. He worked well with Bill in personally setting up the right kind of appearances for him, acting almost as an agent. I think to this day that's meant a lot to Maz.

Sadly, we lost Nellie far too early when he died of a heart attack at one of our alumni golf tournaments several years ago. I did not make that tournament, but Sam McDowell helped host that outing and said Nellie was standing on the tee and just went down. Their efforts to revive him were futile, and nobody seems quite sure exactly how much time went by before he passed. There were heart issues in his family, but I don't know how much that played into his own problems. One thing is for sure. He showed he had the most heart at Three Rivers Stadium in Game 5.

Now we were ahead in the Series three games to two. We were one win away from giving Pittsburgh its first World Series championship in 11 years. The Orioles had those four 20-game winners and supposedly the best pitching staff in baseball. But their powerful lineup could muster a total of only nine hits in the three games in Pittsburgh to our supposedly second-to-them pitching staff. Since the first inning of Game 4, between the efforts of Kison, Giusti, and Briles, Baltimore had gone 17⅓ straight innings without scoring a run.

The scoreless streak would continue through the fifth inning of Game 6, extending the Orioles' futility to 22⅓ straight innings. And they had the superior staff? The Orioles' Gold Glove defense? It committed nine errors in the first five games. We had them on the ropes but understood the importance of closing things out. Everybody in Pittsburgh was rooting for our starter, Bob Moose, in Game 6 but nobody harder than me because I had already had my moment in the sun in Game 3.

I told Moose before the game, "Pitch your heart out, Bob. Win this thing and I'm going to be delighted. I don't need to go out there in Game 7. Go ahead and do it. I will be the happiest Bucco in the clubhouse." I was rooting for him like you can't believe. Because I knew if we lost, it was going to be "hey, tag, you're it."

The rest of the players felt the same way. They wanted it to be over right then. When a team gets a chance to grab the brass ring and get a championship, who would want to take it to another game?

Baseball hardly ever disappoints in giving fans a great Game 6. And ours would do nothing to dispel that notion. In fact, many fans would call it one of the greatest games they had ever seen. Moose, the sixth different starter Murtaugh would use in the Series, would go up against Orioles ace Jim Palmer. By most accounts, it was a mismatch.

We wasted a first-inning triple by Clemente but scored in the top of the second after Bob Robertson singled home Oliver to give us a 1–0 lead. We added to that lead in the third when Roberto continued his torrid hitting with a home run to deep right field to give us a 2–0 edge. On television replays of that shot, you can see Robinson give a quick tip of the cap. I loved that touch of professionalism from Frank for all kinds of reasons, including the fact that before the 1971 World Series began, the media touted it as a contest between two of the best right fielders in the game of baseball. In the meantime, Moose was cruising with a two-hit shutout through five. In the sixth, however, both the Orioles and home-plate umpire John Kibler got the best of him.

Don Buford led off the inning with a long home run to right field to cut our lead in half. After Davey Johnson reached on an error by Hebner, Boog Powell grounded a single into right field. With still nobody out, the Orioles threatening to make it a big inning, and Moose jawing at Kibler about his strike zone, Danny brought in Bob Johnson to face the heart of Baltimore's lineup.

Bob was terrific. He got Frank Robinson to pop out to short, struck out Rettenmund looking, and induced Brooks Robinson to hit into a fielder's choice to Hebner to end the inning without any further damage than just the one run.

After Palmer retired us in order in the top of the seventh, the Orioles got a one-out single from Belanger in their half of the frame. After Palmer struck out looking, Belanger stole second to get himself into scoring position. Johnson walked Buford to put runners on first and second when Danny went to the bullpen to bring in Giusti, our bulldog closer, to face Davey Johnson. Johnson dumped a single into left field to score Belanger, and the game was tied at two.

The score remained tied going into the bottom of the ninth, when it appeared the Orioles might win it. With Belanger on first, Buford lined a shot into the right-field corner. The ball was like a hockey puck coming around the boards when Clemente fielded it and fired a perfect strike from the middle of the warning track on one hop to Sangy at home plate to hold the runner at third.

That was the second of two long throws Clemente made in the Series that didn't result in an out, but I remember both of them 40 years later like it was yesterday. Win or lose, this game was going to go down as the pearl of Roberto's Series, as he showcased every facet of his five-tool talent. He solidified his place alongside Willie Mays and Henry Aaron as one of the all-time great players before a national audience.

With the winning run now at third, Giusti got Davey Johnson to ground out to Hernandez at short to end the threat. Giusti had been magnificent. He had continued his postseason mastery with 10⅔ innings without giving up an earned run. It was just a continuation of what he did all year long when he deservedly was named the National League Fireman of the Year.

Dave was also a throwback to a different time for relievers. A two-inning save was never a problem for him, as he had been a successful starting pitcher for years. He had a great palm ball and a very adequate fastball. So it was a wonderful combination. Though he was a natural for the role of closer, it was something he fell into after our previous closer Chuck Hartenstein struggled in 1970. Dave was given the ball and, with his trademark intimidating countenance, never looked back. The bulldog in our bullpen had found his niche as a closer, and the rest is history.

On the heels of Clemente's great throw and Giusti working his way out of a jam in the bottom of the ninth, it was beginning to feel like destiny was on our side. And in the top of the 10th, we had a great opportunity to capitalize on the previous inning's drama.

Cash hit a one-out single to right field and stole second to put the potential winning run in scoring position. Weaver, partially to fill the open base at first and partially to avoid being punished once again, intentionally walked Clemente. McNally came in to relieve Dobson to face the left-handed slugging Stargell and walked him to load the bases. Unfortunately for us, despite having one of our best hitters up and no place for McNally to put him, Oliver flew out to center field to end our rally.

Bob Miller came in to pitch the bottom of the 10th for us. After retiring Boog Powell on a groundout to Cash to start the inning, the next hitter, Frank Robinson, worked the count full. Miller then threw a perfect slider right on the outside corner, but Kibler called it a ball and Frank took first base. Rettenmund followed with a single to Vic Davilillo in center field, and with Frank chugging to third, Vic made an outstanding throw to Hebner which just missed getting him.

That brought up Brooks Robinson with the winning run on third base. Brooks lifted a fly ball to relatively short center field. Vic got into position and fired a perfectly straight throw home. But the ball hit the grassy portion between the mound and the plate and bounced high enough that Sangy had to go airborne. That allowed Robinson to slide underneath Sangy to score the winning run. I won't blame the surface because we knew about it and you don't want to use that as an excuse, but if Davilillo had gotten a better bounce, we would have had at least a 50-50 shot at getting Frank at home plate.

Far worse than the bounce was the call on Miller's 3–2 pitch to Robinson, because it allowed the winning run to get on base when it should have been two outs and nobody on. Murtaugh, who'd had previous disagreements with the umpiring crew in the Series, was fined by the commissioner's office for arguing with Kibler after the game ended. But it was the call on the 3–2 slider to Robinson that was the straw that broke the camel's back. Danny may have gotten fined, but I guarantee you he got his money's worth. People say that he just sat on the bench and folded his arms, but Murtaugh made the points to his arguments loud and clear.

People have asked me how this game ranked with the greatest I ever saw and I tell them, "It stinks! We lost." But actually, the drama that went back and forth was terrific. It was a grinder's kind of game.

Because we'd had a chance to win the World Series right then, it was a major letdown for us. But it was important for us to get past that. All that anticipation of being a championship team had to be burned out. We couldn't ignore that emotion, so we acknowledged it and ran through it. When that was done with, we had to get our butts ready for Game 7 the next day. After all, we still had a chance to be World Series champions with just one more win.

And I had to get ready for the start of my life.

CHAPTER 10

Thanks Again, Earl

From the moment Game 6 ended, just about all I could think about was the next game. It seemed like time practically stood still and the seventh game would take an eternity to arrive.

I ran into Bruce Kison back in the hotel lobby and asked him if he had anybody in Baltimore with him. He didn't and, because Karen was still up in Canaan hastily making travel arrangements for her and my father to arrive in time for Game 7, we decided to go to a very nice restaurant for something to eat.

You have to picture the setting. Bruce was getting married the next evening, and I of course would be the Pirates' starting pitcher in the decisive game of the World Series. One would think we would have had an awful lot to talk about. But we sat there for about an hour, enjoyed our meals, and hardly uttered a single word to one another. Bruce wasn't going to give me any advice on how to pitch the Orioles, and I sure as hell wasn't going to give him any on marriage. So it was a rather pleasant but quiet dinner.

As we left the restaurant I turned to him and said, "Well, it's going to be fun trying to sleep tonight." It was, indeed, a restless evening. I got up out of bed around 5:00 the next morning. It wasn't even light out, but I got dressed, went outside, and walked the empty, quiet, early Sunday morning streets of Baltimore for a while. I was glad there wasn't a cop around, because it would have been very difficult to explain that I was going to pitch the seventh game of the World Series later that day. I might *still* be in jail. Still anxious, I returned to the hotel and miraculously grabbed a bit more sleep.

At long last, later that morning the team bus pulled up in front of the hotel. Karen and my father arrived shortly thereafter, and it eased some of my tension to see them before the bus left for the ballpark. I was still anxious when we arrived at Memorial Stadium but a little less so than earlier because I was back on the ballfield, where I felt the most comfortable. During batting practice, I stepped into the cage and did my best Roberto Clemente impersonation, the usual arching of my back, cricking of my neck, and rolling around of my head. I had done it 100 or so times before, but now I had a vaster, World Series–sized throng of reporters to amuse with it. It helped ease the tension.

Also during batting practice, I noticed that Danny Murtaugh had made a couple of last-minute lineup changes, which surprised me a little from a timing standpoint. Danny dropped Willie Stargell to sixth and replaced the far superior–hitting Al Oliver with the right-handed hitting Gene Clines against the southpaw Mike Cuellar. Oliver had started in Game 3 against Cuellar, though he was 0-for-3 with a strikeout against him. That likely had a lot to do with Danny's decision. But I didn't remember many of these late changes to our batting order during the regular season. This was not a common thing for Danny to do at all. But those games weren't the last game of a World Series, either, so it was understandable.

I really wasn't too concerned about our batting order. I couldn't have cared less who was in for us because I didn't have to pitch against our guys. Plus, I knew they were all capable.

The game started under a gloomy, overcast sky with a strong breeze going out to left field. The umpires let both sides know to be ready for a long afternoon in case it started to rain. Cuellar looked great early, retiring us in order in the top of the first. The thing about Cuellar was, despite the fact he was wild in Game 3, walking six in six-plus innings, the 20-game winner was more than capable of coming back strong. That was a big deal, because it was Game 7 and Cuellar appeared to be handling the pressure well. He wasn't over-amped or anything and just went out there and did what he usually did so well. I was nervous as hell as I took the mound. I was very jumpy and just wanted to get into the flow of the game. I kept reminding myself that I had just come off a real good outing in Game 3 and I had squared away all that nonsense in the league championship series. So despite the anxiety, I had a good feeling of confidence coming into this game.

My first two pitches to Don Buford missed, but it was not a big deal because now we were under way and I could try to find my groove. I threw the next pitch, a fastball, right down the middle for a strike. That strike was a clearing of the air. That doesn't sound like a big deal, but it was. I thought, *Okay, I can do this thing. Now I know I'm capable.* The count would go full before I walked Buford. The Baltimore crowd roared with anticipation. Through the first six games of the Series, the home team had won each game.

As Davey Johnson stepped to the plate, I was still trying to control my nerves. But I would get a break that helped settle me down a little bit. Davey, on a 1–1 pitch, squared around to bunt and popped the ball straight up. I ran in a few steps and caught it for the first out of the inning. Apparently, the Orioles were playing for one run, not expecting a lot of offense in the game. Despite Johnson being a good major league hitter, I wasn't surprised by the bunt because Game 6 had been a 3–2 extra-inning game, and some of the other games were pretty tight. I guess they figured that if they got one run in the first inning with Cuellar going, it would put them in a good position.

With a man on first and one out, Boog Powell came up to hit. The game plan with Boog was to throw slow curves or anything inside, because he pulled everything. And that was exactly what Sangy and I wanted him to do. My first pitch to him was a perfect slow curve that he pulled foul. But it was just one curve, so I didn't have the mind-set that it was going to be a great pitch for me all day. But it was a good start.

Before the second pitch, Sangy set up like he normally did but then moved in toward Boog just before my delivery. The target was way off the inside part of the plate. It might have been playing into Boog's power, but it was so far inside that he again pulled the ball a long way, but foul, which was our goal.

Now ahead in the count 0–2, I was staying with the same philosophy of giving him nothing away because with his strength he was capable of hitting the ball out of the ballpark. I didn't even want to take the chance of keeping him honest and showing him a pitch outside in case I missed in. I just had to be sure to keep it away from the middle of the plate. A guy like Boog would cash in on a mistake like that. By crowding him all the time, anything he hit hard had a good chance to go foul. The next pitch, in fact, was so far inside it almost hit him.

So to this point, I was still pretty jumpy but was pleased with the way I was pitching to Powell. Perhaps Earl Weaver sensed that my nerves were starting to settle down, because he called for time and came charging out toward home-plate umpire Nestor Chylak hollering, "8.01! 8.01! He's got to pitch on the rubber in front and not on the side." I heard him yelling about 801, but didn't know at first what that meant. I had never looked at a rule book in my entire life. I thought, *What's going on? Is my jock on backward or something?*

In the baseball rulebook, it states, "the pitcher must throw from in front of the rubber." Earl was saying I was throwing from the side of it, which was totally wrong. As long as you're making contact with the rubber, it doesn't matter where your foot is. Maintaining contact is the issue. I didn't understand what the commotion was about. I had pitched almost eight years in the big leagues and always worked off of the first-base side. I never had a problem with it. Chylak and another umpire started talking to me about it and, not getting anything they were saying, I motioned over to Danny to get involved. It was a little unnerving for me. I'm thinking, *Why are we stopping this thing? What good is this little technicality?*

The unflappable Murtaugh strolled out to the mound like he was taking a walk through the park to join a discussion between me, our infielders, and Chylak. For Danny, there was no running out on to the field. He was kind of like, "Okay, Nestor, what's this all about? What do we need to do here?" So after hearing the explanation of what 8.01 meant, I said, "What the hell is this all about? I've been legal for eight years."

The discussion on the mound continued, and realizing how ridiculous this all was, I smiled and realized this was all a lot over nothing. This was not a big issue. In fact, it was no issue at all. I wanted to get on the other side of this thing and get back to pitching. I even reassured Sangy by telling him, "We're okay now. I understand what Weaver's deal is. They're making a bigger deal of it than it really is."

So I moved back to the identical spot on the rubber where I was before. I didn't adjust a thing. Every pitcher does what I did when in the stretch. Some pitchers line up toward the first-base side of the rubber. Some guys put their foot over toward the third-base side and others work in the middle. It's a long rubber. It's like 18" long. The bottom line is the whole thing was nonsense. It was purely a little psychological trick Earl was trying to play on me.

After the delay, which was less than three minutes but seemed more like 10, I threw a couple of warm-up pitches because I hadn't thrown in a while. The first one sailed wildly off of Sangy's outstretched glove, and the crowd erupted in delight. It was right out of central casting. They sensed that the disruption had affected my pitching. After my second warm-up pitch, out popped Weaver again. He just couldn't leave it alone.

He calls out to Chylak, "He hasn't changed! He hasn't moved! *And he's not stopping, either.*" Chylak, knowing that I was pitching within the boundaries of Rule 8.01, told Earl, "He doesn't have to. We checked it out. He's in contact with the rubber."

Perhaps because of all the emphasis Earl was putting on Rule 8.01, Chylak didn't pay close enough attention to what Weaver threw out there at the end of his argument about me not stopping my hands in the set position before going into my delivery. What I was doing was technically a balk. It was a legitimate gripe that could have blown everything up. If I had to start consciously thinking about stopping my hands, it may have completely affected my style of pitching from the stretch. It may have altered my normal way of slowing down and bouncing my hands at the set position.

But Weaver concentrated on the wrong item. Those four words, "He's not stopping, either," were overlooked. And when I look back now, I think, *Oh shit, if Nestor had pulled the plug on that, it may have been a whole different ballgame.*

Later on, when asked about it, Weaver said, "The whole thing wasn't my idea. My players told me about [Rule 8.01]." I guess he thought it was good timing for him to pull his little fit. He had this in his back pocket. It was just a question of when he was going to use it. I've often said in interviews that the delay caused by Weaver's ranting really helped me relax. And every time I see Earl, even today, I say, good-naturedly, "Thanks again, Earl."

But the reality was that, though I was still jumpy, I had already started to settle down and had gotten into a really good rhythm against Boog. I was throwing very well at that point. So it may have been a good line for me to use all these years, but in reality I don't know how accurate it was, because I was throwing the ball right where I wanted to against Powell.

With Weaver eventually going back to the dugout, we started playing ball again. With a 1–2 count to Boog, I just wasted a pitch to show him one down and away in the dirt. It was certainly lower than I wanted to go, especially with a man on first who could have advanced on a wild pitch, but I didn't want Powell to see any pitch he could drive. If I missed, I wanted to miss downstairs. Like Jim Bunning once said, when asked why he always tried to keep his pitches low, "I've never seen a 450' ground ball."

Meanwhile, I was still trying to keep track of Buford on first base because of his speed. I missed badly on the next pitch, another curveball, to make the count full. The curveball is such a delicate pitch and more physically demanding than a slider. That's because if you get your body out in front, the curve will stay upstairs all the time and your arm will never catch up with it. So after being out in front 0–2, it was now a 3–2 count.

But we were able to strike out Powell with a very good slider downstairs. It might not have been as far in as I wanted, but it was good enough. That gave me a jolt of confidence because it was a payoff pitch. If I had lost Powell, they would have had two guys on with just one out and Frank Robinson coming up. Because the only out I had gotten before the strikeout was on a bunt, I really hadn't done much to that point. But getting Powell on the slider, which was my best pitch, was definitely a boost. The whole ballgame can turn around in the first inning, so it was a gutsy call and a big second out. When the fat's in the fire, and it was on that payoff pitch, you don't want to just give in and throw a fastball because, conceivably, it's easier to throw for a strike. Plus, most hitters expect fastballs on 3–2 pitches. So I wanted to go with my best pitch, and for me that was the slider.

I was pumped now. I had completely different body language going. Right after the strikeout, I walked toward Sangy to the grass in front of the mound, shoulders up, a little puffed up, thinking, *Give me the ball.*

It would only take one more pitch to get out of the first inning. Robinson swung at the first thing he saw and hit what looked like a routine fly ball to right field, but it carried all the way to the warning track, where Clemente tracked it down. I was surprised the ball traveled so well, because the wind was going away from right field over to left. Under normal weather conditions, Frank might have hit that ball over the fence. But after a most eventful first inning, the game was scoreless.

I was much calmer at this point than when the game started. You put up a zero in the first inning of a seventh game of the World Series, and that tends to settle you down. I was on the other side of the nerves. Things were under way without any damage. Nobody said anything to me in the dugout, which was the way I liked it when I pitched, even though I am sure some of them might have wanted my take on the shenanigans with Weaver. The Rule 8.01 shit was already ancient history because I had put up a zero, which was much more important.

Cuellar again shut down the Buccos in order in the top of the second. Stargell ended the inning by striking out on three straight fastballs. Willie looked overmatched by Cuellar, taking the first two and not being able to catch up with the third one. The Orioles would threaten to score in the bottom of the inning when, with one out and after getting ahead of Brooks Robinson with a good fastball, I threw four straight balls to put Brooks on first base. It would turn out to be my last free pass of the day.

A routine bouncer by Ellie Hendricks to the sure-handed Bob Robertson was then misplayed to put runners on first and second with one out. Robertson was one of the most underrated defensive first basemen in the game, and the ground ball may have gotten an in-between hop that allowed it to skip by him. There was traffic there, too, which could have served as a distraction, as Brooks took off from first and Dave Cash came over from second not knowing if he or Robertson was in the best position to make the play.

With two runners on and still just one out, I faced the No. 8 hitter, Mark Belanger. Normally I might pitch around him and work on the pitcher's slot instead. But not so in this case. When Cuellar pitched with Houston, he hit a home run off me at Forbes Field. So I knew that he could swing the bat, and as a result I needed to go hard after Belanger. Mark hit a sharp ground ball right up the middle, but Cash made a nice backhanded play, stepped on second base, and threw over to Robertson to get the double play and end the inning.

Cash obviously made a very good play, though credit should also be attributed to our World Series scouts Howie Haak and Pete Peterson. Because they had Cash shaded up toward second base, it kept the ball from getting through and into center field. If Cash had been positioned at his normal spot, we would have been down 1–0 with Baltimore runners on first and third, still just one out, and a good-hitting pitcher coming up.

While my first two innings were filled with drama, Cuellar kept cruising along. By the time it was my turn to hit in the top of the third, Cuellar had retired eight straight Buccos. My strategy was to guess fastball on the first pitch and see if I could drive it somewhere. I knew I wasn't a great hitter, but I was pretty good at making contact. My theory was that, on the first pitch, I was in "rip city," hoping to get a fastball. After that, I would shorten up and just try to make contact.

I took a huge first swing against Cuellar, looking dead red for the fastball. But he threw me a screwball down and away instead, and my helmet damn near flew off while I losing my balance from a healthy cut. After shortening up, I made contact on the second pitch and hit a routine ground ball to Davey Johnson. It was now nine up and nine down for the Pirates.

I started off the bottom of the third by striking out Cuellar. That was just a day at the office, because as soon as I got ahead of him, I just turned over a fastball down and away and he chased it.

THANKS AGAIN, EARL 163

At this point, with the nervousness a memory, the lock was turned, and I was into the ballgame the way I wanted to be in it. In fact, I was so locked in that I wasn't even thinking about the fact I was pitching in a World Series Game 7 any longer. I thought, *Okay, Cuellar's out of the way. Here comes Buford.*

While I was letting the enormity of the seventh game bleed in a little bit in the first inning, now everything was white noise. As far as I was concerned, there was nothing going on except me, Sangy, and Buford. Buford would drive the ball toward right-center field for a single. Clemente made a nice play to cut it off to keep Don at first.

Because it appeared as if Buford was running on the pitch, my pickoff to first base had to be extra quick because Robertson needed the time to fire down to second. Not only that, but Bob didn't have the time to step to the side and get a better angle, so he had to throw over Buford's shoulder. Seeing that and realizing that most of the time one would get thrown out, Buford decided not to slide but to roll-block Cash instead. Robertson's throw was perfect, and Cash luckily tagged him and got the hell out of the way of this charging bull.

I loved picking guys off. It was so much fun. I always had a good, quick move to first base. I could twist my whole body in one swift motion. There were other times when I tried my ultra-quick move when I would throw and step in one motion. It was technically a balk because my body was still lined up with home plate. I was so fast with it that the umpires would only see a blur because the ball was moving in tandem with my arm. So they never could pick it up. Stepping toward first very quickly after releasing the ball helped sell the move.

On the very next pitch, Davey Johnson hit a hot shot close to the line at third, but Jose Pagan was positioned right there and made a nice play. Again, the scouts deserve a lot of credit for their positioning of our guys. If Pagan had been where he normally played, that ball looked destined to be a double down the left-field corner. Cuellar continued his mastery over us by getting the first two outs to start the fourth. But his string of retiring the first 11 Pirates ended with an ill-fated off-speed pitch upstairs to Clemente, which he just pounded over the left-center-field fence to put us up 1–0.

Clemente was a guy who loved to go to the opposite field, but he got a mistake pitch and with the ball carrying to left field, he hit it a long way. It was so much fun watching him play because he could do so many things and hurt the opposition in so many different ways. That home run was just another example. I never wanted to miss anything Clemente did. He was just mesmerizing whether in the outfield, on base, or at the plate. He even had charisma when kneeling in the on-deck circle.

After the inning was over, Clemente received a standing ovation from the fans in the right-field bleachers. That was because most of the people sitting out there had complimentary tickets from the Pirates. To the displeasure of a lot of Pirates family members, wives, grandkids, fathers, mothers, cousins, fans, and close friends, that is where the Orioles' organization stuck them. The usual courtesy is to put the visiting World Series team's comp tickets a little closer to the action, often behind home plate. The Orioles' relatives and friends got much better ticket locations at Three Rivers Stadium.

But I guess if you had to sit in the right-field bleachers, being able to watch the great Roberto Clemente up close and personal wasn't so bad. So now I had a lead, but I had to face Powell, Frank Robinson, and Merv Rettenmund, three hitters all capable of tying it up with one swing of the bat. With Boog, I stayed with my strategy of crowding him with mostly off-speed pitches. He was really the only Orioles batter I had a plan against, because he was more one-dimensional than most of their other guys. He just wanted to pull everything, and that separated him from the others who would hit to the opposite field when the opportunity presented itself. For as great a power hitter as Boog was, it was somewhat easier to prepare for him than the other guys in their lineup. Powell hit a pitch low and in to Cash for an easy out. The plan was working.

Next up was Frank Robinson, and my strategy with him was to start out by throwing a steady diet of fastballs. In Game 3, I had struck him out with a high fastball but also watched him crush a hanging slider off me for a long home run. Many times a pitcher will have a tendency to stay away from home run pitches from a previous game. In this game, Robinson couldn't catch up with my fastball and kept fouling them straight back. Although my curve and slider were working equally well in this game against the other Orioles hitters, my approach with Frank had to be different.

With Robinson, if I made a mistake and hung a slider to him, it would be easier for him to hit it out than a fastball upstairs. With a fastball, you at least get some speed, but a hanging slider doesn't have the velocity of a fastball or the break of a curveball. If you got a slider up, Robinson—or any of those guys for that matter—would crush it. Location is the first commandment in the sliders section of the pitcher's bible. So I threw a few four-seam fastballs and then struck Frank out with a slow curve, which he was way out in front of.

Many times what you try to do as a pitcher is to get the hitter's eyes to think upward after seeing one fast high pitch after another. Then, with his line of vision up there, you go completely away from that and try to get him to quickly adjust to something slow and low. That's a tough combination to adjust to. It can also work in reverse, going from down to up.

After striking out Frank Robinson, Pagan then made his second really good play of the game, charging in on a weakly hit ground ball, picking it up, and releasing all in one motion to get Rettenmund. He made a very tough play look easy. Both sides still only had just one hit after four innings of play.

I was really on my game now. That little pitching clinic to Frank Robinson gave me a real good feeling that I could throw a bunch of fastballs and then all of a sudden throw a perfect curveball. The timing on a curveball was tough enough, but the timing on a slow curveball was even tougher because I had a herky-jerky motion. The timing and release of that slow curve had to be perfect to get Frank to bite like that. And it was.

It looked like we might start a rally and add to our lead in the fifth. Sangy led things off with a single to center field. A lot of emphasis was put on Clemente and me, but Manny had a terrific World Series as well. Up next was Stargell, and everyone, including Cuellar, knew he was capable of busting out of his slump at any time. Pitching him carefully, Cuellar got behind 3–0 but then came back with three straight strikes to strike him out. Cuellar, like the other 20-game winners on the Orioles' staff, just pitched him perfectly all Series long.

Willie did not have a good World Series, but his 48 home runs and 125 RBIs were a big reason why we were there. To this day, I'm so glad he had a chance for a redeemer in 1979 when he did everything to lead the Pirates to a world championship.

Pagan followed with what looked like a sure infield hit. But Belanger fielded the ball hit very deep in the hole near the outfield grass, went airborne, and threw off balance to just barely nip Sangy at second base. Sangy put up a minor argument, but I had no reason to doubt the umpire. It was just a great play by Belanger. He looked like he was posing for one of those old publicity pictures of the jump pass by a quarterback. Those Orioles were just phenomenal defensively.

To this point in the inning, we couldn't capitalize on our good fortune. We got a hit from Sangy, Stargell was ahead in the count 3–0, and Pagan hit a ball that should have been a base hit, but were still clinging to a 1–0 lead. That's how the Orioles won all those games. They were a truly multidimensional baseball team. They had offense, defense, and pitching. Cuellar then struck out Hernandez with his arsenal of pitches to end the inning. Jackie was simply overmatched.

I have so many good memories of Jackie. He was just such a fun, upbeat person and so easy to root for. One of my favorite things was when Jackie was on the bench and the home-plate umpire would squeeze our pitcher's strike zone on a borderline pitch. Hernandez would sometimes shout out to him, "Don't squeeze the Charm! Don't squeeze the Charm!" It was a take on an old television commercial for Charmin bath tissue.

Playing in this seventh game was the culmination of a kind of serendipitous situation for Jackie. He had come over to us in a trade from the Kansas City Royals as a utility man, filled in for Gene Alley after he hurt his knee, and ended up playing marvelous defense for us in the World Series. Had Alley been healthy, he would have been the starting shortstop. Gene was a terrific defensive player, a respectable major league hitter, and clearly the superior all-around shortstop.

The Orioles made a bid to tie things up in the bottom of the fifth when with one out, Elrod Hendricks drove one to fairly deep right-center field for a double. After it got by Clemente running over from right field, it would have gone for an easy triple, except that Gene Clines hustled over and cut off the high bounce by going up and grabbing it with his bare hand, thus keeping the ball from going to the wall. A really good throw by Clines actually made it a close play at second, but Elrod got in there safely. The important thing was Clines keeping Hendricks from getting to third with less than two outs.

The pitch to Elrod was a mistake pitch, a high breaking ball that he just hammered. I came back with the breaking ball to Belanger with better results, as he hit a harmless fly ball to center field. Hendricks tagged but didn't go anywhere. A lot of baseball fans may have been thinking that if Clines hadn't cut the ball off, Hendricks would have tagged from third to tie the ballgame on Belanger's fly ball. The problem with that thinking is that you can never assume that the same thing is going to happen next. Ninety-nine percent of the time something different will occur.

Pause for editorial comment: So why do so many professional broadcasters keep bringing up those bogus scenarios? Because we can't shut up. We're professional bullshitters. We always have to say something. It's just the way it is.

I started the next hitter, Cuellar, off with two balls. Getting behind the opposing pitcher, even a good-hitting one like Cuellar, was cause for some concern. Danny got Luke Walker up and throwing in the bullpen. I had thrown a lot of pitches at that stage of the game. Not that they counted them, but a manager will have an instinctive feel if you're laboring a bit on the mound. He might think, *Is he struggling? Is he laboring?* But back in those days, it wasn't like "Oh my God, there's pitch No. 74!"

But because it was a choppy bottom of the fifth inning, a 1–0 game, I'm behind 2–0 to a pitcher, and Elrod just had that nice poke to right-center field, there was no downside to having somebody warm up. With it being the seventh game of the World Series and not a game in late April, there was no need to rest any of the pitchers for the next day. I came all the way back to strike out Cuellar with a couple of fastballs and a back-door slider to end the fifth. One of the beauties of the slider is that it looks like a fastball. So you start on the outside part and the hitter thinks, *Okay, it looks like a fastball and it's going to stay out there and miss.* Then all of a sudden the slider ducks in and picks up the outside corner. And that's what I threw to Cuellar. I had much success with that pitch.

It was obvious that the strikeout didn't affect Cuellar in the least on the mound. He pitched a perfect sixth, ending the inning by striking out Cash and Clines. It was toe-to-toe with Cuellar now, though he hadn't struggled nearly as much as I had. He had thrown far fewer pitches than I had, and despite being behind a run, he was cooking at this point. I could tell that it was going to be a well-pitched game all the way through, as we were both doing exactly what we wanted to do with the baseball.

In the Pirates' dugout, it was all business. Nobody was talking to me, neither did anyone need to talk to me. When I came into the dugout from the field, I would put my glove down, place my cap on top of it, put a towel around my elbow, and sit on the bench. There was not a lot of noise. I was in my "office," had punched in on the clock, and just went about trying to pitch a very good ballgame. There was never any rah-rah stuff. It was a professional setting, just like I am sure it was over in the Baltimore dugout.

I didn't go up to any of the Pirates' hitters and say, "Now, be careful here. Cuellar's got a good screwball," or "Come on, let's do something big!" I knew they were into it. They were doing their job, and I was doing mine. Cuellar and I were dealing. We'd both shut down our respective opponents in the sixth and seventh innings in order. The tension thickened with every pitch in this still 1–0 ballgame, but because everything was moving along so quickly, I didn't get too mired in it. If I had been on the bench, I would have felt far more pressure because it would have been more of a helpless feeling. I would compare it to pitching a game in April. The pitcher's not cold, because he's working. Everybody else is like, "Goddamn, its freezing!"

So it was tougher for the guys on the bench and the Pirates fans watching at home than it was on me. They were just reacting to what they saw but couldn't do anything about the outcome. I was very much aware that one pitch, one mistake, could tie it up. The fielders were, too, as evidenced by how extra careful they were when the ball was hit to them. Whether it was Clines cradling a fly ball or Jackie squeezing a pop-up in the sixth inning, everybody was making sure to secure the baseball like a quarterback before handing the ball off to a running back.

It was almost like what happens when a guy is pitching a perfect game in the eighth or ninth inning. There's a tremendous amount of tension. Even the umpires are tighter than usual, because there's pressure on them, too. Only Clemente didn't appear fazed by the enormity of this compellingly close seventh game, as he'd shown with his basket catch earlier in the game. But Clemente, naturally, was different. He didn't have to make sure of anything. Being sure was built into him. I used to say, "Hit the ball to right field while I go and get a sandwich. When I come back, you'll be out."

One of the happiest things about the seventh game, second only to winning it, was when I went out to pitch the bottom half of the seventh inning. After my warm-up tosses, Sangy threw the ball down to second, and the infielders tossed the ball around the horn to Pagan at third, who then flipped it to me. At that point, I turned my back to home plate and just paused for a moment or two and did my best to soak it all in. I didn't know if I was ever going to be in this kind of a situation again and I wanted that entire image to stay with me for the rest of my life. And to this day, I have that whole magic feel. Forget about your hard drive—this can never be deleted.

After retiring the Orioles in the bottom of the seventh inning, I remember walking toward the dugout, head down, and thinking, *How about getting me some runs? Come on! Get me a little help here, boys. I'm cooking, but I can use a little breathing room.* And they came through, with "little" being the appropriative word.

Stargell led off the top of the eighth. The Orioles were playing him to pull the ball by putting on a semi-shift. Belanger was up toward second base, leaving the shortstop position wide open. Willie hit the ball sharply the opposite way on the ground and Belanger tried to field it on his backhand side, but it got just under his glove for a single into left-center field. Now we had Stargell on first and Pagan at the plate with Hernandez and me to follow. So there wasn't much offense in back of Jose Pagan. This may have been the reason that Murtaugh put on the hit-and-run.

Stargell took off on the pitch and Pagan hit a high, hanging breaking pitch very well to left-center field, a little surprising because he didn't have a lot of power. Rettenmund, who was playing him shallow, watched the ball sail over his head, short-hop the wall, and carom upward. Merv didn't have to bend or chase it down on the warning track, but he bobbled the ball, costing him a precious second to get the ball to the cut-off man. Seeing the miscue and probably knowing that his No. 8 and 9 hitters were up next, third-base coach Frank Oceak sent that big body of Stargell's around third and toward home.

Belanger made a beautiful relay throw home, but Powell inexplicably cut it off to allow Stargell to score without a play to give us a 2–0 lead. There's been speculation as to whether Boog should have cut it off or let it go through. When you think about it, there was probably no risk for him in allowing for a play at the plate because Pagan was going to stay at second no matter what. There was no way that Pagan would have risked making the first out of the inning trying to advance to third. Also, there was a chance if he didn't cut it off, they would have gotten Stargell at home. Willie was tired by that point. He was probably thinking, *What are you doing to me, Frank? I'm happy to stay here at third.* If there was another base, Willie would have had a pinch runner come in for him.

So why didn't Boog let it go through? He may have heard someone hollering at him to cut it off. Or maybe he felt he was a little bit on the first-base side of home plate and the ball was off-line. We'll never know. So, now with a 2–0 lead, a runner on second and nobody out, we were looking to bring across that critical third run.

It brought up an interesting situation on whether to have Jackie bunt or swing away with me on deck. By bunting, it may have moved the runner to third, but it also would have given us one out with me coming to the plate. And we didn't necessarily want to give an out away. On the other hand, Hernandez was a position player, so maybe we could have gotten a base hit and scored the run that way. Danny had him bunt, so maybe he felt I was a better hitter than I thought I was.

Jackie's first bunt attempt looked like he was trying more for a base hit than just squaring around and giving himself up. His second attempt, while more of a sacrifice, had the same result. Now with two strikes, Jackie swung away and flew out to right field. Pagan was still standing at second base.

Whether or not Jackie had gotten that bunt down, I would have been completely shocked if Danny had pinch hit for me to try to get that third run in. And we had a superb bench that day with Oliver and Richie Hebner ready, if needed. But I was pitching a two-hit shutout. I don't even know if in today's game a pinch-hitter would come to bat in a situation like that. Any team would be chancing it by taking out a hot pitcher for somebody who might not have his stuff that particular day. Why not stay with a known entity as opposed to the unknown?

I guess I was hoping that would be the case for me in this game, even with a closer like the one we had in Dave Giusti. And I would also hope that in a similar situation today that, even with a Mariano Rivera looming in the bullpen, a manager would say something like, "I'm not taking him out. If he blows it, it's his ballgame." It would have been interesting to see what Murtaugh would have done had Jackie got that bunt down. I may have strolled over to the plate thinking, *Oh shit! Danny's probably going to put on the squeeze play. Now the heat's really on!*

But that scenario never played out, and after Cuellar got two quick strikes on me, I got into my special defensive batting stance by opening up almost to third base. All I wanted to do was take a short backswing and make contact. As a result, I didn't strike out a lot. As a pitcher, you want to put the ball in play and see what happens. Something good might happen. It's not going to happen all the time, but there's a better chance of something good happening if you put the ball in play rather than striking out.

I did make contact, but I bounced the ball right back to Cuellar. I was pretty pissed because I thought I was a decent-hitting pitcher and could really have helped my cause. But part of the deal is to let the anger go and get ready to go out and pitch again.

Now we had two outs with Pagan still standing on second and Cash our last chance to get that all-important insurance run. Traditionally, hitters take a pitch to give the pitcher a breather after he bats. But I always told those guys, "Don't wait around. I'm fine. Swing away. Take your normal at-bat." They often took a pitch for me anyway, probably thinking, *Steve's nuts. We know he's crazy.*

Cash would end the inning by hitting a tough chopper to Brooks that he fielded and fired to Boog on one hop. Powell made a nice scoop to secure the third out. It was a good play on both ends and prevented Pagan from coming into score.

After we scored that second run in the top of the eighth, some fans might have thought, *Well, you've got some insurance now.* But I didn't feel any differently with a two-run lead than I did with one. My approach going into that bottom of the eighth was exactly the same as before. The Orioles had a great lineup, and I knew they could score in a heartbeat. Sure enough, Hendricks hit a two-seam fastball through the infield for a leadoff single to center field. Just that quickly, the Orioles were sending the tying run to the plate.

I threw what I believed to be a decent pitch to the next hitter, Belanger, but he just kind of tapped it into center field for a single. When it went off his bat, it sounded like it was hit with a wet newspaper like the *Post-Gazette.* But, as they say, it was a line drive in the book, and now the Orioles had runners on first and second and nobody out. Weaver sent up pinch-hitter Tom Shopay to hit for Cuellar as he tried to seize this opportunity to at least tie the game.

Now, we had a situation. I still had not given up a run. There still had not been any visits to the mound. And there wouldn't be one then or even in the ninth. But we all figured that with the Orioles being the home team and wanting to get their runners into scoring position, Shopay was going to bunt. The wheels were turning. We had both Walker and Giusti up in the bullpen, but I didn't notice that at all. My focus was entirely on the situation at hand.

Surprisingly, Shopay did not square around and took my first pitch inside for ball one. Now the Baltimore fans were going crazy. But we were still expecting the bunt. He still didn't show a bunt on the second pitch, but I got it over to even the count. Shopay, who coincidentally wore No. 28 and was from Connecticut like I was, put down a good bunt on the next pitch, but I got to it quickly by cutting the angle between the mound and the third-base line. Sangy started pointing and hollering, "Third base! Third base!"

But I never considered it. My throws around the infield to second or third base were always a little shaky. Plus, because I had my back to the play, I just shut it down and took the out at first that I knew I had. If I had thrown it down the left-field line, I would never have forgiven myself, especially in a seventh game of the World Series as opposed to a night game in May. Could we have gotten him at third base? Most people say yes. But the two Connecticut guys were both happy. Shopay got his bunt down and moved the two runners into scoring position, and I got the first out of the inning.

So now we had a 2–0 game, runners at second and third, just one out, and the whole thing was in the fire. Weaver was pacing back and forth in the Orioles' dugout like a cat on a hot tin roof. Murtaugh, by contrast, was sitting on the bench, legs crossed like he was getting ready to watch the evening news and signaling ever so casually with his thumb for our infielders to play back and concede a run for the second out. Even then, Danny was cooler than ice.

As it played out, it was a good strategy, because Buford ended up getting a well-hit ground ball to first base that, while scoring Hendricks and moving Belanger to third, also got us the second out and possibly prevented a game-tying double down the right-field line. Had the infield been up, Robertson might have been able to snare it and prevent the run from scoring, but it was not worth taking the chance.

My pitch count was pretty high by now, but when a starter gets to the eighth inning and can sense the finish line, adrenaline kicks in that may not have been there an inning or two before. Sometimes, that gives a pitcher a little more zip on his fastball. For the first time all afternoon, I was slowing down my pace by walking around the mound after almost every pitch. It's a normal tendency for starters late in a tight game. When a pitcher gets in the soup, it's good for him to slow things down a little bit. I had to make sure I had my act together and gave a little more thought to what I would do next. It was different when I was rolling along. Then, it was just get the ball, get the sign, and continue that quick pace. But now I was in a jam with the tying run on third. There was no need to make any quick decisions.

All I could think of was getting one more out and ending the eighth inning with 2–1 lead. Danny was displaying tremendous confidence in me by not even visiting me on the mound. At this point, it would no longer have shocked me if he had brought in Giusti. Dave had been saving games like this since we got him. Back then, two- and three-inning saves were commonplace, so bringing him in to get four outs would not have been a stretch at all.

As Davey Johnson walked up to the plate, Pagan came over from third to talk to me. Jose had been through a World Series in 1962 with the Giants, so it was not a bad time for him to come over and say, "We're still good. Still a run up. Take a deep breath. Collect yourself." The first pitch I threw to Davey, a good slider, just missed for ball one. I stayed with the slider the next two pitches and got ahead 1–2.

I called time to talk to Sangy because, since Davey had seen nothing but sliders and was going to protect the outside corner, I wanted to throw a fastball up and in and try to get a strikeout. I told Sangy, "Set up for another slider away, just in case he's peeking that way. Let's see if we can surprise him and lock him up." It was a good conference with Sangy. There were times when he would come out and we wouldn't understand each other. He was thinking in Spanish and me in English. That rarely worked, but this meeting created a good plan. I threw the high inside fastball right where we wanted it, but Davey didn't bite. Sangy reacted with both fists pumped like, *Oh, man, we almost got him!* Davey showed some pretty good discipline holding the bat back.

Johnson hit the next pitch, a not-so-great slider right down the middle, deep in the hole at shortstop. Jackie made an above-average play by getting to it with the game on the line and fired a strike to Robertson to end the inning. If he hadn't made the play, we would have had a tie ballgame. Instead, we headed to the ninth inning with a one-run lead.

Back in the dugout, I could barely stay still. It was an extended inning in that we got a couple of two-out hits and they changed pitchers, replacing Pat Dobson with Dave McNally, the third 20-game winner to pitch for the Orioles that afternoon. I started pacing back and forth and, while Baltimore made the pitching change, went into the clubhouse to pass the time. When there, I saw a camera setup with Bob Prince preparing what he hoped would be postgame interviews in the winning locker room.

Most players are superstitious and I thought that this scene was, at minimum, a little premature. I walked over to Gunner and asked, "What the hell are you doing down here?" Prince turned it around and replied, "*Me?* What the hell are *you* doing in here? Get your ass out of here and get me some outs so I can go to work. *Okay?*" It was classic Gunner.

Not knowing really what to say, I returned to the dugout with Stargell coming to bat with a chance to break it open with two on and two out. At the very least, I was hoping we could scratch out another run. But it wasn't to be; Willie grounded out to second to end our threat.

As I walked out to the mound to face the heart of the Baltimore order with a World Championship within our grasp, I reminded myself not to try to get all three outs on one pitch. That's a trap. In other words, I didn't want to get ahead of myself. After all, I had it together. I was on a nice roll. I got out of that jam in the eighth inning and was still in the ballgame. The adrenaline was pumping. I was ready to go.

I opened with "old faithful" to Boog, a slow, slop-drop, dead-fish curveball for strike one. It was a good start to an at-bat. Anytime a pitcher starts a major league batter out with a breaking ball for a strike, it really gives him an advantage, because most hitters live on fastballs. Now the hitter wonders if he is going to see *any* fastballs in the at-bat, and if so, when. But if a pitcher misses with that first-pitch curveball, it swings the pendulum the other way. Now the hitter is thinking, *Okay, you missed with a breaking ball, probably your second-best pitch. Now I'm going to sit on a fastball.* So getting that curveball over on the first pitch set up the at-bat.

I then intentionally missed upstairs with a fastball to even the count. Sangy and I wanted to show him the fastball but never intended it to be near the strike zone. A lot of people suffer under the illusion that every

pitcher wants each pitch to be a strike. In reality, though, there are pitches
that you don't want to be a strike. When I was ahead in a count, I might
use a pitch to set up my next one. With my second pitch to Powell, I
wanted to give him a different look than the first one.

I went back to the slop-drop on the next pitch, and Boog hit it about
400 feet. The problem for him was it went around 500 feet foul. It may
have gotten the crowd into it, but it was exactly what I wanted to do. I
knew he was not going to hit that ball fair. Boog just couldn't wait long
enough. It's just the way he hit.

Now ahead in the count 1–2, I tried to get him to chase a slow curve
down in the dirt, but he held back to even things at 2–2. Not wanting
to go full but also not wanting to give him anything I knew he could hit
well, I threw him another curveball, and he hit a routine two-hopper to
Dave Cash for the first out of the inning.

With the dangerous Powell now taken care of, it didn't get any easier
with Frank Robinson, another slugger who could tie things up in a hurry.
Sometimes in a spot like this, it's just as important to be lucky as it is to
be good. Fortunately for me, I may have dodged a bullet with Frank on
my first pitch to him.

I threw a very hittable, waist-high slider to Frank that he just got
under and popped up to Hernandez for the second out. Robinson was
not the least bit fooled by the pitch and put a good full swing on it. He
must have felt he missed a chance to tie the game. That was the type of
pitch that Frank hit a lot of home runs off of. It was very similar to the
one he slammed off me in the third game.

So now it doesn't get any better than this. Two outs. Ninth inning.
Game 7 of the World Series. It was the type of scenario I lived a thousand
times before when I was eight years old, throwing the ball against the barn,
in all those Game 7s I created in my imagination back in Falls Village.

But it was a *slightly* different program now. This was an area where
I really had to contain myself. I was so close to the finish line. This was
really the time to not get careless. I was too close to screw it up. Strength
was a non-factor because of the adrenaline. The last thing on my mind at
that moment was fatigue.

My biggest challenge was to not let anything else bleed in. The tension was there, but the last thing I wanted to think about was winning the World Series. There were 60 million viewers watching it on television, 40,000 more in the park. This could mean a big check. This could be the defining moment of my career. But I had to fight those thoughts. All that shit wanted to bleed in, but I somehow found a way to block it out. It certainly wasn't easy.

Rettenmund stepped in, and although he didn't present the same long-ball threat of Powell and Robinson, he had hit a bunch of home runs the past two regular seasons. I started Merv off with a good slider away from his power for strike one. It was such a good feeling to throw not just a first-pitch strike but also a good one. It wasn't a hanging slider or a ball fouled right back. It was a pitch he would have difficulty hitting solidly.

I came back with the slider, and he hit it hard up the middle. When it went by me, I assumed it would get through for a single. But the first bounce was off the mound, which gave it some height and took some of the zip off of it. That helped Jackie, who was shaded up that way, move toward the ball and see it come at him chest high.

When I turned around and saw Jackie, I yelled, "Catch it!" After Hernandez snared it and straightened up, I hollered, "Throw it!" Jackie fired a strike toward first base, and I turned in Robertson's direction and screamed, "Catch it!"

After that final out was made, all hell broke loose and I leaped joyously into Robertson's arms. It was pandemonium at first base as the rest of our teammates rushed over to join us in a wild celebration. It was pure joy and was a release of everything that had been contained and preserved inside of us. It was a swarm where you just wanted to grab people. And it was justice served cold to Weaver with Jackie making the last play of the game just two weeks after Earl's comment about our not being able to win a championship with Hernandez at short.

Moments later, that swarm moved to the clubhouse because we wanted to be by ourselves. We knew that the fans who had rushed onto the field were jubilant. And that was wonderful, but we wanted to be with the 25 guys who got this thing done and start partying. Now the good times could start. In the midst of all the bedlam in the Pirates' clubhouse, Kison came up to me and said, "Hey, thanks for making it quick!"

Then, off he went to get married. He and best man Bob Moose, still in uniform, rushed to a revved-up helicopter just outside of Memorial Stadium that would take them to a private jet that Bob Prince had arranged for with Jack Piatt, the founder and chairman of Millcraft Industries. Kison was married hours later at the Churchill Country Club just outside of Pittsburgh. Talk about a rookie year! Bruce got called up to the majors, earned a World Series ring and a big check, and then helicoptered out to get married. That's quite the hat trick!

Equally impressive was turning around and seeing my father in there. Somehow, he had talked his way into the champagne-drenched, victorious clubhouse. I was happily surprised to see him there, because it was probably more difficult to do that than to just jump off the top of the dugout at Three Rivers Stadium like he did after my win in Game 3.

Another nice moment for me came from Bill Mazeroski. He was long on the record of judging pitchers by seeing how well they performed with a lead. Maz believed anybody could pitch when he was behind, because the pressure is not on in those circumstances. He had the *most* respect for the guys who pitched well with a lead. So he came up to me and said, "That's the proof of the pudding. You protected that lead. You're in that category now."

After all the locker room celebrating and interviews, we boarded our quick flight back to Pittsburgh. Once there, as we taxied down the runway, there were so many fans that we had to go farther down to get away from them for safety reasons. As we got off the plane with the World Series trophy in tow, there were 14 convertibles sitting there, ready to take us for an impromptu parade from the airport to downtown. The City of Pittsburgh, the Chamber of Commerce, and the Pirates had set this all up, and we quickly began the 14-mile journey.

There were people lined up from the airport to downtown on both sides of the parkway, inbound and outbound. As we came through the Fort Pitt Tunnel, there were just wall-to-wall people. The intent was to do a circle around downtown, but when some of the fans starting grabbing at us, we got concerned for the safety of Murtaugh's daughter, Kathy, who was pregnant.

So we shut down the parade concept and, after stopping over at Three Rivers for a strategy session on a Plan B, headed over to our victory party on a docked Gateway Clipper excursion boat. It was a pretty chilly night, and it wasn't long before the party broke up and my teammates and their wives started to disperse. Having parked our car at a motel near the airport, Karen and I searched for more than an hour trying to get a taxi to get us back there.

Just hours before, I had pitched a complete game to help give Pittsburgh a World Series championship. Now, I was standing there like a street person trying to hitch a ride. Eventually a cab came along. We got a good night's rest and began the ride back home to Canaan the next morning.

On October 25, Canaan had a Steve Blass Day. It was arranged by my old high school coach, Ed Kirby, and a committee of other local guys. The setting was just like a Norman Rockwell painting. It was a gorgeous, crisp autumn day. A sea of people packed the old town from the parking area in front of the train station loading platform where the ceremony was being conducted on up to Main Street and continuing along a small hill leading to a church. The high school band played, Little Leaguers wore their uniforms, and dignitaries from all four corners of the state attended.

Special editions of our weekly newspapers, the *Connecticut Western* and the *Lakeville Journal*, celebrated the occasion with advertisements from every business in town congratulating me. Karen, the boys, and I were chauffeured to this little setting by my friend, Joe Calabrese, in a Chevy Blazer with an enlarged Pirates cap on top to mimic the bullpen cars that were used at Three Rivers Stadium.

United States Senator Lowell Weicker, who would later become Governor of Connecticut, spoke and presented me with an autographed photo of President Richard Nixon. Congresswoman Ella Grasso, who later became the state's first female governor, was there. Bob Steele, a local radio personality out of Hartford whom we listened to every morning of our lives to get the weather and news before going to school, was there. And so was Bob Whalen, the scout who signed me.

Kirby, who sat up on stage with my grandmother and the rest of the family, was the master of ceremonies. He presented me with the only pair of athletic socks that I wore throughout all four years of high school. Every once in a while I had washed them but only when it was absolutely necessary. It was a superstition of mine to keep wearing those same socks as long as I continued to excel. I had put them in a mason jar and buried them underneath the goal post at the football field following graduation. I don't know why I did that. It was crazy, but I did it. And damned if they didn't dig them up after all those years. Of course, we didn't dare open up the mason jar. It might have been toxic.

Everybody and everything was just so wonderful. It was a spectacular, very real celebration with those people. There were none of the bells and whistles that have a tendency to diminish that kind of day. But if I could go back in time, one of the things I would correct would be the length of my speech during the ceremony. I spoke for only about a minute to a minute and a half. I wish I had talked for an hour. I would certainly have no problem doing that today. My speech was short and sweet with the theme showing my love and appreciation for all the support I had received in that area since I was eight years old.

"The celebration in Pittsburgh was wonderful," I said. "But nothing can match the celebration of your hometown because I know all of you. Put me in the grave right now and I would be happy."

It was heartfelt, but I wish I could have talked more. Still, 40 years later, it remains a moment frozen in time.

Above: Father and Son Day at Three Rivers Stadium. Is there anything better than having your two boys on a major league field with you?

Right: Taken at spring training in 1972, this is my favorite family photo.

Above: When you win the World Series, you get to go on a TV show like Sports Challenge, hosted by Dick Enberg. We did just okay.

Below: At Willie Stargell's Sickle Cell Bowling Tournament with Steve Carlton and Gaylord Perry. Two of the three are Hall of Famers. Guess which one isn't.

Above: I am very proud of my charity work over the years. This photo was taken in 1973 with the poster girl for the Muscular Dystrophy Association coin board campaign. We raised $80,000.

Below: I shared my pitching grips with boys at a sports banquet in my hometown of Canaan, Connecticut, after the '71 World Series. This is one of my favorite photos.

Above: At McKechnie Field, I threw my first pitch after working with sports psychologist Richard Crowley. It felt great. Every disease has a cure.

Below: Fantasy Camp at Pirates City. I love running the Kangaroo Court every morning.

Left: Taking an October walk with my dad in Connecticut. We had a couple of beers after. It was a perfect day.

Below: On September 10, 2009, I shot two holes-in-one in the same round. The odds of doing that are 67 million to one. I should have won two cars, but I didn't. I drove home with a $500 bar tab, instead. Everybody wanted doubles.

Above: Posing with Pirates voices (from left) Bob Walk, Greg Brown, Lanny Frattare, and John Wehner. There is nothing better than working with friends. I sincerely believe this crew gave a great mix of professionalism, expertise, and entertainment.

Below: They broke the mold with The Gunner, Bob Prince—an enormous presence for both the Bucs and the city of Pittsburgh. (AP Images)

Above: I interviewed former Pirate John Cangelosi in 1997. I always loved being interviewed. Still do. But I struggled early as interviewer. In fact, I still do.

Below: One of many hugs I've shared with batterymate and good friend Manny Sanguillen.

Above: Opening Day 2009 at PNC Park was Steve Blass Day, celebrating my 50 years with the Bucs. Before the game, I was joined on the field by (from left) Lisa and Chris Blass, Ed and Mary Kirby, Dave Giusti, Karen Blass, Pirates president Frank Coonelly, and Pirates chairman of the board Bob Nutting.

Left: With Karen Louise. After dating for three years in high school and 48 years of marriage, it still feels great to have her hand in mine.

CHAPTER 11

Out of Baseball and Still in the Fast Lane

I was completely out of control.

I will not even attempt to sugarcoat my immediate post-baseball years. I wasn't a saint. There was too much drinking and gambling in the immediate years following my baseball career. I was running so fast, trying to regain that feeling of importance I had when I was living the major league life. Where were the accolades? The attention? The notoriety? The cheering, quite simply, had stopped. I wasn't going to be living that major league life any longer. The life of playing in different cities, having a traveling secretary look after you, and being catered to as a big leaguer was gone. Bang! Eliminated!

It was kind of a double-edged sword being back with Karen and the kids. I loved the idea I was going to be around them, coaching Little League, and spending more time with them. It would have been perfect, except that I missed the clubhouse atmosphere, being around the guys and having fun. There have been times, both light and sometimes serious, when Karen has said of our relationship, "I think I'd rather be your friend than your wife." That remains one of her all-time best quotes.

I think Karen had this perception that after I stopped playing, we would have a chance at a somewhat normal existence. No more road trips or performance stress; we would have most of our summer and evenings together as a family. And these parts were good.

We did some traveling, including a three-week trip out west to see the national parks. We also did some traveling as a couple with some of our friends. What didn't change much from my playing days was that I was still running fast and thinking of myself and skimming with Karen and the boys. I don't know, maybe a midlife crisis, maybe just a lifestyle I couldn't stop and perhaps still can't.

I wasn't seeing signs along the way that I should have been paying attention to. Wouldn't it be nice if looking back after all these years could change things? But unfortunately it can't.

From a pitching standpoint, the end of my career was very much a relief. I didn't have to suffer anymore. That was the good news. But the loss of everything else that went along with it left a major void in my life. I'd had my personal confidence eroded. I was going to have to start my life over again. And that involved having two adolescent sons, a wife, a home, responsibilities, and the disappointment of not being up on that pedestal that you are on as a professional athlete.

There were many nights when, without even thinking about it, I'd stay out and drink rather than come home. It was the elimination of reality by means of the miracle of alcohol, a cruel thing indeed.

All the while, there was a family going on that I wasn't involved with as much as I should have been. It was very difficult on Karen, on us, and on the boys. Christopher internalized a lot of things more than David, who acted out his feelings to the point where we had to change his environment by sending him back to Connecticut with my Uncle Bill and then on to a boarding school in West Virginia.

The way I was internalizing and dealing with the pain stemming from the abrupt end of my baseball career was costing me time with them. On those occasions when I was out drinking until 4:00 AM, I was basically giving up the next day, too, recovering from the inevitable hangover. There was also the new economic reality of no longer getting paid big-league money. In a sense, I had prepared for this by deferring some of my last year's salary with the Pirates. After the dreadful 1973 season, I was thinking, *Okay, if it doesn't work and I'm still wild next season, what am I going to do?*

But preparing for a possible release from the club was only a concept, so when I finally did retire in 1975, all of a sudden, I was like, *Oh my God, this is it! It's here! What am I going to do now?* Maybe it wasn't like graduating from high school again, but a little bit of the concept was the same. *What am I going to do with my life?* I thought over and over again.

We had some money, but I felt a real urgency to go out and get a job. Luckily, within days after leaving Bradenton, a Pirates vice president, Joe O'Toole, contacted me and said he had a friend, George Mitchell, who worked as a national recruiter for Jostens, a company that specialized in making high school class rings. Because of my impulsive nature, I contacted his friend immediately.

Jostens liked to hire ex-athletes because they weren't destroyed by losing a game. Jostens liked the fact that a loss wasn't terminal and you would get back up and go to work again. That's critical in sales. The company had already hired several NFL guys and some baseball players, so this was a viable post-career option for me at the time. I didn't have any other plans, so I went on the interview.

The more I talked, the more I thought, *You know, I don't have many cards to play right now.* So I accepted a job at Jostens, beginning an eight-year period of pitching class rings to committees of high school seniors at 55 high schools located north, east, and west of Pittsburgh. It was actually a big business back then and still is to a certain extent today.

I got to work out of my house, often using the floor in my office to organize my files. Dave Giusti's wife, Ginny, came over to the house a few hours a week to assist me. One of the pluses about my sales job at Jostens was the fact that following my presentations, I was notified within just a couple of days on whether I got the sale or not. From a competitive standpoint I liked that and compared it to the immediacy of baseball. For example, I used to submit my pitch to Henry Aaron and got feedback right away. If I didn't get the sale on a pitch, that was one he hit over the fence. But if he did accept my presentation, it meant I struck him out. I guess with me, everything comes back to baseball.

Balfour was Jostens' biggest competitor and, although I was a sports celebrity in my thirties, my biggest challenge was competing against mostly 25-year-old, good-looking, well-dressed guys with more hair than I had. My celebrity would, at times, actually work against me, as some of the kids wondered how committed I was to what I was selling. Some of them were like, "Is this baseball player serious about selling class rings? Does he care about us?"

So there were challenges to overcome, but I succeeded. I had a good career with Jostens, and the job presented the opportunity to get out and say hello to people who cared about the Pirates, which wound up being a plus experience. I even sold a high school class ring to future Buffalo Bills great Jim Kelly up in East Brady, Pennsylvania.

I still had a little bit of a fantasy that if I left the game for a while that my pitching would snap back into place. A couple of times in an effort to see if I had regained my pitching form, a high school baseball coach I had met out in Monroeville allowed me to borrow one of his players to catch for me and a hitter to stand in the box to face me. But there was no improvement. I pitched perfectly well until the hitter stepped into the batter's box. Then the wildness resurfaced. A comeback was not in the cards.

Because the Jostens job was as a school-related sales position, I was going to have my summers off to pursue other interests. One of those was starting the Steve Blass Baseball Camp in 1976. I wanted to do a baseball camp for two reasons. The first was for the money, because we needed it at that time. But I also wanted to run a camp for the simple reason that I thought I could do it right. I had always been aware of these huge camps. College coaches have them. Current or former athletes have them. But time and again, I noticed that the coach or athlete comes in on the first day, welcomes the kids, and then turns the camp over to a staff that handles the whole thing.

I wanted to have a small camp where I could be there day and night, so if a kid woke up and was homesick, we could give his mother a call while sitting on the steps of the dorm at 2:00 in the morning. I would want to be sitting right there next to him, so if his Mom or Dad needed to talk to me, I would be available. I wanted to really personalize the camp. So I welcomed the kids, lived with them in the dorm, ate meals with them, clowned around with them, and of course, played baseball with them. Another plus for me was having David and Chris with me at many of those camps.

I took in around 60 kids, assembled a staff, and was there from the time they signed in on a Sunday until their folks picked them up the following Saturday. It was a good camp. We had films and fun games, worked on fundamental drills and, on the last day of camp, got on a bus and went to Three Rivers Stadium for a day of fun. The Pirates and the grounds crew allowed me to run fielding and hitting drills with the campers. It was a tremendous thrill for them, because they were on a major league baseball field. The Bucs also gave me promotional items for the kids, put their names up on the message board, and had some of their players come by and talk to them.

It was a hoot having those kids down there at Three Rivers Stadium, so I didn't jump in a hole and feel depressed to be back at the ballpark. When all the dust eventually cleared from my pitching problems, that's one of the things I am most thankful for—it didn't destroy my love for the game. And starting a baseball camp was a significant test, because now I'm 70 years old and still love the game to pieces.

I ran the Steve Blass Baseball Camp for 11 years at the Kiski School in Pittsburgh, whose headmaster at the time, Jack Pidgeon, was one of the most impressive men I have ever met. The camp was later extended down to the Linsly School in Wheeling, West Virginia, when one of Jack's Kiski assistants, Reno DiOrio, became headmaster at that school. Reno has not only become one of my good friends, but he's a man who represents as much character as you're ever going to find. I was very proud of that camp. Much of the camp's success can be credited to the core staff that I had—Duke Strayer, former Washington Senators' pitcher Ed Hobaugh, John Gasper, and Larry Lebowitz. It was a wonderful feeling talking with children just starting to play the game. I emphasized the very basic fundamentals of baseball without cluttering their minds with too much information. That way, they had a better chance of enjoying the game.

Coaching kids was very different from coaching professionals. Although I may have had a strong enough résumé to have gone on to become a pitching coach at some level, it was something that I never pursued. The main reason was because I was so relieved to step away from the pitching part of baseball. The other reason had to do with how I always pitched on gut instinct and not a basic set of mechanics that I could pass on. It was all feel for me; that's hard to transfer to another pitcher.

The baseball camp filled only three weeks of my summer vacation from Jostens. So that allowed me time to help coach my boys' teams as well as play golf. And that free time also came in handy when I felt a need to assist, in a special way, one of my very best friends, Dave Giusti.

I was playing golf on a Friday afternoon in the summer of 1977. It was near the end of Dave's career, and I saw him struggle while pitching for the Cubs on television. I called Karen from the golf course and said, "Dave was there for me every day and every night when I was going through all my stuff. Now he's the one that's having a rough time. I want to go to Chicago, spend a little time with him, and return that gesture to him so he will know that I'm there supporting him."

Karen said, "Absolutely. Go."

So I went home, packed a bag, and flew to Chicago.

That night, in an effort to help Dave blow off some steam, we got together with another one of our friends, Bob Wilkins, and got unbelievably smoked. We got crushed to the point where Wilkins drove home at around 4:00 AM—not a good decision—and instead of winding up in his suburban Chicago home, he found himself in Indiana.

Dave and I went back to his hotel, and I slept on the couch. When I woke up, I didn't have a clue where I was. Dave had already gone to Wrigley Field because the teams played only day games there back then. I thought, *Oh my God, he had to go to the ballpark in that condition. I am so glad I didn't have to.*

After getting myself together, I went to Wrigley to pick up a ticket that was left for me. As I sat in the right-field stands, sweating profusely, and watching the game progress, I kept thinking, *Don't bring Dave into this game.* Naturally, at some point a phone call was made to the bullpen and

Dave started warming up. I felt terrible for him. Not surprisingly, when he was called into the game to pitch he didn't exactly have his best stuff. It was definitely not one of his better outings.

So I went out to Chicago with all good intentions to really help and support him, but my hangover told me it obviously didn't quite work out that way.

While I worked at Jostens, other job offers would come and go. But one of the more interesting ones was from Pittsburgh businessman and financier Frank Fuhrer, who approached me with the idea of becoming the general manager for the Pittsburgh Triangles, a professional tennis team that he held a controlling interest in. I said, "Frank, I'm very flattered, but I don't think I'm qualified."

I may have turned him down then, but Frank was a great contact to have in case something ever happened to my job at Jostens. Sure enough, a few years later in 1983, when Frank got into the beer business, a good friend and golf pro named Sam Depe said to me, "You know, you would be perfect working for Frank Fuhrer. With your name in the Pittsburgh area, you could do PR work for him."

Growing a little weary of trying to make a living by the decisions of 17-year-old kids, I decided to approach Frank. So I wrote a letter to him saying I thought I could be a positive part of his Anheuser-Busch operation. He hired me a few days later. One of the most rewarding parts of my job and relationship with Frank was to help him when he had the concept of Family House, which is like a Ronald McDonald House for families of transplant recipients to stay at while their relative is undergoing the procedure. Frank took an old brownstone in the Oakland section of Pittsburgh, had it gutted, and renovated it into Family House. There were several bedrooms, a common room, and kitchen for the families to share.

Aside from the usual donations that came in, Fuhrer came up with the idea of a charity golf tournament to support the Family House. I told him, "Frank, there are six charity golf tournaments every Monday in Pittsburgh. I don't think it will work." He said, "It'll work if it's the biggest and the best." It was vintage Frank Fuhrer. And, of course, he was absolutely right.

The Family House Charity Golf Tournament became one of the biggest in the country, with professionals coming in from all over the world to play in it. I helped him quite a bit with this venture, as it was a perfect opportunity to use my humor, communication skills, and love of golf for a very good cause. I would go out and try to recruit people to play in it and then would emcee the dinner afterward.

My primary role in increasing beer sales was traveling around with salesmen. Fuhrer liked to say that most of his buyers were "jock sniffers," so my coming along on sales calls was good for business. I was also in charge of Bud Nights at various bars, showing Pirates and Steelers films, giving away hats and T-shirts, and running sports trivia contests. I was in bars practically every night doing promotional work. I was still running hard and doing a lot of drinking with the sales guys, but I was very proud of the work I did for Frank.

I did around 400 Bud Nights while working both full- and part-time for the Frank Fuhrer Wholesale Company over several years, often lugging an old reel-to-reel movie projector and a screen through snowy conditions from one bar to the next. I loved working for Frank. We had a great relationship, and I felt a strong loyalty toward him. That's what made it particularly difficult for me to walk into his office one day with a dilemma.

"Frank, the Pirates approached me to do some cable games for them," I said. "The money would be less than what I make here, so I don't know what to tell them." Fuhrer never hesitated, telling me, "Go for it. I know you can do it. With your personality and knowledge of the game, you'll be great at it. You're a baseball man, not a beer salesman. This could be your calling." I will never forget that.

His response made me feel like a million bucks, because I wanted to give broadcasting a try. But I had this loyalty to him because he offered me a job when I needed one and paid me decent money. When he gave me the validation that being a color analyst for the Pirates was what I should be doing, his blessing meant everything to me. As I left Frank's office, little did I realize the impact that his words of encouragement would have in changing my life forever.

CHAPTER 12

A Second Act in Baseball

"You now can say you've had the best two jobs in the universe," former Pirates manager Jim Leyland once told me. "You went from being a starting pitcher in the majors working once a week to becoming a professional bullshitter. And you get to watch ballgames for free and they pay you to do it."

Leyland was right on the money. Long before I began broadcasting eight years after my baseball career officially ended, I always had a sense it was something I could be pretty good at.

A precursor to what I am doing now as the Pirates' color commentator occurred when I was just a 22-year-old rookie. Somehow, KDKA television, which was one of the three major television stations in Pittsburgh back in the early 1960s, had a morning program called the *John Reed King Show*. I wound up sitting in on the show several times that season, talking about the Pirates and telling baseball stories. I guess I owe John Reed King, who's no longer with us, a good deal of gratitude for giving me that opportunity.

My broadcasting career actually could have begun four years before it did. In 1979, the championship year for the Pirates, KDKA asked me to audition for a color analyst position. The audition consisted of me going to KDKA's studio, sitting in a room with a monitor, and having me broadcast the action on the screen. All they were showing me was raw video footage set from behind the pitcher, a very difficult view. It was a disaster, and I was very discouraged. Surprisingly, KDKA still offered me the position, but I turned it down because the money wasn't good enough to entice me. Nellie Briles wound up getting that job.

My time came in 1983 when I began my broadcasting career with the Home Sports Entertainment network. The cable sports industry was in its infancy during that time, and with fewer restrictions on what you could say and do on the air, it was more fun in some respects than it is today.

At HSE, I worked alongside legendary broadcaster Bob Prince, Willie Stargell, and Dave Giusti. Dave lasted only a few games, never becoming comfortable enough in the booth to make it a career. And Willie, because he had bigger things on his plate, stopped broadcasting during that season as well. So it was primarily just The Gunner and me for the better part of the season. Prince had a tremendous impact on my broadcasting career that first year. He couldn't have been nicer and was always willing to help me learn and improve my craft. And nobody enjoyed doing what he did more than Bob.

The very first game I did with Prince was a momentous one for me. You have to understand that alcohol has always generally been forbidden in the broadcast booth. That is the letter of the law. Of course, most baseball fans know about guys like Prince and Harry Caray, who bent that rule a bit, so it has become blurred at times. In the seventh inning, Prince got on the phone, called down to the press room and said, "Send up two screwdrivers."

Being naïve, I thought something was loose in the booth and he was going to tighten it. Instead, here come the screwdrivers looking like specimens. When I realized they were drinks, I thought maybe there was an orange juice shortage, because there was clearly a lot more vodka in those glasses than anything else. Prince told me that his personal physician told him that he had to switch to screwdrivers or another cocktail of choice because his usual drink, Canadian Club and Coke, was not good for his health. "The damn Coca-Cola's gonna kill you," the doctor would tell Prince. "You've got to get away from that stuff." So that's how he wound up being a great fan of screwdrivers.

I was always amazed with how well Prince did his job. He did anything that was ever asked of him in a broadcast booth flawlessly. There was an instance when a producer said to him, "Say, Bob, we're out of tape. Do you have something you could talk about to fill some air time for us?" Prince replied, "Hell, I can give you seven minutes standing on my head." He was never at a loss. He just had this remarkable gift of filling time or doing whatever they needed him to do.

Another time, because a charity golf tournament we had attended ran late, we didn't get into the broadcast booth until 7:27, three minutes before airtime. The red light went on, and Prince, without missing a beat, began the telecast. "This is the old Gunner here, at Three Rivers Stadium. I was standing around the batting cage talking with Chuck Tanner, and ..." Prince went on for the next several minutes like he had been doing pregame preparation for an hour. I looked at him and wondered, *My God, where does that come from?*

I had been around baseball for a long time by then, but I was not familiar with that part of the business. It was just fascinating watching him. Prince was larger than life. Nobody will ever promote Pittsburgh Pirates baseball the way he did. Gunner's ability to fill time rubbed off on me. These were the early days of cable, and there was not yet a studio to send the telecast back to in the event of a rain delay. So I got kind of a baptism by fire on how to do spontaneous interviewing.

One of my safety nets during those circumstances was almost always being able to interview the Bucs' pitching coach, Harvey Haddix, who had a wonderful baseball career that included perhaps the greatest game ever pitched—12 perfect innings for Pittsburgh in a 1959 contest that he would end up losing in the 13th inning to the Braves 1–0. As a result, I think I know every detail of both Harvey's life and every pitch of his near-perfect game.

Aside from broadcasting, Prince was also a major figure in the Pittsburgh community. Bob was that rare individual who could walk into the boardroom of U.S. Steel and command the room. But he could also do the same thing at a more working-class place like the West Mifflin Fire Department. No matter the setting, he had total recall of names. And he could skewer politicians and get away with it. He was both well-liked and admired.

When I moved into Upper St. Clair in 1972, Prince was firmly embedded in that community. I always remember him giving me a valuable piece of advice. Bob said, "If you're going to live in a community, be a part of it. Show up for the events that are going on in your town." Those were words of wisdom that I still adhere to today.

Prince also carried a great deal of clout. After we called just one game the next season, before HSE pulled the plug on us when their contract with the Pirates expired, Prince made sure we got paid for the entire season. It wasn't a great deal of money or a huge number of games, but the principle of the matter exemplified how powerful he was.

The Pirates didn't have a cable home the following year because the delayed sale of the team foiled any possible deals. So I continued to work part-time for Frank Fuhrer's beer distributorship to pay the bills. But we were back in business the following year and, on April 24, 1986, KBL (clever call letters for a cable network) aired its first game from Three Rivers Stadium. KBL was a strong network with a reach into six states. Those were still the days when most games were on "free" TV, so we carried only around 20 games that season. Again, it was still the advent of cable television.

The founder of KBL and a pioneer of Pittsburgh sports cable production, Gil Lucas, had a gift of putting broadcast programming together and then leaving the talent alone to prosper. Gil had a unique concept in putting together our own broadcasting crew. Lucas came up with the idea of having Mike Lange, the Pittsburgh Penguins Hall of Fame play-by-play announcer, and I do the games together.

Mike was in Boston working a Penguins game the night before our audition and didn't get back to Pittsburgh until around 5:00 the next morning. The three of us met outside Three Rivers Stadium a few hours later. Lucas, forever informal, said to the two of us, "There's a booth up there, No. 43. There's a camera up there, too. Just go up there and see if you think you can work together. See if it works."

Mike and I were beer-drinking buddies, so we already felt pretty comfortable with one another. We sat up in the booth for a couple of innings doing a mock broadcast, and it was wonderful. It was a perfect marriage. So we came back down and told Gil that we thought it could work. And that was the whole audition. We were hired.

Working with Mike, a true mentor for me and later to Greg Brown when he did pregame and postgame work on cable, was tremendous fun because we had a good rhythm doing the broadcasts together. I learned a great deal from him, especially the mechanics of doing a broadcast.

Case in point, when a Pirate hit a dramatic home run and I was getting ready to jump in and scream and holler, he reached over, put his hand on my arm, looked over at me, and said, off-air, "Let the moment be. Let the audience hear the crowd instead of talking over this wonderful moment." Subtle things like that really helped me a lot.

We didn't just give the viewer the game but also entertained them. Every once in a while, I'd get a piece of paper and rip it in half right in front of my microphone. Mike would say, "Is that something off the ticker, Steve?" We'd have these little news items that I would get from *The Star* or the *National Enquirer* or even ones that I would make up. And I'd say something like, "Listen to this, Mike—'Childless Blind Couple Adopts Midget.'" We did that routine quite often and had a lot of fun with it.

The best bit we ever did was a takeoff on the Bartles & Jaymes commercials. We were out in San Diego, and I played the role of the bespectacled guy that did all the talking. Mike played the quiet guy in the background. We went to a Goodwill store and got our outfits—straw hats, suspenders, everything. We wrote our script on storyboards. During the segment, I kept turning back to Mike and would ask, "Right, Ed?" after everything I said.

Of course, his character wouldn't say anything, just like in the real commercial. He just kept tossing a ball into the air. We had to do five takes because it was so hilarious. The crew kept losing it. The spoof wound up getting national media attention around the country, including *This Week in Baseball*. We're lucky we didn't get sued.

Another fun thing broadcasting brought into my life was a ritual that began when my dad visited Pittsburgh. On my drive to Three Rivers Stadium to broadcast a game, I would drop him off at the strip club at The Edison Hotel. He would watch the broads get naked and then, after his fifth beer, when he knew it was getting close to game time, he would walk across the bridge, watch the game, and meet me afterward. We would then go and grab a couple of beers someplace on the way home. It was a beautiful thing—just a father and son having a good time in and around baseball.

In the course of a lifetime, you run across some people that not only wind up being great friends but turn out to be people whom you learn from. Mike Lange is in that category for both Greg Brown and me. I felt like I was beginning to come into my own at that time as a color analyst who not only could describe what I saw on the field, but one who could also entertain. I can appeal to different kinds of people because I'm a storyteller. To this day, I don't know all the rules of baseball. And I don't know all the strategies. But I know enough of those things to get by.

I've also always enjoyed making people feel comfortable, smile, and enjoy themselves. So my broadcasting job is a natural extension of that and conveys my love and enjoyment of the game. My visual image is to avoid having somebody sitting in front of the television or radio with their fists clenched. I want to have people just lean back and listen to us shooting the breeze about the ballgame. In doing so, I will miss some people. My thinking is there are maybe 15 percent of fans who are hard-core and really know the game, probably just as much or better than I do. That's not my audience. My listeners are the remaining 85 percent or so who want to enjoy the game and be entertained at the same time.

The next year, 1987, the Pirates' flagship station, KDKA, was having on-air auditions for a full-time color commentator position. Jim Rooker, one of its broadcasters at that time, thought I would be ideal for the gig and encouraged me to give it a shot. KDKA was looking for a fourth guy because it had Lanny Frattare, John Sanders, and Rooker but needed a fourth guy so they could have two on television and two on radio. With just three announcers, they were flip-flopping and moving around too much.

I went down to Houston and sat in on one of the broadcasts. Because of my experience with HSE, I was very comfortable with the whole setup. I was throwing some of my best material out there. I remember saying after someone made a catch in right field, "My goodness, look at the size of that glove. Two cows died for that thing." They liked my comedic commentary. After the game, they asked me if I could come back and do another game. Of course I said yes, and it evolved into them asking if I could do 10 more games. That's how it started taking off with KDKA, and soon thereafter they offered me a contract. I have been a fixture on the Pirates' broadcasts, splitting time between television and radio, ever since.

I was now one of the busiest people in Pittsburgh. At one time, I had a contract with KDKA for radio and TV and one with KBL, and I was still working part time doing promotional work for Fuhrer. Plus, in the summer, I was running my baseball camp for three weeks. So I wasn't just running fast with the drinking, gambling, and all that stuff. I was working like a dog career-wise as well. And it was probably at the expense of things at home. I was self-absorbed like I was when I was pitching but now in a different way.

By this time, Karen couldn't take it anymore and moved out one day in June. I came home from a road trip, and she was gone. It was like getting hit by a truck. I said to myself, *Where is everybody? What's going on here?* It was a dose of reality that knocked me off my feet. But there was still this overriding thing that I needed to keep pace with what I was like when I was playing. After 12 years, when she thought I would have spent more time with her and the boys, she had finally had enough.

I wish I could say I immediately sat down after Karen left me and thought about all those years when she was dealing with not only my over-the-top pace but also raising the boys, running the house, and wondering how and where her life was headed. But I didn't sit down with that reality check. I was by myself, so I just ran faster for a little while. It would take a long time for me to realize that running fast does not always get you where you want to go.

That point would be driven home on a fateful night that August. There was an off-day before a series opened with the Astros in Pittsburgh. Larry Dierker, a broadcaster with Houston at the time, Dave Giusti, Jim Rooker, and I had played golf earlier in the day. Afterward, we were drinking pretty heavily. After they closed whatever place we were in, I dropped Dierker off at his hotel.

Driving home at 3:00 AM, I crashed into a tree and totaled one of Fuhrer's company cars I was driving. The police came, took me to the hospital, and administered blood and alcohol-level tests. Ultimately, they gave me a DUI. I called Frank and said, "I totaled the car, but I'm okay. I'm home now. I'm sure you are going to hear about it on the news tomorrow, and I just wanted to let you know."

Sure enough, it was on the news the next day and on the front page of the *Post-Gazette*. I honestly don't know if the accident slowed me down any, but it sure got my attention that perhaps I needed to take another look at my life. One thing was certain: I needed to regain Karen's trust to get her back.

I finally convinced myself that "me and her" was more important than "me and the fast track." She was tough to convince, but sparing the details, after 10 months of her being away, we got back together, and it's been better ever since. Not perfect, but better.

Somebody once said that you can't look back and fix all the hurt and damage from a lot of years ago. But it's never too late, if you've got the time, to try. And that's what I continue to do.

Because I wasn't injured in the accident, I went right on with all of my commitments. In a way, my full-time color commentator position at KDKA was good therapy for me. I got myself down to just one job, and it included working with three true professionals.

With Lanny Frattare, it was the beginning of a 23-year stint together. I first met Lanny in Charleston in 1974 while I was trying to work through my control problems and get back up to the majors. It was kind of an interesting atmosphere in which to meet anybody because I didn't want to be there. It was not my favorite place, and I was going through my own particular hell at the time.

I was impressed with his abilities, preparation, and commitment to his job. Knowing that I had this fantasy of becoming a broadcaster myself one day, I paid attention to him. I was impressed by what he did, so I made an effort to get to know him a little bit. Between starts, I used to sit up in the booth with him for a few innings and do a little color. With my best deprecating humor, on the days I started, I told him I would come up and see him around the third inning. That was kind of a lighthearted comment I would make, one of the few I made throughout that depressing year.

After the season was over, Frattare had to drive through Pittsburgh on his way from Charleston to Rochester, where he lived. I invited him to stay at our house for a couple of nights, and he took me up on my offer. The stay ended up being a nice thing for him. The first day he visited Three Rivers, and Bob Prince asked him to come up and do an inning of Pirates baseball. Afterward, he called his parents and told them he had reached his goal, since age 12, of broadcasting in the major leagues. And the rest is history. He replaced Prince two years later and became the Pirates' play-by-play announcer for the next 33 years.

The day after his debut, Frattare had it in his mind to go back out to the ballpark again. But I had something else in mind for him. He woke up and I told him, "Get your shoes on. We're going to seal the driveway today." So his room was free at my house, but it was labor-intensive.

I have the ultimate amount of respect for guys like the Lanny Frattares, the John Sanderses, the Mike Langes, the Tim Neveretts, the Bob Princes, and the Greg Browns of the broadcasting world. They weren't handed their jobs like a lot of us former major leaguers. When they were working their way to the major leagues, they had to lug electronic equipment around and do a lot of games all by themselves. In those smaller markets, there were no studios to throw the broadcast back to during rain delays. They had to come up with a lot of their own thoughts and information to keep their listeners tuned in.

Neverett is a great example of that journey to the major leagues, having worked in several markets for two decades before ultimately landing a full-time play-by-play position with the Pirates in 2009. Considering the difficulty he must have encountered in coming to a new town, learning the names of the areas in and around Pittsburgh, and indoctrinating himself as much as he could about the history of the Pirates, his ability to step right in on the broadcast is very impressive. (Note: Hey Tim, thanks for hooking me up with coauthor Erik Sherman.)

My relationship with Lanny over the years we worked together was an interesting one. When I first started, I didn't really know too much about what I was doing, but Lanny was always there to help me. He gave me opportunities to get my thoughts in on the air, and I've always appreciated that.

But it wasn't always easy because, at times, Lanny was his own worst enemy. He had standards that were so high that they could not be met all the time. He may have hit them a lot because he was very good—always very prepared, speaking with great inflection, and providing a sense of drama in calling a game—but I think he was hurt by the demands he placed on himself. I think that frustrated him a great deal, and there were occasions when that spilled over to the people he worked with, including me.

There was one Friday night not long after I started broadcasting when Lanny was so down amid some media criticism, that he considered quitting. I felt the need to step in and try to help him, so I called him the next morning and asked, "Do you mind if I stop at your house for a minute?"

He was kind of weary, but said, "I guess that would be alright."

I went over and said to him, "Damn, you're good. You've got to stop being so tough on yourself. Give yourself a break here. We're not trying to change the world. I don't know if anybody can be absolutely perfect in any aspect of their life. You're great. Lighten up."

I don't know how well I said it or if it was convincing or not, but I felt like maybe I could help him appreciate himself a little more by building him up. I want to be clear. Frattare was very good most of the time, but there were periods when I would come to the ballpark and ask myself, "Which Lanny will I be working with tonight?"

Those were the times when he was very much into himself because something was bothering him. I don't know if there were issues away from the ballpark or if they were baseball-related. His personal life, of course, was none of my business. But what I will say is that when the national anthem was finished playing and the red light came on for Lanny to begin announcing a game, there was nobody more professional.

In fact, I believe Frattare has a chance of ending up in the Broadcasters wing of the Baseball Hall of Fame. Thirty-three years of broadcasting with one team the way he did gives him that chance.

He also had one of the great calls in Pirate history on July 12, 1997, when Francisco Cordova and Ricardo Rincon pitched a no-hitter and Mark Smith hit a walk-off home run in the bottom of the 10th before a packed house at Three Rivers Stadium. The way he ended it, without missing a beat, was perfect: "Here's the pitch to Mark Smith. Long drive to left, it's outta here! No-hitter! Home run! You got it all!"

It was Frattare at his best.

Lanny and I didn't give each other feedback because we had different personalities. We didn't socialize a lot, nor did we ignore each other away from the ballpark. There were functions and birthday parties we saw each other at here and there, but we had different directions away from the team, which was fine. That's the way life works. But perhaps most important, we had a sense of loyalty toward one another. For example, I went to his charity golf tournament for years, even helping him with live auctions. I know he appreciated that, and I was always happy to do it.

One of the reasons we worked so well together on broadcasts was because Lanny enjoyed my sense of humor while he did his usual great broadcast of a ballgame. His style was straight and professional, so when I could interject, it made us a good team.

One instance when Lanny indulged my humor was during a rather dull game in Philadelphia in the early 1990s. He asked me if I had ever been on a horse. So that was my entrée into telling him about a charity harness horse race I was in the week before down at the Meadows, a local track. Jim Leyland, ElRoy Face, Maz, and I, among others, were riders.

Describing the race, I told Lanny they gave me this horse called Whistling Billy. The trainer and owner of this horse told me he would get out front early, but then he had a tendency to get a little bit lazy. They advised me to whistle at him, hence the name Whistling Billy, to get him going again.

I continued with the story of how Whistling Billy and I sprinted out of the gates like we were shot out of a cannon. We were about five or six lengths out in front of everybody, and I thought winning the race was going to be cake. But then all of a sudden the other horses started creeping up on us. Whistling Billy started backing up a little bit, so I started whistling.

"Whew, whew, whew, whew!"

But the other horses were still gaining on us. Now I was whistling my ass off. I could hardly breathe. I'm whistling like I've never whistled before. Louder and louder! "Whew, whew, whew, whew!"

But we finished dead last.

By this point in my story, Lanny is on the floor laughing, trying to gather himself. In the meantime, the Pirates' Mike LaValliere had just hit a very critical home run. Lanny scrambled to get out of laughing mode and back up into his chair, face the microphone, and describe the home run. But damned if we didn't completely miss the moment because of Whistling Billy. When we finally did collect ourselves, it was too late to give justice to the call of LaValliere's home run.

Another time, Lanny and I were broadcasting a game at Shea Stadium during a rain delay, filling time. There was a camera in the booth, so we were standing with our backs to the field. Out of nowhere, there was a loud crack of thunder and lightning while we were on live, and I practically jumped out of my skin. Lanny started howling, then turned to me and said, "That really bothered you, Steve." And I said, "Only me and the laundry man understand how much." That was another one that buckled his knees a little bit. So aside from the differences in personality, we were together for 23 years and established a pretty good rhythm.

I am blessed to have so many friends and am particularly lucky to have had one of my best ones—Greg Brown—by my side in the broadcast booth for the past 18 years. What a treat it is to work with a best friend, because it opens up the lines of communication so well. I can say anything to Greg, and he can say anything to me right back. Someone might think he's walking on thin ice when he challenges me, a former ballplayer. But that has never been the case. And that's not just on the broadcasts. We'll talk to one another about everything—our lives, dreams, fantasies, memories, and so much more. It's truly wonderful. Greg also indulges me. I'll step on his lines, come in at the wrong time, or won't be carefully listening and go off on a tangent that doesn't relate to what he said. But instead of becoming frustrated, he'll just give me a little nudge, and that's appreciated.

Greg runs the show as the play-by-play guy. His preparation is so good that I may say that I'm not crazy about a player in a certain scenario, and he'll turn to me and say, "Wait a minute! Look at this. You might be wrong here." So, basically, after all these years, I am still learning things from Greg.

Like with Lanny, Greg and I also have a good rhythm together on the air. When I sit next to Greg in the booth, he has a sense of when I want to get in and will let me do so. We almost don't even have to look at each other. Greg also has an appreciation for the fact that I love words. A philosophy of mine is that the better vocabulary you have, the more efficient with words you become. As a color man, you want to get in and out; you don't want to talk all around something. The better you are with words, the better and quicker you'll get to the heart of your subject.

Another important thing Brownie taught me is that if I lose the moment, I shouldn't try to get it back. In other words, if there's something I want to get in on a particular play but something else happens in the interim, I shouldn't try to come back to it two innings later because, by then, the moment is lost.

My favorite moment up in the booth with Greg occurred on a very hot Sunday afternoon in St. Louis' Busch Stadium that, in the summertime, can get as steamy as any ballpark in America. Tommy Sandt was our first-base coach and was standing near Mark McGwire of the Cardinals. I started the game wearing a shirt and tie but eventually started to make myself more comfortable. I started by taking off the T-shirt under my white dress shirt. Then I took off the shirt itself but left the tie around my neck. So there I sat, like a big, fat, slick seal with a necktie on. Sandt caught a glimpse of this spectacle and then got McGwire's attention, pointing up to me while they both laughed like crazy. As the television cameras took a shot of me like this, Brownie said, "Whatever happened to dignity? Whatever happened to professionalism?"

Off the field, one of the things Greg and I have fooled around with is the Abbott and Costello "Who's on First" routine. We've read it from a script at banquets and in front of other gatherings of fans. A couple of times, it has gone over extremely well. Greg constantly begs me to have us go up to my cabin, lock ourselves up for two or three days, and learn it by heart. He says, "We can make a killing on the baseball banquet circuit. We can make a fortune!"

And he's right, but I can't get myself to sit down with him and memorize it. I don't know if he could, either. But if we did, it would be hilarious, because when we've done it from the script, it's fun acting it out. I love the way we do it.

Greg and I have done nearly 2,500 regular season games together. But there was one game, or better yet, one home run call, that best exemplifies how deeply we care about the Pirates. The call, in YouTube lore with more than 25,000 views, occurred on August 7, 2010.

Pedro Alvarez, considered by the Pirates a building block to better days ahead, hit a walk-off home run before a sellout crowd at PNC Park to win a game. I was on the radio with Greg and, like a fan in the stands, went crazy and probably sounded like I was out of my head for a moment. But afterward, Pedro came to me and said, "My Dad listened to your call and really, really liked it."

Every once in a while, you get caught up in something that just hits you, and you do stuff without thinking. My over-the-top reaction to Alvarez's home run was just so spontaneous. At that moment, I wasn't a broadcaster but rather a Pittsburgh Pirate. I just went nuts and make no apologies for it. Every once in a while, you hit a pure vein like that and, for me, it was that night. Damn, that was fun.

Brownie is the same way. Some people say, "Greg, why are you so overly enthusiastic about the Pirates?" But he, too, makes no apologies for it. Nor should he. It's okay to be a fan every once in a while. It's so funny, because Greg will go nuts about a call or a Pirates win, sometimes sounding like he's completely out of control. But then, 10 minutes later, after the game, we'll go down and have a glass of wine and he'll calmly say, "Good Pirate win, yep."

Greg has such passion for what he does. He's done everything for the Pirates. In my book, *he's* a Pirate for life. I also think he's a great candidate for the Pride of the Pirates award that honors an individual for a lifetime of service. He has such intense energy and loyalty toward the organization. I feed off of that. We all have days when we're not at the top of our game, perhaps even down a little bit. When I have one of those days, I'll come down to the ballpark and he'll pick my ass up in a minute.

Every once in a while, we'll stand by a ledge at PNC Park, look out at the river, sneak a pregame cigar, and talk about anything other than baseball for about 15 minutes. He'll listen to my jokes that he's heard a thousand times before. And he's never failed to remind me that I've made a very handsome living out of four lame jokes, six exaggerations, and two good hours on an October Sunday afternoon many, many years ago. But he's very kind about it. He indulges me wonderfully. He's very patient with me because I've got my line of nonsense that hasn't changed much in 30 years, and he's been around to hear all of it too many times.

Bob Walk is another friend who is practically a Pirate lifer, having pitched 10 years for the club and then worked the last 18 as a color man up in the booth. On occasion, I've done play-by-play with Bob if Greg or Tim Neverett ever had to miss a game, and it always goes very well. Our broadcasts together are like two guys talking, with little mention of statistics. We just shoot the breeze about the ballgame. We've received some nice comments about the work we've done together.

Walk has a *tremendous* instinct about the game, the strategies, and about what should and shouldn't be done in a ballgame. When I watch the Pirates' road games on television, because I don't travel with the team anymore, I learn things that Bob sees that I don't. I think that shows the deep balance we have on our broadcast team. Bob and our other color guy, John Wehner, are very knowledgeable about the rules and flow of the game on a technical level. Not that they can't tell stories, because they can. But it's a nice balance because while they're into the Xs and Os of a game, I'm all about the stories, the history, and the tradition of the Pirates and the city of Pittsburgh, itself. The really knowledgeable, hardcore fans get what they need from Walk and Wehner. And the other folks get the lighter stuff from me, so I think we have a little bit for everybody who's interested in Pirates baseball.

When "Walkie" was a Pirates player, I had to interview him once, and he got me good. I was such a naïve and nervous interviewer, exactly the opposite of how comfortable I was in getting interviewed. Rooker, a fellow broadcaster at the time, set the whole thing up. He had talked to Walk beforehand and then encouraged me to get him as the pregame show guest. I took the bait. I walked over to Bob and asked him, "Would you be my guest on the pregame?"

"Sure," he said. Rooker knew what one of my stock questions was going to be, and Walkie was ready for it.

"Hey, Bob, what would you be doing if you weren't a baseball player?" I asked.

Walk said, "Oh, I'd be an anthropologist. I'd be over in Egypt by the Pyramids."

And stupid and naïve, I just ran along with him, having no idea he was putting me on. Walk could hardly keep a straight face. I turned around when we got through and Rook was just pissing in his pants laughing. Walk got me good there.

Jim Leyland was the Bucs' manager then and always said that Walk was one of his favorite players. So was Wehner. Both had played for Leyland at one time or another, and they weren't guys who were gifted with phenomenal natural talent. But they maxed out their abilities and were "grinders," and Leyland has the ultimate respect for players in that category, which impresses me.

Our current broadcasting crew is like a band of brothers and has certain traditions. One of them is to come out to my cabin after the season ends as a way of unwinding. One time, we all sat around a huge bonfire that our resident pyro Brownie made. I said, "Man, is it hot." We were all liquored up, so I just took off my shirt and threw it in the fire. "Well that's better," I announced to the group. Then Walkie did the same thing. Of course, it's nothing unless you do something to excess. So I took off my pants and socks and threw them into the fire. Whatever piece of clothing I threw into the bonfire, Bob would match it. This continued until we both sat there in our underwear.

I was okay because I had some extra clothes stored in the cabin. But Bob had brought only a small suitcase. The only thing I still wonder about was whether Walk's wife, Lori, was curious as to why Bob's suitcase came home a lot lighter.

Even a potentially dangerous situation turned out to be hilarious with our broadcasting team. During the 1994 strike, the club had us go up to Buffalo to do some minor league games. To kill some time one afternoon, we went downtown to see a movie. Greg; our broadcast coordinator, Jon Mercurio; our VP of broadcasting, Mark Driscoll; and I went to a not so very nice area where the theater was located.

Halfway through the movie, Greg went into the bathroom. As he was finishing up in the urinal, he peeked over his shoulder and noticed a guy had walked in and pulled out a good-sized handgun while he was at the sink. Because the theater didn't have more than 10 other people in it, Greg very quietly but quickly made his way back to his seat and whispered to us what he had seen. I immediately leaped from my seat and said, "Let's go. We're outta here."

We tried to be completely quiet and discreet after we decided to sneak out a fire exit door near the front of the theater, concerned that the guy would come after us if he figured we knew he had a gun. Just as we began walking quietly down the aisle, I grabbed my box of Raisinets and put them in my pocket. It made a rather loud sound as they bounced around the box. Once outside the theater, the guys laughed their asses off at the thought that I couldn't leave the box of Raisinets at my seat even if our lives depended on it.

Our broadcasting team has never been completely about just goofing around all the time. In a business that is highly competitive and, at times, cutthroat, we're very close. There is definitely a serious side that shows how much we care about one another.

One gesture turned in by Greg and our director of broadcasting, Marc Garda, I will never forget as long as I live. The night before my dad's funeral, they worked a home game. After it was over, they got into a rented car and drove 500 miles, starting around midnight, all the way to Canaan, Connecticut. They stopped in a McDonald's parking lot to change their clothes into suits and ties, and then drove straight over to the funeral. Then afterward, they took the rented car back to Bradley

Field in Hartford and flew home. They will always have my loyalty and friendship. They own me.

Another time our group separated the funny from the serious stuff involved a terrific young man named Shawn Gaertner, who had worked with Garda in various roles, such as the ticket office and the community service department with the Pirates. Shawn was a very real, honest, principled, and fun guy. Greg and I learned that Shawn was in a local hospital dying from melanoma. After a game, we got in our cars, drove over to the hospital, and went to see him. Shawn's family was there, and they gave us a few minutes alone with him. Shawn was close to passing away.

We went in there, held his hand, and talked to him. When we came back outside, I talked to the family and tried to convey how proud they should be of raising a young man of that quality. You don't fool around with that stuff; you don't say something like that unless you mean it. You understand what that means to a family. So I searched for the right words and conveyed to them in a respectful way, "You raised a winner." Marc would later say how much our visit meant to Shawn's family. But it meant just as much to me to be able to be there with them at that most difficult time.

As my boss for the last 14 years, Garda and I have had a terrific working relationship. I think part of the reason why is because he knows he can always count on me if he needs something done. Garda, in turn, when necessary, has been quite tolerant of my work on the air. An example of this came during a night game when I was on the radio. Kevin Young was playing first base, and a ground ball was hit deep in the hole to our shortstop. It was a difficult throw over to Young, but Kevin straddled the base and awkwardly made contact with it to get the putout. I said, "Well, we're on the radio, folks, but if you can visualize it this way, think of a dog straddling a fire hydrant." I turned around to Garda and asked him if that was okay to say on the air. He looked at me, rolled his eyes, and said, "Well, it's out there, Steve. Nothing we can do now."

I'm close to the edge lots of times on the air. Sometimes I'll back off; sometimes I'll test the edge. If I test the edge, I'll do it and then look back at Garda. He'll either have his hands over his eyes and his head down on the table, or just say, "Yeah, it's you. I know, it's you."

But that's a part of my job. I am supposed to add color to the broadcasts and tell stories. It's not always easy. Nineteen straight losing seasons and some difficult games along the way make it a challenge. But that's what I signed up for. You grind it out. In the big picture, I'm working three hours a day. Tell that to people who punch in and double down on the night shift. There are some times when it's not a lot of fun. But I still like getting in the car, driving to PNC Park, and watching our Buccos play a major league game. I choose not to make it any more complicated than that.

It's because I care so very deeply about the Pirates and the fans. I want badly for Pittsburgh to have a winner again. So when I'm broadcasting a one-sided game that the Bucs are losing, it's like having bamboo slivers stuck in my eyes. Brownie tells me all the time that if the Pirates had been more competitive the last 19 years, I might still be doing road games. I know Greg feels it sincerely, and I'm very flattered. I consider it a compliment.

But, actually, there were other reasons why I stopped traveling, and the Pirates' woes weren't one of them. I was starting to realize how much time I have left on this earth, and it got so that I hated the mornings and early afternoons on the road waiting for the ballgames to start. I loved being around the guys, being at the ballpark, and having a couple of beers afterward with Bob and Greg or whomever I was with.

But, oh, those empty hours. I'm an early riser; I get up at 6:30 most mornings. My routine was to have breakfast, take a walk, and go back to the hotel around 8:30 or so. So I still had the rest of my day. I hated that. I wanted to stop wasting any more hours or days in a hotel room. I started thinking about what I owed to my wife, my family, and my immediate friends around the neighborhood.

But mostly, it was about that time factor. I'm looking down at the finish line, to be quite honest. I was in my mid-sixties, had been on the road for a lot of years, and, even though I loved everything about the road trips, with the exception of the flights, I wanted to catch up with my life a little bit.

One of the things about the road that I do miss is going back to the room after a few beers and watching infomercials on TV. There's nothing better than the late-night drunk ordering of "bargains." A lot of years ago, I ordered three sets of Ginzu knives, but that wasn't good enough. The last couple of years I traveled, they used to have Chef Tony's masterpiece series. I ordered three sets of those—one for me, one for my son David, and one for the cabin.

Another time I ordered the pants stretcher, so I could crease my pants without ironing. On a sober Wednesday morning when it arrived, I unwrapped it and it looked like a sex device for little people. And an additional bonus for this particular order was that it also included discs of the top 100 love songs of 1946.

I also have the complete set of the *Dean Martin Celebrity Roast* tapes. It reached the point where Karen finally had to call someone in Tennessee to make the company stop sending them, because I would get one every month. She told the poor customer service person she would come to Tennessee and hunt him down if they sent me more of that stuff.

But one of the best things I ever ordered was this tool set that came in a metal container. The actual tools were packaged separately. I unwrapped them, but when I put them in the tool box, I couldn't lift the damned thing. It must have weighed 150 pounds. It was a wonderful tool set, but I just couldn't lift it.

It's just so much fun and makes so much sense to order this stuff. It seems like the right thing to do at 4:00 AM when you're half in the bag. Plus, I love getting stuff in the mail. I would think, *I'm half-smoked right now and I really like the idea of buying this product. I know I'm going to forget about it, so what a great surprise it's going to be when it arrives.*

I think ordering things from TV is the neatest concept. It's almost like getting stuff for free. I mean, when Chef Tony gets on there and cuts that penny in half with one of the knives and then goes right to slicing tomatoes, it's like the best thing you've ever seen in your life. You've *got* to order it. And it's the *masterpiece* series, not just the regular series.

I showed great discipline in ordering the masterpiece series because when I did, the person taking the order said, "And by the way, we also have this...." But I cut her off. I said, "No lady, you're not going to trick me. I just called for the masterpiece series. Let it go. It's over. Just send me the three sets. What do you think I am, some kind of sucker!"

My infomercial ordering occurred mostly on the road, but every once in a while, I'd do some ordering at home. But it was safer on the road, because there was no chance of Karen waking up and coming down the stairs to stop me.

So there were certainly things I missed about the trips, but it was just time to come home. That said, I paid the price emotionally over it. On April 6, 2005, the Pirates completed their first homestand of the season and were headed to San Diego. It marked the first time in 20 years they would start a road trip without me. As the team and the broadcasters were walking toward the buses for the trip to the airport, I had a twinge.

When I got through pitching, it was a relief to get away from the game because of all that I went through with my control problems. But at that point in my broadcasting career, I was at the top of my game, the exact opposite of when I stopped pitching. Despite the fact that leaving the road was my decision, walking away hit me very hard. I got pretty depressed about it. I felt that I wasn't going to be a part of the team for the first time in two decades.

It was not how I thought I was going to feel. I thought I would have a tremendous feeling of relief and freedom. Well, I had the freedom, but I wasn't getting the feel from the freedom that I thought I was going to get, making it a very difficult time. One day, being particularly sad, I went over to our country club and, because I couldn't sit still, played dozens of holes of golf all by myself. I just played all day, going through 18 holes and then just starting all over again. That helped me that particular day.

My feeling of being left out didn't go away all of a sudden, but it did finally work itself out. It was almost like a grieving period that I had to go through. I have always hated change. Now, I'm absolutely fine with just working home games. When the team takes off in those buses, I go to the golf course, see the grandkids, or just come home. And I'm perfectly happy with it.

I am truly thankful to the Pirates for allowing me to stay on the broadcast team by just doing the home games. They didn't have to do that. My being able to do the home games helped get me through that transition of not going on the road. It would have been devastating to have gone cold turkey and stopped broadcasting altogether.

I get asked all the time how much longer I want to broadcast. John Wehner, who would likely be promoted to a full-time color analyst should I retire, jokingly says to me every now and then, "You're looking a little peaked, Steve. You feel alright?" We kid about it a lot.

Karen and I have talked a lot about it, too. For a while, we thought I would do it until 70. But now the more we think about it, we realize it's kind of an ideal scenario. Our feeling is that if our health is good, why fix something that ain't broken? It's a pretty damn good gig. I am working just half the time, we get to go to Florida during spring training, and we have more time together when the team goes on the road. It's all positive now, as opposed to what a strain it was on both of us after I first stopped traveling.

So my retirement plans are still open-ended. I have a contract through 2013 and would love to keep going as long as I can.

It's that damn mistress of baseball. I can talk about gripping the ball all I want, but it's the ball that's had a grip on me since I was eight years old. And, oh boy, what a firm grasp it is.

CHAPTER 13

Defeating the Damn Thing

"Excuse me," a funky-looking guy right out of the 1970s called out to me at McKechnie Field one Friday morning during spring training in 1998. "Are you Steve Blass?"

"Yeah!" I shouted back in a manner I might use to direct my Fantasy Campers. "Why? Who are you?"

"I'm Richard Crowley. I was looking for Mark Wohlers, but you're the guy I should be talking to. I have worked with Steve Sax on his 'yips' problem, and I heard you wrote a letter to Wohlers about his control issues."

With that brief exchange, a conversation ensued that would mark the beginning of the end of my quarter-century struggle with "the damn thing," later known around baseball as Steve Blass Disease. It was also the start of a wonderful friendship.

Richard Crowley, the acclaimed sports psychologist who also goes by the nickname "Yips Doc," had a quirky personality that amused me. He was so damn sure of himself and spoke with a very strong Boston accent. I decided to talk to this guy because I could sense he was kind of a fun character to be around.

"I never heard back from Wohlers," I told him. "Maybe he never received it."

"Well, I flew here from California to offer my help to Mark after reading a *New York Times* article about him. And that's how I found out about your letter to him," Crowley said. "I think I can help him find the strike zone again."

Wohlers had been the Braves' closer the previous three seasons with a 100 mph fastball but inexplicably began battling wildness similar to what I went through at the end of my career. Despite spending two weeks in Florida in an effort to introduce himself to Wohlers, Crowley wouldn't meet him until the day Mark had to leave for a road trip. Richard, supremely confident that he could help Wohlers, wouldn't get the chance before his scheduled trip back home to the West Coast.

But Wohlers' inaccessibility and ensuing trip gave Crowley the free time to find me and set the stage for our chance meeting. I told him a little bit about my own struggles that led to early retirement.

"Oh, we can fix that," Richard said. "No problem."

I'm thinking, *Are you out of your freaking mind!* But as our conversation went along, his simplistic approach really appealed to me. I'm a minimalist to a fault. I typically don't consider a lot of factors and just try to get to the heart of a matter. Richard is the same way. Still, I was skeptical. I thought, *Oh my God, here we go again.*

I had long before stopped entertaining inquiries about my situation. I had had enough of that stuff. I wasn't rude to people when approached but would just respond briefly that I didn't want to get into any new projects. If Richard hadn't seemed so confident about fixing me after all those years, the conversation would have ended right there. When he offered to give me a session, gratis, I told him I needed the weekend to think it over and would let him know if I wished to proceed with it that Monday at 11:00 AM at McKechnie Field.

My first impulse was to discuss it with Karen when getting home that night. I laid the whole scenario out for her. "Do it!" Karen said. "If you can clean out some cobwebs and get some understanding, maybe you can get to the point where you can throw a little bit or get on the other side of it more completely."

With Karen's encouragement, I was excited about moving forward and having the session with Richard. I showed up an hour early to the field, and to my surprise, so did Crowley. We found a vacant back room at McKechnie and got to work.

"I don't care what caused this 'thing,' Steve," Richard began. "We're just going to get rid of it. We're going to replace bad with good. And we're not going to get rid of the bad by just shooting it, because there would still be a carcass. We're going to use acid on it and make sure it's gone."

What appealed to me was how he didn't care about a guy's personal life and any traumas that he thought may have brought on his troubles. This hit home with me, because one of the common theories about how my problems started revolved around its timing being right after the shock of Roberto Clemente's death. I had never bought into that because Roberto's death was no more shocking to me that it was to my other teammates. And the 24 other Pirates didn't get any "personalized diseases."

Crowley explained that it was a pure coincidence that high-profile players like Wohlers, Chuck Knoblauch, and Mackey Sasser all had dealt with significant off-the-field traumas either before or during the time the "yips" developed. His reasoning was that thousands of other athletes had personal problems and threw just fine.

Richard basically told me to get an image in my mind of losing the strike zone. After I had that, he told me to tell my imagination, which is located on the right side of the brain, to change that image with the help of some simple exercises using numbers, colors, and positive mental pictures. For all those years, I thought "the thing" was psychological. Actually, as Richard explained, it was more like a "pattern" where I would start out calm and confident when throwing in the bullpen. But once I crossed this invisible line called "The Game," this pattern woke up like a sleeping giant. The tension would take over by getting into my thoughts, running down to my arm, and taking away my control over both of them.

It was not psychological, because nothing like this has ever been described in psychology. Truth be told, the "thing" is unexplainable. That is why instead of trying to explain it, Richard's goal was to just fix it.

My problem was not logical, so it could not be found on the left side of the brain, which most of us use to try to solve our problems. If it was, I would have been able to make the adjustment on my own by having my pitching coach point out some mechanical issues I may have been having in my delivery by watching videotape of myself pitch.

Of course, I tried all that logical stuff, as well as numerous other mental exercises, during the last two years of my career, and nothing worked. Richard explained that because I still had this weird thing going on despite my efforts, the problem was both illogical and irrational. The good news was that Crowley had found a way to tap into a process to go to the right brain for things that don't make sense.

We were breaking a pattern, and it was easier to get rid of than I ever thought possible. By changing my bad images to good ones, it was like I had come out of a spell. One of several positive images that I used as something of a mantra was a daffodil. That may sound silly, but the image needed to be something I found pleasant and nice. Who could argue with that choice?

I couldn't wait to throw the baseball off the mound again. Richard and I went out to the mound at McKechnie Field after our 90-minute session was over. With the exception of a grounds crew guy, there wasn't a soul in the place. Standing on the mound, I turned to Richard and said, "Toss me that ball."

"Oh, you want this ball?" Richard asked slightly hesitantly. The ball was one that I had autographed for him. He flipped it to me and took out his camera. He wanted to take a picture of my first pitch after being cured of "the thing."

There was no catcher to throw to, but I went into my delivery and, without holding anything back, turned it loose, turned to Richard, and said, "I just threw my first strike." It was a tremendous feeling. It was like, in a baseball sense, I had been like Rip Van Winkle, asleep for a quarter century but now feeling as good as ever.

Though 56 years old at the time, my first impulse was to consider trying out for an Independent League baseball team. My fantasy was to go to someplace like Montana and pitch one inning of organized baseball.

The plan in my head was to meet with the owner or manager of such a team and just say, "My name's Joe Smith. I'd like to try out." I was very serious about giving that a try. In fact, I went home and discussed the idea of doing that with Karen.

Although Karen never said that I couldn't pursue that fantasy, she gently brought up some concerns. The most obvious, of course, was my age. Though she readily admitted that my body acted like a 30-year-old one and I never had a sore arm, I would be twice the age of most of the hitters I would be facing.

Another concern was "going back into baseball." It immediately sent up alarms in her head because of my past history. She remembered very well how painful the end of my career was for the both of us, and to open up those challenges again seemed like risky business. Karen brought up the idea of me throwing at Fantasy Camp or asking the Pirates if I could pitch batting practice as another means of satisfying my itch to pitch. Finally, she pointed out how very comfortable I was in the broadcast booth doing Pirates games. And Karen was comfortable as well seeing me do that. So after talking it out, we reached the conclusion to leave things well enough alone.

Three weeks later, I did a second session with Richard on the patio where we were staying in Florida to ensure that no doubts had crept into my head about my pitching, which Crowley said was very typical of the players he worked with. In fact, I did have some doubts I would fall into that "dark hole" again. I felt good. I felt it was going to work, but I hadn't really proven that to myself. The "fix" had been so easy. I still had doubts to some degree that it was going to continue to be alright when I went back out to the mound.

After that second session with Crowley, we met a few days later at 7:00 AM at Pirate City, the venue for the team's fantasy camp, with Pirates coach and former minor league catcher Trent Jewett. Trent continues to be one of my really good friends, the kind of old-school baseball guy who was nice enough to come out there that early to catch for me. I believed and still believe that Trent Jewett should be a major league manager.

The three of us walked over to Batting Cage No. 1. Richard stood in the batter's box as the hitter. We got a bag of balls, and I just aired it out. I must have thrown between 50 and 75 pitches that day. And that was with no conditioning on my part. To no one's surprise, my groin and ass cheek muscles hurt afterward, because I had just gone out there throwing the ball cold. But that's how good my body was for pitching. My arm was still very much alive.

"Shit, with that slider," Jewett joked, "you could pitch on the Triple A ballclub [the Nashville Sounds] I manage." Although it was, I'm sure, said tongue-in-cheek, his saying that made me feel like a million bucks.

Jewett and I continued to meet at Pirate City every few days that spring at the same hour of 7:00 AM to keep the fans and the press from finding out. My pitching again was an extremely personal thing. I wasn't trying to sell it to anybody. I wasn't trying to impress anybody or get any publicity. I just wanted the joy of throwing a baseball again. It's hard to describe that feeling, but that's what I had had since I was eight years old before "the thing" came along. When that joy went away, I felt as bad about that as I did about not being able to pitch in the major leagues any longer.

Pitching was something I enjoyed doing so much that I wanted to continue doing it after my playing days were over. Before "the thing," way back in my heyday, I would sometimes think, *Boy, when I get through playing, I would love to go down and pitch BP every day.* I knew former players who had done that. Bobby Del Greco did it for the Pirates for years. Vernon Law is 82 years old, and he still throws BP at fantasy camp as well as to high school kids. I always thought that was a great thing. As a BP pitcher, after I would get done throwing, I could still shag fly balls. I always loved chasing down fly balls.

I would give my left arm to go down to PNC Park and throw batting practice every day to the Pirates. I would love it. I would give $10 million to feel good enough to do that. But I still don't. I worry that I might hurt one of them with a pitch that would get away or embarrass myself by not throwing strikes. That's my little devil that I live with. I'm not obsessed by the dream of throwing BP, but damn, that would be fun.

After a few more pitching sessions with Jewett, I had a catch with Bob Walk, one of my broadcasting partners and a former major league pitcher himself, just outside of the Pirates' clubhouse. We were just screwing around, killing time before a broadcast. Bob said, "Damn, you're throwing pretty free and easy." It was just a catch, nothing structured or anything, but I was throwing the ball just the way I wanted to.

The next spring, *USA TODAY* ran a large article on the first page of its sports section titled, "Yipes, He's Got The Yips." I was interviewed for the article and mentioned what a tremendous help Richard was to me with my own "yips" issues. The writer of the story contacted Crowley and asked him what he thought about Wohlers' situation. Richard told the reporter, "He's quite salvageable."

This was not long after I had talked with Reds general manager Jim Bowden and recommended they make a deal for Wohlers. I said, "I know the guy has talked with Crowley, and I think he's worth a shot again." He took my advice and, on April 16, 1999, the Reds acquired Wohlers and cash from the Braves for John Hudek, a journeyman pitcher.

With Wohlers on their team, the Reds were a little more than curious about Richard now. According to Crowley, Reds management forced their team medical director and chief orthopedic physician, Dr. Timothy Kremchek, to call Richard and ask him a most important question.

"Mr. Crowley, are you a 'crackpot'?"

Richard calmly responded rather matter-of-factly, "Yes. Do you have a second question?" It was vintage Crowley.

The Reds had Richard fly up to Cincinnati the next day to work with Wohlers. Crowley was eager to help, even blowing off a scheduled trip to Paris. By working with Crowley, Wohlers may not have regained the closer status he once had with the Braves, when in 1995 and 1996 his strikeout-to-walk ratio was an impressive 4.2:1, but his wildness was definitely gone. His walks-to-innings pitched totals dropped significantly over the following three seasons.

I met Mark for the first time prior to interviewing him while he was with Cincinnati in 2001. I just walked up to him and said, "Hi Mark, I'm Steve Blass. It's time we said hello. You and I need to talk."

He knew who I was from both the *USA TODAY* article and from Crowley. I said to him, "I'd love to interview you on the pregame show. I don't want to deal in negatives. When we do this, we will just deal in positives."

It was a little different with Rick Ankiel, another pitcher felled by the dreaded "Steve Blass Disease." I didn't approach him for an interview until *after* he had reinvented himself as a legitimate power-hitting outfielder at the major league level. When I did get to him, I said, "Hey Rick. Steve Blass. I'd like to talk to you, and we won't talk about all the 'nonsense.' I know better than anybody what you've gone through, and I couldn't be happier for you."

It was interesting when I finally got a chance to meet both those guys, because I was saying to myself, *They may want to avoid me. They're probably not going to want to talk to me.* But it was interesting. I had good talks with Mark and Rick. I didn't want to talk about any bullshit. I didn't particularly enjoy going into detail about my stuff, and I was sure they didn't want to about theirs. They were probably wondering what the hell was going through my mind, especially now that I'm a part of the media. Would I abuse this connection that we had?

I just kept our talks and interviews light and breezy and, basically, threw them softball questions. I have a connection with them in that I know what they went through, so we acknowledged that fact and moved on to discussing current and more positive things. Even now, when I see Rick, I just like to check in, say hello, and see how things are going.

Rick, of course, had a fabulous rookie regular season as a pitcher in 2000 with the Cardinals. But it was his highly visible meltdown during Game 1 of that year's NLDS against the Braves that would start a pitching descent that he would never recover from. In fact, I was watching that game in my family room with Karen. As Ankiel started to implode, throwing one pitch against the backstop en route to walking six batters in 2⅔ innings, I turned to her and said, "Karen, the phone is going to ring in five minutes or less."

Damned if it didn't ring less than two minutes later. "Disease Central," I said after answering the phone. I swear, it is like I have a rarely used 1-800 number that is called whenever any pitcher has this stuff come up.

"Steve, this is Paul." Paul Meyer is an old friend who was covering the game for the *Pittsburgh Post-Gazette*.

I said, "I knew it. I knew a call was coming, Paul. I'm watching it, too."

But the interesting thing was, any time I got one of those calls, it was never from the principal involved. It was either from a writer or a friend. The writers would often ask, "What advice can you give them?"

Before I met Richard, my stock answer was, "They don't want to hear from me, because I didn't beat this 'thing.' I'm the last guy they want to talk to. The only advice I have for them is to try everything, so that when they're 80 years old they don't say something like, 'Oh God, I wish I had tried that.'"

The next year, in 2001, I started pitching in the presence of then–Pirates pitching coach Spin Williams. I didn't work with him on anything particular. It was more just throwing on a pair of shorts and a T-shirt while on the road with the team and throwing for fun to a catcher. I also wanted to show Spin how live my arm was. Without the fanfare, pitching for fun became a trend for me. The idea of pitching in an actual organized game was not something that had really entered my mind.

But that would all change at Pirates Fantasy Camp in 2005. It had been seven years since I first started working with Crowley, and for the most part I had satisfied my itch by throwing to Jewett and Williams in side sessions. Without having pitched in a game setting to that point, I couldn't know completely if I had beaten "the thing," but I was satisfied that I had addressed it and felt better about my situation. I had kind of talked myself into believing, *Okay, I beat 'the thing.' Now I don't need to do any more with it.*

So throughout a lot of fantasy camps in previous years, I hadn't felt the need to pitch. Deep down I wanted to, but there was still some apprehension so I didn't do it. I guess that, despite my sessions with Richard and pitching for seven years on the side, I was still a little bit afraid that I hadn't really 100 percent beaten it, and I didn't want to be embarrassed. I still had a vivid recollection of pitching great in the bullpen at the end of my career but then falling apart once I entered a ballgame.

I know this may sound silly, because it was just fantasy camp, and what risk would I really be taking by getting back on the mound to confirm victory over "the thing"? Even I would say to myself year after year, *Jesus Christ, I pitched in the big leagues for 10 years. Why am I concerned and having anxiety about going out to pitch in a fantasy camp? My arm feels great, my body's good, I never had a sore arm, so why not do this?* I didn't like the way I felt over not giving it a try.

I guess I have to give a camper who gave me a lot of shit during Pirates Fantasy Camp 2005 a certain degree of credit for getting me back out there. He wasn't a bad guy, but he was just getting off on his back-and-forth with me. He would become really agitating and challenged me to pitch against him. I started thinking, *Geez, should I do this?*

The next day, a Saturday, the former major leaguers would play each of the eight camper teams in a three-inning game. That was a total of 24 innings for us old timers. In the sixth game, the "agitator" was slated to bat second in his team's lineup. Chuck Tanner, the camp commissioner, walked over to me and asked, "Do you want to pitch to this guy or not?"

In the past, I would have given my standard reply of, "No, I'll pass. I'm fine." Not this time.

I told Chuck, "I would like to pitch against him because he's been a pain in the ass all week. He's one guy where I'm just going to air it out, and if I hit him, I won't give a rat's ass." All that was on my mind was just to go after this guy. It wasn't an evil thing, and there was no anger. But because I didn't really care if I hit him with a pitch or, for that matter, threw the ball to the backstop. I wasn't concerned about being wild.

Despite being in that frame of mind, I still had some anxiety, so I thought about Richard's teachings. One of his ideas was to have a word or phrase, like a mantra, used while in the windup as a relaxation technique. Remember the daffodil? My phrase *that* day was, "Screw it."

So I went into my delivery, said my phrase to myself while in the middle of my delivery, and just turned the pitch loose. I fired a pitch right down the middle for strike one. It felt good, with less anxiety, and when I got to two strikes, I blew his ass away.

Chuck came out to the mound and said, "Okay, Steve, you want out of here?"

I told him, "No, Chuck, let me try it again with the next guy."

And it just went on from there. I kept getting guys out. The more I pitched, the better I felt. From the mound, I would sometimes glance into our dugout and see all those guys whom I played with years before on the Pirates. I sensed they were thinking, *God, how good is it to see him do this. Isn't it great to see him out there having fun again?* Heaven knows, it was great to believe they were feeling that way. I was just having the time of my life. Even though it was still risky to a small degree, I wanted the ball.

I completed the first game without giving up any runs, and Chuck came over to me said, "Hey, great job! That was fun, wasn't it?"

"Yes it was, Chuck. I feel great! Let me go back out there in the next game and see how long I can run this thing."

Tanner let me start the seventh game. The result was the same. Three more shutout innings. I was floating on air. I came into the dugout, looked over at Tanner, and said, "Still good, Chuck, still cookin'."

I went back out there and pitched the eighth and final game of the day as well. The result? Another three-inning shutout.

So in my first mound appearance in 30 years, I had pitched a total of 8⅔ innings without giving up a run. And, maybe just as important, during the course of the entire outing, walked a couple of guys and didn't panic. At 63 years old, I was dealing again. And my arm felt great.

It was like breaking scar tissue. I had incorporated what Richard had been working on with me, and it worked. His teachings didn't eliminate the anxiety each inning I went out there, but they allowed me to deal with "the thing" head on. It was an unbelievable feeling! I couldn't wait to drive back out to Anna Maria Island to have a drink with Karen and tell her all about it. Pitching had been an utter joy for me and, on that particular day, I got that joy back.

I called Richard after the game and told him all about it. He said, "Yep, feels good, doesn't it?"

I felt like I was 18 years old again. I was so caught up in that feeling of euphoria, I didn't think, *Oh my God, I'm bitter that I didn't find the answer sooner.* I may have been wistful, but not bitter. That's because, in the big picture, my life has been a joyride. That bump in the road that I had in the final two years of my career gets minimized with each passing year.

I enjoyed this wonderful day for what it was. I'm an in-the-moment type of person. Every once in a while, I might put my feet up and say, *Damn it. I could have pitched for a lot more years and maybe won another 100 games.* But my career was long over, and it was a good one. I won more than 100 games, appeared in an All-Star Game, and was a part of a world championship team. So I did all the things I dreamed about, times 10. The Bucs gave me a chance to live this dream when I was 18 years old. And I'm still living it. How good is that?

What if "the thing" had occurred to me at the start of my career like it did with Ankiel or, even worse, before it ever began? What happened to me with "the thing" is a fact. It happened. And if I had dwelled on it, I might still be in some kind of an abyss. I choose not to do that.

It does make me sad sometimes that I didn't find the solution while still in my prime. I wish I had, because I had the perfect body to pitch until I was 40. And I loved it so much. Nobody had more fun. But who knows? After all, I still get a little bit of anxiety, even now, when I go out to pitch in a fantasy game. I guess there's still a little twinge in me that is concerned "the thing" might all of a sudden just reappear.

So perhaps another session with Richard is in order. And come to think of it, maybe we can work on my golf game while we're at it! The work I have done with Richard, though life-changing in some respects, hasn't been a total cleansing. It's that concern over the reemergence of "the thing" that probably is the reason I tell Karen to stay away from my Pirates Fantasy League games. I once told her, "I don't know if I want you there, because if it did reappear, for whatever reason, I wouldn't want you to endure the pain and discomfort of watching that again."

I will never, ever forget what she went through. I would have no issue if she wants to sneak into a fantasy game sometime without me knowing about it, but that's her business. I know she tried that once but got caught in traffic and didn't make it in time.

After that fantasy game in 2005, I wasn't sure if even *I* ever wanted to see myself pitch again. That gem was just so meaningful to me that I didn't want to tempt fate with being embarrassed again. On the other hand, whenever I wear the uniform, go on the field, and put the glove on and smell that damn leather, I get the itch again to go out and pitch. As a result, I still find myself a little bit between being concerned over the return of "the damn thing" and how wonderful it feels when I take the mound.

Richard Crowley helped close the door on years of anguish and not only improved my feelings about baseball, but also improved my life. When Crowley helped me pitch again he also helped my marriage. The results of our sessions took away the nightmares and my preoccupation of being a competitor who could no longer compete.

Richard Crowley helped me in many other capacities in my life besides pitching a baseball.

CHAPTER 14

Pittsburgh, A Love Affair

F alls Village, Connecticut, may still be "home" to me, but since 1964 when I was called up to the Pirates, my life has been in Pittsburgh. I've spent a good deal of time in all different kinds of cities—New York, Chicago, Los Angeles—but Pittsburgh is so great for me because it's manageable without sacrificing any of the activities, sports, arts, and other amenities of a major city. Despite growing up in a very small town, I can keep up with a city like Pittsburgh and not be overpowered by it. Plus, you can drive 10 minutes and be out in the country. That is one of the great charms of this place.

The people, of course, are the true foundation and essence of Pittsburgh. Because I've been in this town for nearly half a century, I've met a ton of them. They have always made our family feel welcome, a part of the city, and I've tried to say thank you to as many of them as I could.

I've been around a long time and have a high degree of recall. I enjoy relating to folks that I've been with just one organization for 50 years. That means a great deal to me. I'll end a lot of speeches by saying, "You may thank me for being here, but thank you for letting me be a part of your lives in some small way."

Naturally, my love affair with Pittsburgh flows from my association with the Pirates. It's never been lost on me that, as an 18-year-old, it was the Pirates that gave me a chance to live my dream. Some say to me, "Well, another team could have done that." But another team didn't. The Pirates did. I wasn't that blue chip bonus baby or anything like that. But Joe Brown cared about me. Danny Murtaugh cared about me. My teammates cared about me. Because of what the Pittsburgh Pirates did for me, they will have my loyalty for the rest of my life.

In March 2008, it was that loyalty, love, and appreciation of the Pirates that was laid bare before the entire organization. Pirates president Frank Coonelly and general manager Neal Huntington were both beginning their first spring training with the team and wanted to change the culture of the clubhouse. The team had struggled for a long time, and the front office wanted to instill a pride and passion that had been missing for years.

That was when Joe Billetdeaux called me and said, "The management guys would like to have you address the ballclub."

I said, "What about?"

Joe said, "About being a Pirate and your years with the team. Basically, what it means for you to be a Pittsburgh Pirate."

I said, "Wow. The major league team?"

"Yep," said Joe. "It's going to be in the lunch room at Pirate City later during camp."

I said I would do it, and for the next two weeks I practiced my speech during my morning walks on the beach. I was taking this one particularly seriously because, even though I had given a lot of speeches in my life, I had never addressed a major league baseball team without any humor. In fact, it was the hardest I have ever worked on a speech in my entire life. Thankfully, I eventually got it to where I liked it.

When the time came to give the speech, I walked into a packed lunch room. The whole baseball team was sitting around, some on the floor and the rest in chairs. There were the major league roster, the spring invitees, and the coaches, so about 60 guys in uniform. The Pirate brass included Coonelly, Huntington, Maz, Virdon, owner Bob Nutting, and minor league coordinator Kyle Stark. Everybody was there.

I walked out into the middle of that room. There was no podium to lean on nor microphone to hold, just a baseball I had grabbed somewhere.

There were no notes because my speech was well rehearsed and would come from my heart. It would turn out to be the finest thing I'd ever done in front of a group.

I hadn't pitched in more than 30 years, but I still went around the community, the restaurants, the grocery stores, and the gas stations with the pride that I had been a Pittsburgh Pirate. I wanted to convey what it should mean for them to be Pirates and the unique opportunity each of them had before them.

My speech went like this:

> *Listen up guys. This isn't bullshit. I lived what you're living. I'm not some googly-eyed sports psychologist that is stand-ing here telling you that you can't hit the slider because your mother didn't love you enough.*
>
> *You guys have worked your asses off to get here. Think of the guys who are falling by the wayside. Not only opponents but friends of yours through a bad arm, a personal situation, or by just not having enough ability. You are carrying the banner for those people who had the same dream that you did but didn't make it and had their hearts broken. You represent them. Opponents. Teammates. And it is your responsibility to be as good as you can. Because the worst thing that can happen is that you get to the big leagues and become content.*
>
> *Content on a big-league team is cancer. You might be able to fool the fans a little bit, your teammates a little bit, your manager, and your city, but you can't fool yourself.*
>
> *Think about it. How many levels are there as a major leaguer? Just getting there is one thing. Proving you belong is another. And finding out you're good is yet another level.*
>
> *Don't you want to find out how good a major leaguer you can be? Because when you're 85 years old, sitting on that back porch at the home, you don't want to think, "Boy, I made the big leagues, but I wonder how good a major leaguer I could have been."*

Don't be content to just be here. Find out how good you can be. You know what? There are some guys who said they are motivated by their brother, their dad, their coach, their manager, a friend. And I respect that.

But think about it. What if you get traded? What if your manager gets fired? What if your coach passes away? What if your brother moves to a different city? What if your Dad is no longer there for you? What if your friend is gone? Who are you left with?

It's you. You are your motivator! You!

And to me, the greatest motivational tool in the world costs $39 at Home Depot. It's a bathroom mirror, because that sucker won't lie to you. It's brutally honest. It will ask you questions only your gut can answer. And that's when it gets down and dirty. You will see that mirror every morning and every night.

But it's also your best friend, because when you do what you think you're capable of and you do it to the degree that you need to at the major league level, you look at that sucker after a ballgame, and it's smiling right back at you.

I cared enough to the point where I went through hell. I would challenge each and every one of you to go through what I did and experience that. They say what doesn't destroy you makes you stronger. I don't know if that's the truth, but I went through hell for baseball because I wanted to be entirely convinced that it was over.

So when you struggle and go through a slump, try everything you can. Because one little thing might change everything.

Do I care about the Pittsburgh Pirates? I can't tell you how many nights when I was going bad, I would sit up in my backyard at 4:00 in the morning with tears running down my eyes because I knew I wasn't going to be a Pittsburgh Pirate anymore.

So do I care? Yeah, I care. And I hope you care enough
to find out how good a major leaguer you can be.

I had a sense these guys were locked into what I was saying. And as the speech went on, that motivated me to just dig my heels in as deep as I could. Before I gave the speech, I wasn't aware that my talking with the club was an attempt to change the culture. I'm glad they didn't tell me. As far as I knew, they just wanted me to speak and tell the club what being a Pirate meant to me. Coonelly would later say that in all the locker rooms and clubhouses he had been in during his time in sports, he had never been so moved in a situation as when I gave my remarks.

I use the phrase "living my dream and still living it," every now and then. It sounds like a bunch of words at times, and I probably overuse it. But that expression was the foundation of what I said to that baseball team. A few years before, in 2001, I had received another phone call from the front office, this time from then–team owner Kevin McClatchy.

I was announcing a Bucs game at Shea Stadium when McClatchy called up to the press box and said, "Send Blass down here." I thought, *Oh boy, am I in trouble.* The owner of a ballclub doesn't usually summon an employee unless there's an issue.

I went down to see him, and Kevin informed me that the next April I was going to be receiving the Pride of the Pirates Award, which is given annually to recognize members of the Pirates family who have given a lifetime of service to the ballclub. It means a great deal to me, because the Pirates are the only organization I've ever known. It's a tremendous honor, because they don't give other honors out. It's one of the smaller trophies I have out of the stuff I've accumulated, but it probably means more to me than any of them.

Another honor that blew me away was a 50th Anniversary Ceremony the Pirates had for me at PNC Park on Opening Day, 2009. I was contacted in spring training by Christine Serkoch, Director of Special Events. Chris said, "We'd like to acknowledge your 50 years with the club. And after you give a speech, we'd like you to throw out the first pitch."

I said, "Yeah, that would be great! That's quite an honor. How many people can I bring?"

"We'll give you a World Series Suite room for entertaining," Chris said. "You can have as many people as you want."

Then I had an epiphany. I thought, *What if I could invite my high school coach, Ed Kirby, and his wife, Mary, to come out?* So I called Chris and she said, "Yes, the Pirates will take care of it." That meant the world to me.

From there it took on a life of its own. They wound up giving us two suites because all 40 people we invited on a work day showed up. One of the first things I noticed when on the field during the ceremony that day was a big sign the Pirates had affixed under the broadcast booth. It was a shadow print of me in my pitching motion with a caption underneath saying, "Blass 50 Years." They would leave it up there for the entire 2009 season.

The celebration was just wonderful. There were a lot of people important to me on the field during the ceremony. Some of them included my wife, Karen, my son Chris and his wife, Ed and Mary Kirby, Dave Giusti, and Manny Sanguillen. And after my speech, I threw out the first pitch to Sangy, a hard strike right down the middle to show the fans I still had something left.

Greg Brown was the emcee and did an unbelievable, emotional job from my standpoint. I didn't have to broadcast, so I was up in the suite with Nellie King and nearly 60 family members and friends, who I was so happy were there. It made me feel like a million dollars. It's a day I won't forget. It never gets old seeing the guys you won a championship with.

And the 1971 team was able to do just that at a grand celebration in the summer of 2011 at PNC Park to commemorate the 40th Anniversary of our World Series championship over the Orioles. The great thing about it is you start reminiscing about the great stories and wish the guys who have passed away could be there—players like Clemente, Briles, Moose, Ellis, and Stargell. Plus, our beloved skipper Murtaugh and his coaches Don Osborn and Frank Oceak.

The only downside is this Internet is killing us. Because of the embellishment used in some of the stories we tell, our actual stats are right at everyone's fingertips to cross-check claims of grandeur. We can get busted right on the spot because the Internet holds the truth. What a cruel device the computer is. The technology is killing a lot of our great stories.

Those reunions also mean a lot because when you win a World Series together, it's the single most important point in your whole baseball career. Its significance will never go away. We've all aged and you're aware of the years, but it seems like we become kids again at those reunions.

One of the highlights of this particular reunion was when Richie Hebner approached Charlie Sands, who has had all kinds of physical issues and challenges, and reached into his pocket, pulled out his funeral home business card, and said, "My goodness, Charlie, hey, great to see you, but keep in touch." So, 40 years later, we were just boys being boys, returning to that clubhouse atmosphere.

What made it even more special that particular summer was the fact that the Pirates were playing so well. It was one of many sellout crowds that season, and the atmosphere and energy level were phenomenal.

I have always said that when we got a team that matched the beauty of PNC Park, it would be a carnival every night. And it was for the first four months of the 2011 season. So that reunion, in June, was right near the peak of that run. It was just one more reminder of what a great baseball town Pittsburgh really is.

Another reason why those championship Pirates teams from 1960, 1971, and 1979 have stayed relatively close is because of the strength of our Alumni Association. We think we have one of the strongest alumni groups in all of Major League Baseball because of how the late Nellie Briles was so committed to elevating the program when he was at the helm.

Nellie was such an integral part of our alumni. He also was heavily involved with the Major League Alumni Association, giving the Pirates a strong identity with our national arm. He was just tireless with his work and quickly became recognized as one of our greatest ambassadors. It's ironic, because he didn't play with the Pirates for very long. But in a short time he became a highly visible and effective member of the Pirates' organization.

Tragically, Nellie had a heart attack on February 13, 2005, at the Pirates alumni golf tournament in Florida. I was not at the outing but heard that the guys were in the middle of a round and Nellie just went down. Attempts to revive him failed, even though an ambulance got there very quickly. Trying to make some sense out of it, the only thing we came up with was there had been a history of heart issues in his family. At age 91, dying suddenly on a golf course is not a bad way to go. But not at 61, like Nellie was when he died.

Nevertheless, Nellie Briles' legacy within the Pirates' organization lives on. After Nellie passed, Joe Billetdeaux came to me to take over Briles' role as head of the Alumni Association, and I accepted. My duties included going out and representing the ballclub when people would approach Joe with community-related requests.

In one sense, it was a good job in that I felt I made a positive influence on the community and represented the Pirates well. But the bad news was that it maintained my out-of-control pace. I was out a lot again, away from home, my wife, and family, doing more and missing more things than I should. It gave me an excuse for not slowing down. So I stepped down from that position for personal reasons.

Nellie's imprint on the Alumni Association continues today under the leadership of current president Kent Tekulve and the tremendous support given by Sally O'Leary and her *Black and Gold Newsletter*, a publication that is the gold standard for any major league alumni group.

Sally is just phenomenal. She started with the Pirates in 1964, so we were rookies together. She is like the Earth Mother of the Pittsburgh Pirates and the unofficial historian. Sally knows secrets that could bury all of us, but she's been very kind over the years.

Our former players are also active in improving the lives of others both through the Alumni Association and Pirates' Charities. Our Alumni Association, for example, wound up having an affiliation with the State Correctional Institute at Greensburg Prison because of the friendship Briles had with pitching great Sam McDowell's brother, Bill, who had a prominent position at the facility right up until his death several years ago. The inmates there raised money for Make-A-Wish by receiving pledges from employees at the prison and some outside businesses. So we as an alumni group go there in early December each year and shoot baskets in a competition among ourselves that is called Shots-For-Tots.

There is always a Make-A-Wish child there, and we typically end up raising between $5,000 and $8,000. A lot of people don't realize that Make-A-Wish is not just for terminal kids. It's actually for children with life-threatening diseases, so, thankfully, some of them do recover from their illnesses. We now are doing the Shots-For-Tots in memory of both Nellie Briles and Bill McDowell. It's one of those feel-good things that when you drive home from the event your heart feels good.

The Pirates' Alumni Coordinator, Joe Billetdeaux, will ask former players to make appearances at various functions to help raise money for Pirates charities. Sometimes, the team holds auctions and will put up for bid something like a round of golf with former Pirates players. So, once or twice a year, Maz and I, for example, play golf with fans who had a winning bid to play with us. The Alumni Association's biggest annual fundraising event, by far, is the Pirates Alumni Golf Tournament, which raises close to $100,000. At the end of the year, that money is distributed to different causes that we, as former players, have a personal interest in.

For example, Frank Thomas supports Meals on Wheels. Maz has a foundation for his high school. I lend support to Family Hospice. There are a ton of charitable tournaments around Pittsburgh, and the city is tremendous in the way that it raises money for worthy causes through golf. Aside from helping charities through the team, I also give back, as a former professional athlete should, to the Pittsburgh community in other ways. Shame on us if we can open corporate doors and don't.

Karen and I got very involved in Family Hospice, which provides end of life care in homes, assisted living facilities, nursing homes, and hospitals. For four years, I was involved with the Pittsburgh Muscular Dystrophy Foundation, where I led a coin board campaign in various bars and restaurants which raised close to $80,000.

But the charity that I'm most involved with is the Cystic Fibrosis Foundation. Greg Brown and I are honorary chairmen of the 65 Roses Club. The club's name derived from how a child with CF once tried to pronounce "cystic fibrosis." It came out sounding like *sixty-five roses*. Every major league team now has a 65 Roses Club. People who are a part of the club pledge $1, $2, or $5 for every home run that their favorite team hits in a season.

The reason I got involved with CF is because I have a nephew, Robert John Blass, who has cystic fibrosis and has beaten the odds in terms of life span. Sadly, a lot of these kids don't make it past age 20. It's a very cruel disease. But there's been a lot of progress, so by raising funds for its foundation, it's another thing I feel very good about doing.

Aside from supporting charities, I also give back by becoming involved in some of Pittsburgh's more educational foundations. I am an honorary chairman for Junior Achievement, which is a youth organization that focuses on educating kids about the free enterprise system. Essentially, it gets children prepared for entering the workforce once they are finished with school.

I am also very involved with the sports museum inside Pittsburgh's John Heinz History Center. I'm on its sports committee, along with Mike Wagner from the Steelers and golf greats Arnold Palmer and Carol Semple Thompson. One of my most prized possessions, the glove I wore during the 1971 World Series, is on display there.

Another way I keep in touch with my former mates while engaging with Pittsburgh fans is through the Pirates Fantasy Camp in Bradenton, Florida, every January. A lot of teams have one now, but ours is out of sight thanks to the blueprint created and carried out by Briles right up until his death. I've never been to another fantasy camp, but we've had people at ours that say it compares very favorably with others they have been to. And a lot of that had to do with Nellie.

Briles put it together to such a point that when the campers arrived on the first day, he would lead those Pirate lovers right into the major league locker room and present that whole big-league aura in such a way that blew them away. He just did it so unbelievably well that we haven't changed his camp itinerary one bit in the six-plus years he's been gone. Kent Tekulve has done a great job in carrying the torch ever since.

I have always been a class clown, so at fantasy camp I am in charge of the "Kangaroo Court." Every morning, I take note of campers' missteps such as missing a belt loop in their pants or having crazy-colored baseball shoes. I get up in front of the group and just rip on them with no conscience whatsoever.

I remember asking on one of the first days of camp one year, "Any gynecologists here?" One guys raised his hand, and I said, "That's it! I'm taking Babe Ruth's picture down. You're my new hero. You have women come to your place at 8:30 in the morning, take off all their clothes, and give you money. You're my hero!" Just ridiculous stuff like that gets them going for the day. Not all of it has a sexual connotation. I will just take off on anything, because I'm so caught up in my presentation. I'm saying this nonsense to heads of corporations, neurosurgeons, and other fans who plunk down around $4,000 to be there. Nobody gets spared, and they all love it.

Thank God I don't have time to explore their backgrounds. I just pick them out as they stand out there and jot down demerits with my pencil and paper. It takes on a life of its own after a couple of days, as guys begin coming up to me and start ratting on their friends and roommates. As soon as the tattling begins, I will get up there and say, "Joe Smith, your buddy Bill told me this about you. So that's a dollar fine for you. And by the way, Bill, that's a dollar for you, too, for ratting on your buddy."

Another time, a camper named Julie Jacobs, who has attended Fantasy Camp with her father for at least a dozen years, was fined a buck for not wearing a cup. But she defended herself by saying, "Actually, I have two cups." So I said, "That's a five dollar credit!" Julie, it should be noted, is a catcher who is as good as or better than a good number of the other campers.

I'll even use props when addressing the troops. I'll go out there, holding a big bucket used to put the balls in, and yell, "Sangy! Sangy! You forgot your cup." It reminded me of the time in reference to our pitching signals where one's a fastball, two's a curve, and three's a change. That night his jock broke and "Commander Cody" dropped down and I threw 34 straight fastballs. So nobody's immune to the ribbing, not even the staff. I get particular delight out of fining Maz and Virdon—two of my heroes. It brings me full circle from an 18-year-old who was in awe of them.

The Kangaroo Court is just a wonderful way to start the morning because everybody's hooting and hollering and laughing and having a great time. And I love it as much as anybody.

One of the funniest things I ever overheard at fantasy camp one January afternoon was from behind the right-field fence at one of the four fields we use at Pirate City. During one of the games, while walking back toward the clubhouse to get a pair of sunglasses, I noticed a car with Pennsylvania plates. There was an elderly couple in front of it, leaning against a fence and looking out at the game the campers, dressed in Pirates uniforms, were playing.

The wife turned to her husband and said, "My God, I hope they get better by April." I was trying to walk, but I practically pissed in my pants laughing so hard at her innocent comment. If someone ever put out a tape on the raw footage of our fantasy camp, I would never be able to go out in public again.

Another venue for staying close with some of my teammates, the "Buccos Stag," as we like to call it, coincided with a historic day on the golf course for me. In 2009, at the Greenburg Country Club just outside of Pittsburgh, I sank two holes in one in the same round, which is crazy. *Golf Digest* contacted me afterward and said the odds were 67 million to one against that happening.

Our foursome started on the 13th hole and, on 15, I knocked in my first hole in one of the day. The neat thing is that after I made that first one, I called my golf-loving son Chris on his cell phone. We laughed and hollered about it, and he was very happy for me.

Then we went all around to the front nine and, on the 7th hole, I hit one straight down the hill with a 7-iron on a par 3. The ball dropped to the left of the hole but then bounced sideways to the right, down onto the green, and into the cup for my second hole-in-one. I went totally insane. I took off my glasses, threw them away, and then took my 7-iron and tossed that up as well. I then got flat on the ground like a kid and rolled down a hill. At almost 70 years old, I damn near killed myself.

After brushing myself off a little bit, I called Chris back. But this time, after telling him I had just sunk my second hole in one, he hung up on me, thinking I was already drunk.

One would think after sinking two holes in one that it might merit winning two new cars. But, no, that was not to be. The prize for the first one was a computer. Because I don't use computers and don't even have an email address, I knew I wasn't going to benefit from that. The award for the second one was a $500 Visa gift card. I knew Karen was going to get that one. So, basically, as it played out, I drove home with a $500 bar bill because everyone wanted doubles to commemorate the two holes in one.

When I got home, Karen was watching television and asked me how I did. I told her, "Ah, I made a few good shots. I was okay." Then she read all about it in the next morning's *Post-Gazette* and shouted, "What's wrong with you? Why couldn't you tell me about this last night?" So it was pretty wild and got a lot of attention. And it was great to have done it with some of the other Buccos like Maz and Tekulve there.

The next day, I wrote a note to Titleist, but I never sent it. I wish that I had, to see their reaction. It went as follows:

> *Dear Titleist,*
>
> *I used your Pro-Vs and made two holes in one in one day. It made me wonder if it would have made a difference if you had had Pro-V baseballs back in 1973 when I really, really needed to know where the ball was going.*
>
> *Sincerely,*
> *Steve Blass*

Golf has been a big part of my life for years. My average is around a 10-handicap, so I have had my moments. But aside from how the game gets my competitive juices flowing, I also enjoy it for the social aspects and for how golf tournaments can raise money for good causes.

I am very proud to have a golf tournament of my own. A number of years ago, Champ Perotti, a good friend of mine from back home in Canaan, Connecticut, approached me about getting involved in a project that would recognize what I've done in my life while doing some good back home. So, in October 2006, the Steve Blass Charity Golf Tournament was born.

We play at the Egremont Golf Course in Great Barrington, Massachusetts, which is just over the line from Connecticut where I grew up. They do a bang-up job there for us. Frank Mazzerelli runs and operates the country club to the point where he's not just the pro but even helps cook the meal for the tournament after we get through playing.

Originally, Champ and I thought the tournament would just support the Little League field named after me in Canaan, which I am quite proud of. But, as we found out, the Little League field program didn't need a great deal of financial support. It kind of runs on its own nicely. Champ asked what I thought about using some of the funds raised for special projects like helping challenged kids in the area. Of course, I thought that was a great idea.

We chose The Region 1 Athletic Fund, believing it would make another perfect recipient for our concept. So, if there are locally challenged children who might want to go horseback riding, on swimming trips, or do other casual things and maybe are not so much in the mainstream, we can help their parents financially. Also, if a kid wants to go to a special athletic camp and has unique equipment needs, we can help out with the costs of that as well. It is a wonderful concept of helping challenged kids to become a part of something that is sports-related, and I am very proud to put my name and time into it.

The tournament itself is great fun. It gives me a chance to go home to that Norman Rockwell setting where some guys come and play in flannel shirts and jeans. My annual foursome consists of me, my son David, my brother Terry, and my best man, Del Kinney. While David and Terry like dressing casually for the event, Del, a golfing purist who has played in national senior tournaments, does not, I repeat, *does not*, arrive at the tournament in a flannel shirt and jeans. Back in the days before Karen and I were married, Del and I had talked about cutting a path through the country with him as a PGA golfer supporting us in the winter and me as a major league baseball player supporting us in the summer. Just control the American sports scene. (Personal note to Del: By the say, I upheld my part.)

After the golf itself, I get up after dinner to tell a bunch of stories about what I've done, where I've gone, and what's going on in the big leagues and with the Pirates. I get to do my shtick, going back and forth with my old high school coach, Ed Kirby, on how I tried to organize a revolt to get him removed because he made me run up that bank by the high school field time after time. It's all a joke, of course, and everybody has a good laugh.

Because of the generosity of my Pittsburgh connections by way of the Pirates, Penguins, and Steelers, as well as corporate donations, I wind up sending a lot of memorabilia to that tournament that can be auctioned or raffled off. For example, we might raffle off a Sidney Crosby jersey that would fetch $2,000 or $3,000 in Pittsburgh. Instead of having somebody bid on it, it gives everybody a chance to be involved and win something great.

Also, we've got a great goody bag that our guests receive when they register, thanks to a lot of my friends in Pittsburgh. We even keep the auction part of the event lighthearted, offering up two or three items while keeping it affordable for our guests. To kick off the festivities, I might say, "Alright, I've got a Mario Lemieux jersey here. We're going to start the bidding off at $15,000." Of course, I get the traditional laugh. We might end up getting a few hundred dollars for something like that, which is fine because it makes it reasonable for the folks to bid on it and still puts a few bucks in the pot. The bottom line is that we all enjoy it, and we help make a difference in the community.

Giving back is one of the things in life that drives me. And when given the opportunity to use my celebrity and ability to entertain to help a worthy cause, I often make the time to do it without asking for anything in return. One way I explain my community involvement when people ask is to break it down and simply say, "I show up." Any time I wind up doing something good in our community, or helping just one individual, it makes my heart feel good. The Thompson Run Club in West Mifflin, a working-class town outside of Pittsburgh, is a perfect example. For years, the Thompson Club Stag was a wonderful banquet that was somewhat irreverent, to say the least. But it gave some of the local celebrities like me the chance to tell all of our filthy sports-related stories, and the guys in the audience loved it.

The guy who ran it, Darrell Hess, raised money from the event to help out part of the Pittsburgh suburbs that had gone through tough times when the steel industry left the area and took a lot of jobs with it. It was totally out of line in terms of political correctness and went on for some 50 years. But it got to the point where, in this new age of technology, guys with phones could hold them up and take pictures or record the verbiage, the dialogue, and the terrible stories. So the Stag had to stop because people risked losing their jobs and careers. In a way, it had to come to an end. But it was great fun while it lasted.

At the other end of the innocence spectrum, I love giving talks at Little League banquets around Pittsburgh. The kids have such a pure love of baseball, and the Pirates and I get a hoot from their enthusiasm and exuberance.

Even at PNC Park, I can't help myself. I'll go up to a kid and tell him, "Hey, that's a good looking Pirates T-shirt you've got on. By the way, have you ever seen a World Series ring?"

And my colleagues kid me, saying things like, "Oh, you forced your ring on another kid, didn't you?"

But I defend myself by saying, "When I was 10 years old, I would have loved to have seen a World Series ring."

So I swallow the grief I get from Greg, Bob, Tim Neverett, John, and Marc Garda, because I feel as if I relate to those young fans. To see a kid's eyes light up, it's still a big deal for me. Ain't any bad news with that. The kid had a good time, I hope as much as I did.

One of the other primary reasons I love Pittsburgh is our neighborhood in the South Hills that we have called home since 1972. Our neighbors always made our family feel welcome. Our neighborhood is unique. So many families have remained there that we have many lifelong friends. Even though the legendary parties have slowed down a bit, we could not have made a better choice of where to make our home. They mean the world to us. Pittsburgh is that kind of town. If you as an athlete reach out 10 feet, people will come 100 feet to meet you. It's a great city from that standpoint. As a ballplayer and then as a broadcaster, I never lost track that the least I could do was return as much of myself as I could to them. And I have enjoyed it to the fullest.

In its heyday, we had Fourth of July block parties that would go on for two or three days and wind up having at least a couple of hundred people at certain times of the day or night. We would get the fire department involved and it would bring a truck, spraying the hoses all over and getting the kids going crazy. I would have the Pirate Parrot stop over, and before long he was like the Pied Piper with the kids. We had softball parties with broken ankles and collarbone injuries suffered by the guys trying to pretend they were much younger than they were. There was square dancing, egg tosses, water-balloon fights, and once even a magician that was so drunk when he arrived that while trying to do a special trick he fell into a hedge. So basically, he made himself disappear. It was a terrific act. The point was that everyone in the neighborhood got involved, and it was and, to an extent, continues to be a wonderful tradition.

Halloween is still a huge holiday in our area, and I really am like a big kid when that holiday rolls around. I love to dress up. I don't know if I'm a latent cross-dresser or not, because I once wore a dress to fantasy camp, but that's a whole different story. Years ago, I got a very realistic looking gorilla suit. For years, I alternated between sitting in a chair on the front porch and jumping out at the kids when they came by, and then simply filling the gorilla suit up with newspaper the next year. So the kids never knew what was coming. While they would wait for the newspaper-filled gorilla to jump, I would surprise them by jumping out of my door at them. Over the years, that took on a life of its own because the kids who grew up with that now have kids of their own. They bring their kids up the driveway and tell them not to be afraid of the gorilla, because it's not real. So now I am hearing these kids that I used to scare advising their own kids about it.

One of my special Halloween highlights in our neighborhood occurred when for a change of pace I wore my gorilla suit in the house. One of our neighbor ladies who didn't live close by knocked on the door and, wearing a trench coat, opened it up and flashed me. She wasn't completely naked but enough that it very much excited the gorilla. Now the gorilla was turned on, lumberjack style. I lunged at her in the gorilla suit, and she started running. So what you had was this woman running up toward Giusti's house in her trench coat with a gorilla literally in hot pursuit. There was no resolution, of course. The gorilla had lost a step by then, and she was much quicker and got away.

I'm a sap for the holiday season. In fact, Thanksgiving means a great deal to me. I think that's our one true holiday, where you don't have to give a gift to everybody. At Christmas time, I help organize caroling parties. So for a lot of years, when our boys were small, we'd get all the neighborhood kids bundled up, meet down on the street, and go to several houses to sing some Christmas carols.

But over time the kids became a bored with it. So I made up my own version of the "Twelve Days of Christmas," just funky things that I knew the kids would like. I changed the verses to things like "Nine pots of ear wax, Eight bowls of toe jam," and all that kind of stuff. Then the kids loved it. They would ask me to sing it with them as early as August. I still love the concept of traditional caroling. It's an old romantic fantasy that I have.

On the serious side, every once in a while a neighbor runs into a streak of bad luck with health issues. Because we've known most of them for a lot of years, it takes only a half hour to go over and say hello or to send a note. I've received a note or two myself, so I know what that means. When you do these things, it makes your heart feel good. So it does as much for the giver as the recipient. There are a lot of my friends who do what I do and some who do quite a bit more.

The Pirates will get letters on occasion about someone's sick uncle or a great Pirates fan who has fallen ill and ask if I can give him a shout-out on the air, send him a note, or maybe go to see him. I try to do my part.

We had a neighbor, Roy Augenstein, who was critically ill and was days away from death. I went and sat with him. I brought him a baseball. He was not conscious and was heavily sedated. I didn't know what to say because I didn't know if he could hear me, but I talked to him anyway. I don't know if it was the proper thing to do, but since he was just such a phenomenal baseball fan, I put the baseball in his hand and said to him, "I've had some tough times along the way, Roy, and it seemed like when I had a hold of a baseball it helped me. I hope it helps you, too."

I sincerely hope that my involvement with charities, foundations, letter writing, and visits have brought comfort to the people who needed it the most. I truly love the great city of Pittsburgh and have felt that love right back.

So here I am looking down the barrel at age 70. There are still some goals that I wish to accomplish. Of which, in addition to meeting Doris Day, would be to have the means to live on Anna Maria Island, where Dan and Patty Talley have been great hosts for more than 20 years. But I am at the point in my life where I can also reflect on all the good fortune and blessings that I have had. After all, I've had such a phenomenal run in my life of 70 years.

It's true; I had a couple of bad years. But it would be almost hypocritical to bitch and whine about how my career ended, because my plus side of the ledger is so phenomenally weighted in that direction. I lived my baseball dream and continue to do so today.

I've got wonderful grandkids. What grandparents don't think it's one of the finest aspects of their life to be around their grandkids? They are absolutely the joy that I always thought they would be and that I heard everybody talking about. And recently we added a great-grandchild to the mix.

As most dads would say, I'm very proud of my children. I truly admire the way David has faced his challenges and come out on the other side. He's one of the hardest workers one could imagine. And Chris has done a great job with his life. Some of my happiest days are with him on the golf course. I look forward to a lot more of them. I am proud of the way my sons have started their own families. With each year that passes, I'm more aware of all they've accomplished.

And it all starts and ends with Karen, my wife whom I have been with through 48 years of marriage and high school. We, like most families, have our issues, but I feel like we're all in a good place and it only will get even better from here. I'm extremely proud to be its patriarch.

Finally, I have many dear friends who care about me, which I consider to be the ultimate test as to whether one's life is a success or not. I've had these subconscious thoughts about staying busy as long as I can because I've heard from friends that once you stop, you start to die. I never want to become that bored guy who sits in a chair in the morning thinking, *Oh my God, what am I going to do today?*

Also, it's tough for me to shake off my unattainable goal of having everyone in the universe like me. It's almost an obsession of mine to try to make people laugh or smile. In other words, I continue to try to be everything to everybody, and that can be very time-consuming. On the other hand, it's not all that bad. It has brought me great joy, and I'm pretty damn happy. The gift of being able to put a smile on someone's face is pretty remarkable. I understand that my hectic pace has cost me in some areas, but that's the way it is.

So the bottom line is that I'd like to slow down a little bit and not say yes to everything that comes my way. But as my Uncle Jack famously once said, "When we live, let's live in clover. Because when we're dead, we're dead all over." So even though I may have loosened the laces on my running shoes, I still have them on my feet.

Do I have advice for anybody? Yeah. Be kind. It'll make your life sweeter and you'll sleep better. All the rest is details.

Oh, and one final thought:

Let's go Bucs!

Afterword

I had no idea what to expect.

When I first began working on *A Pirate for Life* in the summer of 2011, unsure what the level of reader interest would be, I turned to my coauthor, Erik Sherman, in the first floor hallway of my house and told him, "I don't care if you and I are the only ones to buy this book. I am ready to tell my story and get it out there."

I also wondered if I had enough material for a book.

Erik was very confident on both measures. He assured me that when he was through with me, there would be more than enough material for my autobiography.

And, yes, he thought there would be a great deal of interest in my life story.

A Pirate for Life was released on May 1, 2012. I realized immediately from the Amazon ratings it reached that it was a hit. In fact, it would become Triumph Books' best-selling sports book of the season. But seeing numbers on the Internet is not as real and is far less personal than what I experienced on my summer-long book signing tour.

The signings were amazing. I did eight signings altogether around Pittsburgh at various locations. People would come up with their book, and many of them had a great story about me personally, guys I played with or against, or about the Pirates in general. It was interesting. I wish that somehow, magically, I could have had the book signings *before* I wrote the book! I would have had some different material to use.

I had never experienced a book signing event before. I had no idea what kind of an atmosphere there would be, whether they would have me set up in a corner with a bottle of water and a chair and a pen, or how it would be promoted and marketed or how many people might be there. For the most part, the signings were very well attended and I was set up in many locations with a wall of my books in the background, which was neat.

But the coolest thing was walking in just before the signings began. If there was a signing, say, from 2:00 to 4:00 PM, I would get there at 10 minutes to two. I would come in through the front door and walk by the line of people. While it was not to the degree of feeling like a rock star, it was still an energizing entrance, with many folks enthusiastically saying things like, "Oh, here he is, here he is!" And I would shake hands and exchange pleasantries with them. So I made sure I was never too early.

The book signings were so much more enjoyable than just the standard autograph sessions I have been a part of, where you scribble your name, look up, and say "Hi, how are you? What's your name?" And they move on. This was now a different kind of dynamic, far more personal.

A lot of people were like, "Here's what I was doing during the last out of the World Series you pitched in." One told me that Danny Murtaugh rented a house right next to his in Munhall. Not a lot of kids came up alone with a book, but rather a lot of parents with their children.

Some of the feedback was not even so much about baseball. It was more like, "Here's what I was doing when you guys were playing." Or "Here's how we grew up in Pittsburgh rooting for the Pirates."

It was mostly veteran Pirates fans and it was great to hear their stories.

One of my favorite interactions was when a woman came in and said, "The day after you won the World Series, I gave birth to my son. And guess what I named him?"

So I said, "Steve?"

"No, Freddie."

I said, "Freddie?! What are you, a Red Skelton fan? Freddie the Freeloader? C'mon! Not Steve? Not Roberto? Not even Honus? You know what, I'm gonna sign this book, "To Freddie."

And she goes, "That's what I want!"

It was a good little exchange. It wasn't the normal, "Oh, you were so wonderful, a great pitcher, blah, blah, blah." This was so much more fun.

After one signing, a bookstore manager said to me, "We have a lot of authors who scribble their name and go to the next person. But you really enjoyed interacting with your fans."

So the interactions with the fans made the time go fast, and I enjoyed the signings a lot more than I thought I would.

There was one book signing that I set up on my own, at the David M. Hunt Library in my hometown of Falls Village, Connecticut, in early October. I couldn't wait to see what my hometown people thought about the book. The ego in me, I wanted to get their reactions.

However, knowing this to be a small town, I wondered how many people would show.

The library's director, Erica Joncyk, called and said, "We'd like to have a little presentation before the book signing. We're going to set up a tent with chairs and a podium for you to speak from and then have a catered wine and cheese program back inside the library during the book signing."

I said, "My God, I hope we don't prepare all this and four people come."

The day arrived—a classic crisp, overcast New England autumn day with the foliage in all its brilliance. Karen and I parked up along the side of a road by a small Catholic church and walked down a small hill as a couple of people drifted by. I saw about 100 or so white chairs under a tent and some big pictures of me in the background behind a podium area with a microphone. There was a guy with a video camera set up in the back of the seating area.

This was a small area, maybe 100 feet by 100 feet. I walked up and there were a lot of people I knew, including my basketball coach, Roland Chinatti. Later, my baseball coach, Ed Kirby, wandered in, and then some family and a smattering of people before we got started. All the chairs were filled, plus some people standing in the back. I hadn't prepared a speech at all, not even my usual safety net of bullet points that I run out there for most of my speeches.

But this wasn't going to be a formal presentation, and I didn't give it much thought. It was going to be about the book, so I didn't talk much about the Pirates. It was one of those times that I really felt good because I ended up just rambling along, rambling along, and rambling along some more. Originally, I figured the talk would be about five minutes long before we'd all go inside and begin the book signing. Instead, it went on for close to an hour. It was so much fun.

The response to my speech was good, and when I mentioned somebody's name, the great thing was they were usually there, whether it was my high school coach or catcher or my brother, Terry, who was his usual straight man self sitting in the front row.

The great thing about the talk was that it was so personal.

Near the end, Erica nudged me and said, "We have to get going here. We've got a lot of books to sign." But I was cooking, just rolling. I was giving them my best stuff when Karen said it was time to start the signing.

"They're not going to want to read the book if you keep going," Karen said. "It's time to get in there."

While I was walking towards the library entrance, this guy came up to me and said, "Steve, I'm David Elliott."

I said, "Oh my God! David Elliott. We were Little League teammates at eight years old."

Not only were we Little League teammates, but his dad was a doctor, so he was in a little different social strata than I was. Still, we hit it off. His family had a beautiful lake house on Twin Lakes, which is about five miles from where I lived. I would ride my bike up to that lake house and we would throw a rubber ball against his barn, much like I would do by myself at my own house. David would be the Boston Red Sox, and I would be the Cleveland Indians, and we played games against each other all day long a lot of days.

I had always wondered what happened to David Elliott. I just thought the world of him when we were kids. I half-wanted to shut down the whole book signing and spend an hour with him. It caught me. It took me back in time to when I was a kid and the joy of Little League and being back by his barn playing ball. It just snapped me back as abruptly as any time warp that I've ever experienced. I just wanted to stop time right there and talk to him. But I couldn't.

I said, "David, are you living here now? Did you become a doctor?"

"No, no. It's a long story."

I said, "Can I give you my phone number?"

He asked, "Do you do email?"

I said, "No, but Karen's right there. Go over and get her email and, please, tell me how to contact you."

When we got back home, there was an email from David.

It began, "No, I didn't become a doctor, Steve. I got into business and I wound up being the CEO of a Fortune 500 company. I now have an office in Pittsburgh with a new company. And I still have a place on Twin Lakes with my family."

I was blown away by his email.

I have since scrawled out a hand-written letter that Karen emailed back to him because I deeply want to maintain contact with him after all these years. That was one really neat part of going back to Falls Village for the signing.

It was also wonderful because people came up to me and talked not about Pirates baseball, but about Falls Village. About growing up. Person after person came up to me with all these great stories about growing up there, like when I came over to someone's house and watched cartoons, or played catch out in the yard, or when we listened to the stories that our teacher, Carolyn Howe, used to read to us upstairs at the library so many years before when it was used as a school.

One old classmate asked me what I remembered about the first grade. I said, "I remember that picture of George Washington that was probably in every first grade classroom in America. And playing ball out there in the schoolyard, when it looked as big as Yankee Stadium to us, but was actually only about 70 feet from the street up to the back of the building." And I remembered batting cross-handed because I didn't know the difference. All of those childhood memories just came rushing back, which was a great feeling.

The day was completed by Champ Perrotti, who runs my charity golf tournament. Champ hosted a wonderful, informal lobster fest in his barn. He and his wife, Delores, put together the event with a couple of good friends of mine, Mickey and Tanya Riva. The Rivas drove down that Saturday morning from Maine with 40 pounds of lobster and clams to provide for the party. When they do it, they do it right. It was just a fabulous day.

The return to Falls Village was everything I thought it would be and more. It was warm and wonderful and had that small-town country feeling that I love.

I've had some Pirates fans write to tell me how much they enjoyed the book. Well, that was the idea. The intent was to make this a love letter to baseball, and Pirates fans in particular. But love letters aren't always flowery. Love is supposed to be multi-dimensional, so I'm glad they learned about the Pittsburgh clubhouse and some of the irreverence, because you can't be irreverent amongst yourselves and scream and holler obscenities and not have someone kill somebody. You can only do it if you're pretty close to people and the lines are completely open.

The theme I kept getting from friends after the book was released was that they couldn't believe the full disclosure, how I really exposed myself.

I started to think, *Maybe I gave them more than they needed to know.*

The other reaction, especially from women around Karen was, "Karen, how the hell did you put up with this man for all those years?"

Not that it's all bad. A lot of people put a baseball player and his wife up on a pedestal. The perception is that it is a dream life—you've got money, so everything is smooth sailing. We pulled the rug out from underneath that, while at the same time conveying that it is a great life. My goodness, I couldn't have dreamed of this much comfort, this nice a home, and what we have. But it parallels a lot of people's lives, just at different levels. We have our ups and downs at this particular level, other people at higher or lower levels. Most people just don't write about them.

I was always raised with my New England mentality that you do not air your dirty laundry. And I adhered to that all my life until I wrote this damned book! It was like, *Here's my laundry out on the line. I'm flapping in the breeze. Here I am!*

I also hoped that the book would help fans and friends understand what baseball life is like not only for the player, but for his family and the people around him. After all these years, I finally detailed to my wife and my sons some of the things that I hadn't at the end of my playing days because, as I said in that lengthy first chapter, I had tried to internalize a lot so I wouldn't bring that burden and that downer-type thinking to them. With the passage of time, it was nice to convey some of how I was really feeling at the time.

The neat thing about my sons is that they now not only have a better feel for those two years where it was just awful, but also after reading the book they have a little feeling of the highs of getting to the major leagues, being successful, and pitching in the World Series.

So it wasn't lopsided. That was the mission statement of the project. Originally, Erik and I had two working titles for the book: *They Named a Disease After Me* and *Up and In, Down and Out*. But *A Pirate for Life*, chosen by Triumph, was much better because it focused on my entire life, not just my career.

One of my favorite letters I received about the book came from a Falls Village man named Dick Heinz. It reads as follows:

> *August 26, 2012*
> *Hi Steve—*
> *I'm one of the Falls Village boys. I don't know if you remember me. I was listening to NPR earlier this summer and heard an interview with the great Steve Blass. And I mean that sincerely. The interview was something about a syndrome, but in the end, Steve, you said that you wished that once in a while someone wanted to talk about the good things in your career.*

Well, I just want to let you know that I brag about knowing you and never mention anything about any damned syndrome.

I can remember playing on the green in Falls Village when you were in high school and you stopped to throw the ball with us. It was not enough just to see you make it to the majors, but then the '71 World Series happened. I don't mean to make small what happened prior to 1971, but here I was that October, watching you come out for the third game with the Pirates trailing by two. That's how I set this up when telling the story. To watch you blow down the Orioles was awesome and I was jumping around like a mad man with the final out.

I played for the Little League Indians and later played softball with your dad and two brothers. I loved your dad. Watching your dad jump into your arms (after Game 3) is something that still brings tears to my eyes.

Not even looking ahead to the final game, but the Bucs made it to Game 7, and the world then knew who you were. Game 7 was a beauty. You won the World Series. You turned the World Series around and closed it out.

1972 was an outstanding season. You may remember that you had an All-Star season that year.

So, I just want to say thank you for being a hero to us skinny kids from Falls Village who got to live that dream with you. You can stop by my house for a beer any night. It would be an honor.

—Dick Heinz

I guess that's why Falls Village means a lot to me.

Of all the reviews and letters, there have been exactly two negative ones. Not too bad. Even Shakespeare had his critics.

A former military guy wrote that he threw the book away because of the bad language. He acknowledged that he knew the colorful language made the book more realistic, but he didn't want his son reading it.

I thought, *Well, you've got white-out.*

Actually, I wasn't surprised that there were a few people who were offended by some of the language. I understood that. But again, why write a book if you're going to sugarcoat it? So it doesn't bother me. I apologize for offending some people if I did, but I don't lose any sleep over that.

The book continues to take on a life of its own. When we started, I was at Ground Zero. I didn't know what to expect about the reaction, about sales, about anything. I did not write the book to make money, but back in those nasty, little dark recesses of my heart, I felt, well, it would be nice to make a few bucks off this, too. However, it was not paramount.

Everywhere I go in Pittsburgh, people will ask me, "How's the book doing?" Or "I read the book." Or "I like the book." It's been very gratifying. I guess we sold close to 10,000 books by the end of the baseball season. To me, that's fabulous.

One bookstore manager in Sewickley, Pennsylvania, told me that *A Pirate for Life* had outsold *Fifty Shades of Gray* in her store. So I told the lady, "Yeah, it's because my book has pictures!" That was my most unique signing.

Another time, I told some golf buddies, "You know, we've had four printings."

One of them replied, "What are there, 25 books in each printing?"

"No, no, 20. You're giving me too much credit," I told him with self-deprecating humor.

During the summer, when I went to the ballpark to broadcast, I averaged signing two or three books each night that people would send up to the booth, much to the chagrin of my broadcast partners. They'd say stuff like, "Steve, I'm trying to get ready for a ballgame. Do you mind signing that and getting ready so we can talk?"

I got the expected ration of crap, though it could have been much worse.

My broadcast buddies actually had a lot of fun with the book, sometimes referring to me as "Hemingway" when the camera panned over to me while I did radio. They also did a great job of promoting it on the air, doing so in a variety of different ways.

There was the straight way, like "Steve wrote a book, it's fun, a good read, and you ought to pick it up." Then there was the humorous way, like "Blass is over there in the booth, it's the sixth inning, and he hasn't seen one pitch because he's signing another book. We'll be introducing you to the next color man for the Pirates shortly."

With that group, you never know. As Marc Garda, our boss, has said, "I've got five monkeys that I try to keep in a barrel—my broadcast team. And they keep trying to jump out and run away. So, my job is to keep five monkeys in one barrel for six months and it's not easy."

The great thing about Marc is that he's not only my boss, he's my friend. Plus, he's got a very warped and wonderful sense of humor that I appreciate.

I'm glad I got on the other side of the book because it was one of my intentions to be able to convey my story while I still had the recall. The only issue I have is that I thought when I completed the book that it would really free my mind from all the stuff that I wanted to remember. Well, it hasn't. There are still fruit flies. There is still a lot of clutter.

So, of all the things I accomplished by doing a book, the only thing I didn't do was clear my mind because it still goes a mile a minute from the moment I wake up. I don't know if that's a good thing or a bad thing. It's just a thing.

Some people have asked me if, based on the success of this book, a sequel is in the works. To that I answer there will not be. But if there was, I have the perfect title. I would call it *Fifty Shades of Blass*.

• • •

When I first learned from Triumph in late summer that they planned to publish a trade paperback version of *A Pirate for Life* and wanted to add an afterword, I imagined a good deal of it would recap a special season for the Pirates.

After all, by August 8 the Bucs were a season-high 16 games over .500 and had spent a total of 22 days in first place in the NL Central division.

So, what happened?

Well, there were three tiers of disappointment during the last two months of the season. We thought we'd do the division. Thought we'd do the wild card. Thought we'd do .500. As it turned out, we didn't do any of the three.

The severity of the disappointment varies from fan to fan, individual to individual. This is going to sound so much like a spin, but when the dust settles on a major league season, it's not about *when* you win ballgames or lose ballgames, it's about *how many* wins and losses you have when it's over. It's just count 'em up! And that's one of the unique things about baseball. It's 162 games. That's the bottom line.

There are just so many games. You can't fool people. Every major league team has talent, but you've got to sustain it for six months. The Pirates in 2012 had the talent to win games. We just didn't have enough talent to keep winning games late in the season.

So was it a collapse? That's certainly a term that can be applied. But my point is, what if the Pirates played like they did late in the season early in the year and buried themselves? And then came on like we did in May, June, and July and played good at the end? It would have been too late. At the end, it's only the total number of wins and the total number of losses that matter. And you've got to be good enough to have a lot more wins than losses. It's as simple as that.

What happened to this club? We didn't hit, pitch, or play defense as well as we needed to down the stretch. And we didn't play as well fundamentally as we did when things were going well. Why? Run off the reasons. We just simply didn't. And if you want to get better, you've got to do those kinds of things for six months instead of for four months. People analyze this thing down to the nub, but I take more of an overview. Maybe I'm too simplistic, but to me that's my interpretation of the season.

The outrage from the fans and the media exists because the collapse happened at the end of the season. But there's an interesting question that arises with respect to the fans' perception of the 2012 season that should be considered.

Psychologically, what if the Pirates had the two bad months early, and the four good months later? Would there be excitement instead of disappointment looking forward into 2013? It's an interesting thought.

Would there have been outrage at the beginning of the season? Yes. But the team emotionally and psychologically set things up for that outrage because it happened at the end. I'm not surprised at the fans' reaction, and I don't blame them one bit. Our success through two-thirds of the season set up the possibility for disappointment if we didn't continue that success—and we didn't.

In a sense, we were victims of our own success because we didn't maintain that high level of play. We just weren't good enough in 2012.

The one beacon of light that come out of the season is that for years, Pittsburgh showed an indifference towards the Pirates. Now there's anger. And that's better than apathy because now I think they're going to demand better. We won more games than we did the previous year. But I understand the anger. And I respect the anger. Plus, the fact that 2012 piggy-backed 2011's late-season collapse just "doubled-down" the emotional reaction of the fans.

The Pirates won just 57 games in 2010, then 72 in 2011, and 79 in 2012. So in two years, Pittsburgh has improved by 22 games. Statistically, we can say that, but don't run that by the fans. They will laugh at you, punch you, or turn and walk away. I understand that because I can remove myself from the emotion, but I don't want our fans to remove themselves from it. From an organizational standpoint, the ascent is meaningful, but it's a tough sell to our fans.

While the winning lasted, the season was a carnival atmosphere and we ended up drawing more than 2 million fans. We always said when this beautiful ballpark was built that if we could get a team to match its brilliance, PNC Park would be a circus. And it was.

May, June, and July were incredible. Sellout after sellout. People were in the streets and around the ballpark for hours *after* the game in the bars and restaurants. They didn't want to go home. The place was rockin'! And we seemed to find a different way to win most every night. It was so much fun.

It was so enjoyable for me to drive from my house to the ballpark to see kids playing catch in their yards with an Andrew McCutchen, Neil Walker, Garrett Jones, A.J. Burnett, or Pedro Alvarez jersey on. The town got caught up with this ballclub.

I love the Steelers. They open training camp each summer at Saint Vincent and for years and years that cornered the media. But this year, it was about baseball. There was still attention around the Steelers opening camp, because this is a great Steelers town. But we were the hot topic and it was great.

The Steelers' mystique is enormous all around the country. But the Pirates' mystique is strong, too. Everywhere you go you see Pirates gear and hats, T-shirts, and jerseys. I think Pittsburgh has always had a reputation as a hard-working town. People respect that more than the glitzy, glamorous stuff that surrounds other teams. But there's been a migration from Pittsburgh. People relocate and still have these loyalties. So it's a combination of those factors.

Despite the collapse, there were most definitely some significant positives in player development that show the Pirates are moving in the right direction. For the first season since the days of the Pittsburgh Lumber Company in 1966, the Buccos had three players—McCutchen, Alvarez, and Jones— hit more than 25 home runs.

We came out of spring training with no real expectation of being a team that was going to hit a lot of home runs. We finished with 170, which was 67 more than in 2011 and the most by the Pirates in 13 years. We just hit a ton of home runs. I have no idea where the power came from. But it was there. So that was a real plus to start going toe-to-toe with other teams and scoring a bunch of runs. It was totally unexpected.

Alvarez, however, is not a surprise to me. He's got that power capability. He's going to strike out a lot, but hopefully he can build his confidence even further with this year's results. You hope that's a stepping stone because he's a game changer. Everybody around the National League says when he makes solid contact, there are very few hitters that have the ball jump off their bat like Pedro. He's got enormous power.

I love Jones because he's bounced around a little bit. He's got a wonderfully positive attitude and has a good perspective of who he is and where he is. I was very happy for the year he had.

As for Andrew, he is on the verge of being a very *special* player. How good can McCutchen get? We don't know. He can take off and be a superstar. He could be a Hall of Famer. The sky is the limit. He's got a lot of physical abilities. Fundamentally, maybe he could be a better base stealer and a more consistent center fielder, but if he just works at those things a little bit, it could elevate him to superstar status.

I hope Andrew strives to find out how great he can be. When he hangs them up, and sits in that proverbial rocking chair I talk about when he's 80 years old, I don't want him wondering how good a major leaguer he could have been. I want him to say, "Boy, I was the best I could be regardless of what level I achieved."

The Pirates also had a tremendous pitching staff for four of the six months of the season.

A.J. Burnett was very solid. He could have had 20 wins, but he had some games when he didn't get much run support and pitched extremely well. His 16 wins were the most by a Pirates pitcher since John Smiley more than 20 years ago.

James McDonald was like Dr. Jekyll and Mr. Hyde. He was tremendous the first half of the year. Probably should have been on the All-Star team. But then it just got totally away from him. He's a big question mark for 2013.

Out of the bullpen, Joel Hanrahan was terrific. His 36 saves were fifth-best in the National League. I've got no problems with him closing. I don't know what he's going to do after 2013, whether he'll test free agency. While I don't get consumed with following potential free agents, I hope we are able to keep him.

The Pirates' individual achievements are fine, and looking forward they give the club a lot to be encouraged about, but I don't get too caught up with that stuff. I get caught up with wins and losses. It comes down to this. If you're not going to hit, you better pitch. And if you're not going to pitch, you better hit. Our problem in 2012, as it was in 2011, was they both went south at the same time. We didn't have one dimension carrying the other.

Despite the rough close to 2012, I still love the organization and the game of baseball. It is different from any other sport in the world.

One of the biggest differences was pointed out by the great writer Roger Angell, who wrote one of my favorite baseball quotes that goes as follows: "Since baseball time is measured only in outs, all you have to do is succeed utterly; keep hitting, keep the rally alive, and you have defeated time. You remain forever young."

I just love getting in the car, going to PNC Park, and watching the Pittsburgh Pirates play baseball. The 2012 season was an exciting campaign for the most part. Between the book coming out and the way the Pittsburgh Pirates played, I couldn't wait to get out to the ballpark. It was disappointing at the end, but I saw a lot of great baseball and I look forward to seeing even more in 2013.

Steve Blass
Pittsburgh, Pennsylvania
November 2012